MATTERS of CONSCIENCE

A PRACTICAL THEOLOGY FOR THE EVANGELICAL CHAPLAIN SERVING IN THE UNITED STATES MILITARY

DR. MICHAEL C. WHITTINGTON

CHAPLAIN, COLONEL, USAF (RETIRED)

———————

DR. CHARLIE N. DAVIDSON

CHAPLAIN, LIEUTENANT COLONEL, USAF (RETIRED)

ENDORSEMENTS

The success of military chaplaincy depends on the freedoms of its members to fulfill their calling from God. Matters of Conscience proposes that a chaplain's ultimate allegiance must be to Jesus Christ. Otherwise, his commitment to the Constitution — and to those he ministers to — is disingenuous. Matters of Conscience explores the biblical foundation of servant leadership and Christ-centered worship "within" the chapel walls, then dives deeply into how theology can be applied during both peacetime and war to help those spiritually wounded by the effects of battle.

David L. Young, Brigadier General, USAF (Ret)

I have nothing but the highest respect for those men and women who serve in the United States Armed Forces. This powerful book speaks to the value of Christ-Centered ministry to these heroes. The authors have proven themselves in the military and in the church as leaders in Christian ministry. They have been on the front lines of handling the tough issues with the Bible in one hand and the Constitution in the other. Every Christian interested in reflecting the love of Christ to our troops should read this book.

Jonathan Falwell, Pastor, Thomas Road Baptist Church, Lynchburg, Virginia

Outstanding book! Well-documented and written by two veteran chaplains; just the right blend of scholarship and practical theology for the military chaplain! Matters of Conscience is not only an enjoyable book to read but would be a great textbook for any course within the academic disciplines of military history, chaplaincy studies, and American religious history.

Ronald Hawkins, Liberty University Vice President for Academic Affairs and Vice Provost

Whittington and Davidson have blessed us with wise advice and insight in Matters of Conscience! ...This work will be very valuable for chaplains, commanders, and anyone wanting to understand the role of the chaplain in the Armed Forces of the United States

John Weida, Major General, USAF (Ret)

Truly outstanding ... the authors' use of Scripture, history, and experiences on the battlefield make this a tremendous tool for anyone trying to learn about the Chaplain Corps... Matters of Conscience is a must-read for any pastor with a heart for ministry in the military services.

Charles C. Baldwin, Chaplain, Major General, USAF (Ret)

America's finest need to know they are not alone – God is with them! And the mere presence of the chaplain is a reminder that God is at their side... For this reason alone, Matters of Conscience is a must-read for every Christian interested in protecting our troops' religious freedom.

Robert F. Dees, Major General, U.S. Army, (Ret), Author, *The Resilience Trilogy*

MATTERS of CONSCIENCE

By MICHAEL C. WHITTINGTON & CHARLIE N. DAVIDSON

ISBN: 978-1-935986-63-8

LIBERTY
UNIVERSITY.
PRESS

Lynchburg, Va.
www.Liberty.edu/LibertyUniversityPress

PUBLISHER'S ACKNOWLEDGMENTS

A special thank you to all the individuals who assisted in
the creation of this publication:

Proofreader:	Whitney Delaney
Editorial Assistant:	Arielle Bielicki
Project Editor:	Leo Percer
Editorial Manager:	Sarah Funderburke
Cover Art:	Carrie Bell
Layout and Graphics:	Rachel Dugan

ACKNOWLEDGMENTS

Generally, authors of Christian books close their acknowledgments expressing their sincere gratitude to God – perhaps remembering the words of Jesus, "The last shall be first." Breaking precedent, however, we want to begin with the Lord. The last fifteen months have assured us both that God can do anything, "Far more than you could ever imagine or guess or request in your wildest dreams! He does it not by pushing us around but by working within us, his Spirit deeply and gently within us" (Eph. 3:20, The Message). This scripture resonated within us, and served as a beacon of light when we felt lost, wondering if we should quit the project and go our separate ways; but God had other plans for His servants, and with that, we tried to salute smartly and press forward. So we begin our brief acknowledgments with "Thank you, Lord."

Much of our time was spent in research. With Charlie in Lynchburg as a resident professor at Liberty Baptist Theological Seminary, the campus library provided easy access. Michael, however, living in Nashville, Tennessee, had to get special permission to use the resources at a local university. And it just so happened, one of the best divinity libraries in the nation is located at Vanderbilt University – Jean and Alexander Heard Library. With no direct ties to the school, he was graciously authorized access to this prominent library.

We are also grateful to the Liberty Press publishing team, with special thanks to Sarah Funderburke (Liberty University Press Manager). Since *Matters of Conscience* is one of the required texts for a newly-developed graduate course in Chaplaincy Ministry at Liberty Baptist Theological Seminary, the relentless efforts of the editorial team allowed the course to be deployed on time.

We are also indebted to Chaplain, Major General Charles Baldwin for sharing two first-hand accounts of ministry of presence; both riveting examples of the need for the chaplain to reflect the light of Christ.

When a project demands over a year of an author's time, it is generally one's wife and family that bear the greatest burden; in this case, Michael's wife Debbie, and Charlie's wife Roydene. We all process life differently and your authors are no exception. Charlie can attest to the fact that Michael "thinks-out-loud" but it was Debbie who heard his every thought; and by listening with her head as well as her heart, she provided valuable insight into the whole of the book.

So there you have it, our recognition of those who deserve our gratitude. There is however, one more person we would like to thank. You! This book is a work of flawed men who were often hard pressed to hear the Lord's voice. At the risk of sounding pious, there were those rare moments when we listened to that "still, small voice." And that's where you – the reader – come in. May God help you discern which is which!

Authors, Matters of Conscience

To Christian chaplains who remain true to Jesus Christ while facilitating the religious freedom of all military personnel.
You are "Chaplains of Conscience."

CONTENTS

Acknowledgments 6

Foreword 11

Introduction – Chapter Overviews 14

PART ONE – THE BOUNDARIES

Chapter 1 Was America Founded as a Christian Nation? 35

Chapter 2 Pluralistic Quagmires 65

Chapter 3 Censoring Military Chaplains – A Case Study 85

PART TWO – MINISTRY "INSIDE" THE WALLS

Chapter 4 Servant Leadership 97

Chapter 5 A Practical Theology of Worship 119

Chapter 6 Building a Protestant Program 141

PART THREE – MINISTRY "OUTSIDE" THE WALLS

Chapter 7 The Enigmatic Role of the Chaplain – Officer or Clergy? 173

Chapter 8 Controversial Matters of Faith 195

Chapter 9 Ministry in the Foxhole 221

Epilogue 243

Meet the Authors 246

Bibliography 249

FOREWORD

I have the greatest respect for our nation's military chaplains. In simple terms, where would we (our nation's troops and families) be without them? I found that when troops are hurting, they don't first cry out for the general. They cry out for the medic and the chaplain, desperately seeking first aid for the body and for the soul. As the Commander of the United States Army Second Infantry Division in South Korea, I had one *acid test* I would give to my chaplains, "Do your soldiers recognize your voice in the dark?" The soldier manning a lonely outpost in the middle of the night with the chaplain at his side completely understands this powerful metaphor. Or in the words of the authors,

> *Ask the soldier in battle who just lost his buddy in a firefight. Ask the Air Force pilot steadying himself the night before his first combat mission. Ask the young marine returning home from a lengthy deployment discovering his wife is gone, or a commander searching for just the right words before delivering a death notification. Ask the young sailor working launch-and-recovery on the flight deck of an aircraft carrier. Ask them if they understand what their chaplain brings to the table – a "visible reminder of the Holy."*

As the commanding general, why did I ask this question of my chaplains? Because America's finest need to know they are not alone – God is with them! The mere presence of the chaplain is a reminder that God is at their side. The chaplain's presence calms the airman working the mid-shift just south of the Arctic Circle on a frigid winter's night. He provides some much needed levity to a team of sailors repairing an aircraft carrier's catapult. And he lifts a soldier's spirit with a simple prayer and a pat on the back.

Regrettably, some of my soldiers had never even seen their chaplain, much less recognized his or her voice in the dark. Often these same "voiceless" chaplains were the ones who would not swing at the pitch when "thrown a softball" by a commander asking for them to provide a relevant word in time of need. These are the chaplains who had neglected their own spiritual walk, who had forgotten who they were as God's servants and why they were called to stand with our troops. To quote Chaplains Whittington and Davidson, *"Somewhere, along their journey, they lost their way."* For this reason alone, *Matters of Conscience* is a must-read for every Christian interested in protecting our troops' religious freedom. It is a must-read for every minister considering military chaplaincy. And it is a powerful reminder to every chaplain to remain true to their conscience and their calling.

For the evangelical chaplain, *Matters of Conscience* pulls no punches, "…in order for the evangelical chaplain to fulfill his calling from God, his ultimate allegiance must reside in Jesus Christ or his commitment to the Constitution is disingenuous." And these authors know a thing or two about a military chaplains' calling.

Our authors of *Matters of Conscience are immensely qualified.* Colonel Michael Whittington and Lieutenant Colonel Charlie Davidson are retired Air Force chaplains with over fifty years of active duty service between them. Whittington served at the highest levels of the Air Force Chaplain Service in four overseas military theaters (Europe, Middle East, Far East, and Pacific) including joint tours working directly with soldiers, sailors, marines, and airmen. Davidson also served overseas, experienced multiple deployments, and had the distinction of being the first Air Force chaplain during Operation Iraqi Freedom to be awarded the Bronze Star under combat conditions, in hostile and dangerous situations. In short, both of these committed chaplains know the chaplain business and provide wise, experienced insights to the reader.

Though university professors, Dr. Whittington and Dr. Davidson have devoted most of their lives, in the trenches, introducing God to the soldier and the soldier to God – sharing the love of Christ in austere conditions both at home and abroad. *Matters of Conscience* reflects both of these callings – academia and pastoral ministry.

This well documented book is divided into three parts, each integral to the next. *Part One* addresses America's Judeo-Christian heritage and its relevance to the constitutional boundaries of the chaplaincy. *Part Two* and *Part Three* suggest how the Christian chaplain can work within these limits; *a field manual* governing the day-to-day activities of a military chaplain.

A significant portion of *Part Three* deals with the chaplain's role in controversial faith issues. Is he first an officer or a minister? Is his allegiance to the Constitution or Jesus Christ? Do recent changes to the policy directives on issues such as prayer in the name of Jesus, repeal of "Don't Ask, Don't Tell," and the repeated warnings against proselytizing military personnel trump the biblical command from 2 Timothy 4:2, to "preach the word, be urgent in season and out of season, convince, rebuke, and exhort"? Must the Christian chaplain be politically-correct to be successful in the United States military? Or is it possible, for the chaplain to be faithful to Jesus Christ while, at the same time, providing for the soldier's religious freedom? Such questions certainly require a wisdom befitting of Jesus' challenge in Matthew 10:16, "Behold, I send you out as sheep in the midst of wolves; so be shrewd as serpents and innocent as doves."

Matters of Conscience not only provides the chaplain with practical solutions to a challenging ministry environment, but also educates the non-chaplain reader. While galvanizing the reader with a renewed appreciation of our religious heritage, the authors convey riveting true stories of ministry played out in complex social and political military settings.

The military chaplain lives, works, trains, and deploys with the troops. The good ones don't have to introduce themselves. Even in the darkest hour, soldiers recognize their voice.

In *Matters of Conscience*, you will hear another voice, the voice of chaplains who seek to exercise their God-given and Constitutionally-supported responsibility to the military they serve. And once heard, perhaps you will stand at their side, lifting them in fervent prayer. It is, after all, a matter of conscience.

Robert F. Dees
Major General, U.S. Army, Retired
Author, *The Resilience Trilogy*

INTRODUCTION
CHAPTER OVERVIEWS

Let us as a nation join together before God, aware of the trials that lie ahead and of the need for Divine guidance. With unshakable faith in God and the liberty which is our heritage, we as a free nation will continue to grow and prosper.

– Ronald Reagan, 40th President of the United States
Proclamation 4826, National Day of Prayer, March 19, 1981

Who's Flying Lead?

It was a clear sky on the Monday morning of January 18, 1982 when four Air Force Thunderbirds crashed almost simultaneously into the Nevada desert on Range 65, now referred to as "The Gathering of Eagles Range." The world renowned aerial demonstration team was training at Indian Springs Air Force Auxiliary Field[1] preparing themselves for their next breathtaking performance at Davis-Monthan Air Force Base, Arizona. On this brisk winter morning, Thunderbird numbers "1-4" (famously known as the *Diamond*) were flying line abreast doing a loop – a four-ship pattern calling for the T-38s to climb in a side by side formation for several thousand feet, pull over in a slow, backward loop; and then, hurtle down to the earth at a dizzying 400 miles per hour, leveling off at 100 feet above the ground. This incredible feat thrills audiences all over the world, even aviators familiar with the sight and sounds of the jetfighters.

At the time of this disaster (the worst in the Thunderbirds' storied history) Chaplain Whittington was stationed at Gila Bend Air Force Auxiliary Field,

---

1 In 2005 the name of the training base was changed to Creech Air Force Base in honor of General Wilbur L. "Bill" Creech (1927-2003), whose influence was instrumental in securing congressional support for the Air Force's Aerial Demonstration Team following the tragedy of 1982.

Arizona.[2] When news of the tragedy reached the Sonoran desert, reporters from local newspapers and television stations were asking what seemed to be a logical question, "How could four T-38s malfunction at the same time?" Of course, the answer was, "Four T-38s did not malfunction, only one – the lead jet."

What the reporters did not know was that in order to fly in such a tight formation (eighteen inches wingtip-to-wingtip) the other three pilots had to be focused exclusively on the lead jet to gauge their proper distance. Visually cueing off the lead aircraft, the wing and slot pilots were unaware of their position relative to the ground. The left wingman, with his hand on the stick, looked right. The right wingman, with his hand on the stick, looked left. And the slot (Thunderbird "4") gained his perspective by focusing on the lead jet and the two wingmen. Only the lead pilot looked forward and on that fateful day in January, Major Norm Lowry's lead jet malfunctioned.[3] Within a nanosecond Thunderbird "1" crashed headlong into the desert floor followed by the other three jets. A local resident said he heard the scream of the engines as they plunged downward to the ground, then "boom-boom-boom, boom-boom-boom as they hit the ground one after another."[4] By following the lead pilot – however trustworthy – all died.

The imagery speaks volumes to the constitutional promise of religious freedom and the Christian chaplain's ministry. Whether or not chaplains fulfill their calling to God and country is determined by *what* or *whom* they follow. The probing question to the reader is: "Who is flying your lead? What *person* or *principle* is worthy of your ultimate allegiance?" It's a fair question. In fact, it may be the only question for the military chaplaincy, in general; and the Christian chaplain, in particular. There is only one question, but there are two

---

2 Gila Bend AFAF, located in the Sonoran desert of Arizona, was the other remote CONUS auxiliary Air Force field. In 1982, the small outpost of 500 AF personnel supported the largest gunnery range in the free world. Local reporters regularly covered the air-to-ground training of the AF fighters from Luke and Davis Monthan AFB.

3 The Air Force concluded that the tragedy was a combination of a mechanical failure in the lead jet and the strict discipline of the other three pilots. See "Crashing in Formation" (February 1, 1982), *Time Magazine* 119, 19.

4 The eyewitness account was from Loren Conaway. See "The Thunderbirds' Diamond Crash" (January 18, 1982) at http://www.check-six.com/Crash_Sites/Thunderbirds-Diamond_Crash.htm.

answers. And both answers will determine whether or not the chaplaincy will survive in its present form.

One Question, Two Answers

From 1996 to 1999, Colonel Whittington served as chief of the Education Division of the Air Force Chaplain Service Institute (CSI) and toward the end of his assignment, as director of CSI.[5] It was a wonderful assignment that deepened his respect for his chaplain colleagues – Christian, Jew, and Muslim. It was also a sobering reminder that some Christian chaplains (like the Ephesians of old) had abandoned their first love.[6] Some of the Christian chaplains focused on rank and position to the point that they forgot who they were and to whom they belonged. Their theological center (Jesus Christ) had been replaced with their own vainglorious drive for promotion and political correctness. Somewhere along their journey, they lost their way. It would be enough of a tragedy if they were the only victims but when chaplains lose sight of their calling, everyone suffers, especially the troops. Make no mistake; the chaplains' relationship with Jesus Christ (or lack of) will form the paradigm for their entire career, the lens through which they view their ministry. And this Christology will find expression in their relationships with commanders, colleagues, and troops. However "politically incorrect" it may sound, one's effectiveness as a Christian chaplain to facilitate the soldiers'[7] religious freedom will be in direct proportion to his[8] allegiance to Jesus Christ, the lead pilot – the first answer to the question, "What *person* or *principle* is worthy of your ultimate allegiance?"

One might argue that since the vast majority of military personnel are

---

5 CSI was the Air Force Chaplain School. All three Chaplain Schools are now jointly located at Fort Jackson, S.C. in the Armed Forces Chaplaincy Center.

6 Yet I hold this against you: You have forsaken the love you had at first. Consider how far you have fallen! Repent and do the things you did at first …" Rev. 2:4-5 (NIV).

7 With few exceptions, *Matters of Conscience* will use *soldier* as a generic term to represent all of America's warriors – soldiers, sailors, marines, airmen, and coastguardsmen.

8 As in the case with the use of the word "soldier," *Matters of Conscience* will use the masculine gender throughout the text as a generic pronoun representing male and female chaplains; both of whom continue to serve God and country with distinction.

Christians, the chaplaincy as a whole should reflect a similar allegiance to our Christian heritage. At the risk of alienating our fellow conservatives, the response must be a resounding "no." A quick perusal of all three policy directives governing the military chaplaincy will disclose what even the least informed soldier understands – military chaplains facilitate our religious freedom. The First Amendment[9] is the *sine qua non*[10] for the chaplaincy, our reason for existence. Repeal it and the chaplaincy would vanish overnight. To continue the Thunderbird analogy, the Constitution is the lead jet; the First Amendment, the pilot – the second answer to the question, "What *person* or *principle* is worthy of your ultimate allegiance?" Tamper with this and the chaplaincy will go down in flames.

A "Practical" Theology

How will addressing a *practical theology* of the evangelical chaplaincy help it survive? When discussing the theological underpinnings of the Christian chaplain, it is important to understand what is meant by *theology*. Even a cursory search of the word would expose a dazzling array of definitions, but if one takes the time to read carefully, a common thread emerges in all of them – relationship. Not a relationship connected by a family's surname, but a fellowship[11] joined by core values.

The word "fellowship" may sound too religious to be appreciated by the average soldier, but every warrior understands loyalty to one's friend.[12] At the heart of all of the armed services' core values is loyalty. It may be expressed differently in the three policy directives[13] but the meaning is the same: "I have your back." The directives governing the chaplaincy are uniquely written to

---

9 The First Amendment begins with the words, "Congress shall make no law respecting an establishment of religion, or prohibiting the free exercise thereof...."

10 Latin: "without which [there is] nothing."

11 Greek: *koinōnía* (*fellowship* as in 1 Jn. 1:1-3); *koinōnoí* (*partners* as in Luke 5:10). For a thorough study of its New Testament usage, see Frederick Hauck, *Theological Dictionary of the New Testament*, volume III, (Grand Rapids: Wm. B. Eerdmans Publishing Company, 1965), 804-809.

12 *Cf.* Jn. 15:13

13 See AR 165-1, AFI 52-1, and OPNAVINST 1730.1D

serve our warriors on land, in the air, and at sea but are perhaps best explained by the Army in its description of the chaplain's purpose: nurture the living, care for the wounded, honor the dead.[14] How can the chaplain "nurture, care, and honor" void of relationship? And how can the Christian chaplain, whose core faith resides in Jesus Christ, have a relationship void of Christian values? And how can the chaplain impart these values without the recognition that they emanate from Jesus Christ?

At its core, then, a practical Christian theology demands that the chaplain's ultimate allegiance be centered in Jesus Christ; and, a practical theology of the Chaplain Corps demands loyalty to the First Amendment. The two are not mutually exclusive; on the contrary, we would argue that the two are inseparable. A failure to understand this verity will destroy the chaplaincy as we know it today.

How then can the two be complementary? That's the question we hope to answer in the following pages. There is a scarcity of published works on the U.S. military chaplaincy and the majority of those are historical in scope. *Matters of Conscience* is a practical guide for today's military chaplain, an attempt to blend history and theology into a biblically-based, hands-on resource divided into three parts.

Using a scriptural metaphor found in James 1:22 – "Be doers of the word, not hearers only" – *Part One* is the hearing; *Part Two* and *Part Three* are the doing. The first section speaks to the historical and constitutional boundaries of the chaplaincy and the policy directives that govern the day-to-day activities of its chaplains. The rest of the book suggests how the Christian chaplain can work within these perimeters; a field manual, if you will. All three parts are needed for the chaplain to fulfill his calling from God and country. One must be aware of the boundaries to safely reach his destination, but the rubber-meeting-the-road is where ministry is validated. By providing the following chapter overviews – a map for the evangelical chaplain's journey – your authors hope to encourage the reader to walk with us.

---

14 AR 165-1, Chapter 1-5.b.

Part One – THE BOUNDARIES

The military chaplaincy is arguably the most specialized, yet far reaching ministry within Christendom. Granted, the Lord calls some to be evangelists, some to be pastors, and some to teach[15] but only the military chaplain is called to be all three, to all people, at all times, in all places – in war and peace.

The conservative Christian chaplain makes two promises. The first is a confession of faith: "I believe that Jesus Christ is the Son of God."[16] The second is an oath of office: "I do solemnly swear that I will support and defend the Constitution of the United States against all enemies, foreign and domestic...."[17] Though the eternal trumps the temporal, both promises call for the ultimate commitment. To be willing to sacrifice one's life for faith or patriotism runs counter to the natural instinct of "survival at all cost," but the human spirit is more than natural, it is supernatural. We are created in the image of God and as such we have the capability to rise above our egocentric nature and, if need be, sacrifice our lives for God or country.

For that reason, we consider the military chaplaincy the most noble of all Christian ministries; however, if you feel the nudging of the Holy Spirit to pursue this calling, do so with your eyes wide open. Know the boundaries levied by the Department of Defense to meet an ever changing congressional docket. As for the reader who finds himself already engaged in the chaplaincy, pay attention to the policy directives of your respective branch of service. Boundaries can be moved, regulations change, and policy directives are rewritten regularly. Should the time come when the chaplain's ultimate allegiance to Jesus Christ is usurped by the government, there is only one honorable option, resign your commission and return to civilian ministry! Callings are seasonal but one's faith in Christ is timeless.

---

15 *Cf.* Eph. 4:11

16 *Cf.* Acts 8:37

17 "Oaths of Enlistment and Oaths of Office," *Center of Military History, United States Army* at http://www.history.army.mil/html/faq/oaths.html.

Chapter One – Was America Founded as a Christian Nation?

What happened on America's journey from 1620 to present day?[18] Even the most ardent critics of Christianity admit that our Founders were religious men and that our nation of laws was predicated on the biblical truths from Holy Scripture.

In his insightful book, *American Gospel*, author Jon Meacham proposed that colonial America was "a place of people whose experience with religious violence and the burdens of established churches led them to view religious liberty as one of humankind's natural rights ...."[19] Though adamant in establishing a government free from the entanglement of religion, there is no doubt that the Founders' Judeo-Christian[20] ideals were imbued into the Constitution, where religious freedom was "a right as natural and as significant as those of thought and expression."[21] However, in today's largely uninformed and indifferent society, there is a skewed disconnect from our national heritage.

Much of the rhetoric in the public square seems to revolve around the question "Was America 'founded' as a Christian nation?" There is no shortage of passion on both political sides of the dispute but what if the question only blurs the real issue? Perhaps the better question is, "Was America predominantly 'Christian' at its founding?"

Chapter Two – Pluralistic Quagmires

Who is America? Its people have never been the selected aristocracy of the world's nations, but as we read on the base of the Statue of Liberty, we are "the tired, poor, and huddled masses" of the world's peoples. No one individual

---

18 Fleeing from religious persecution, a small group of people (known as the Separatists) signed the Mayflower Compact, the first governing document of Plymouth Colony, on Nov. 11, 1620. This is an appropriate date to begin America's religious journey.

19 Jon Meacham, *American Gospel* (NY: Random House, 2006), 84.

20 Yale Professor of Law, Stephen L. Carter suggests "the rhetoric of the Judeo-Christian tradition may have originated in efforts to overcome entrenched anti-Semitism in the nineteenth century" though he also notes the important similarities between Christianity and Judaism. It's an excellent discussion of the validity of the description, and deserves the reader's attention. Stephen L. Carter, *The Culture of Disbelief* (NY: Harper Collins Publishers, 1993), 87-89.

21 Meacham, 84.

person or group makes up America. As a nation of immigrants, we have accepted a form of pluralistic rule for centuries, as the Army Deputy Chief of Chaplains, Charles McDonnell, reminded his audience in 1987,

> We live in a nation where religious, cultural, ethnic, and linguistic pluralism is the rule. Our national motto E Pluribus Unum describes the American phenomenon. We are many seeking a [sic] oneness which is not a homogenized, unified religion, watered down beyond recognition; but a [sic] oneness of purpose, of toleration, of spiritual identity. I have a right to be unique – and to defend the rights of others to be unique.[22]

Soldiers work, worship, and fight side-by-side. The word unique may be overused in our vernacular but when describing the military community, it is on-target. The military, in combat or training, is unlike any civilian setting. This is as true for chaplains as it is for soldiers. Military clergy have learned to adapt and thrive within such diversity while retaining their own faith identity. Each one's uniqueness can contribute to the strength of the whole or create such havoc as to destroy a team's unity. So, is there unanimity among our Christian chaplains and, if so, how does this occur? Generally speaking, "yes," but it is an agreement based solely on the individual chaplain's personal faith and denominational core belief.

Christianity is steeped in tradition, and every Christian movement – from the apostolic period to present day – has delineated its differences with a litany of credos.[23] Though these traditions are critical to their denominational identity, when the layers are peeled away and the core is uncovered, there is a common belief (*kérygma*) that every denomination considers immutable: "Jesus is Lord."[24] This ancient *credo* served as the only doctrinal test of fellowship for

---

22   Charles McDonnell, "Multi-Cultural and the Unit Ministry Team," *Military Chaplain's Review* (Fall 1987), 77. Taken from a speech delivered by Chaplain, Brigadier General, Charles J. McDonnell at a conference on "Multi-Cultural Ministry in the U.S. Army Chaplaincy" in Atlanta, Georgia, Spring 1987.

23   There are some denominations who claim they have no creed, but in fact, they have certain beliefs that serve as "tests of fellowship" to which all participants must adhere to be counted as *bona fide* members; *de facto*, an "oral" creed.

24   *Cf.* Rom. 10:9; 1 Cor. 12:3

the New Testament church and serves today among many Christian chaplains as the baseline for cooperation among a diversified Protestant chaplaincy.[25]

The greater pluralistic challenge seldom takes place with the soldier or commander in the field; it occurs when you sit around a chapel table with your colleagues from diverse Christian traditions trying to professionally hammer out the theological differences when having to plan a worship service or produce a strategic plan. If given the opportunity by the Senior Chaplain, each chaplain has to work conscientiously through these differences before arriving at consensus.

For example, by the end of my first year as an Air Force chaplain, I (Whittington) discovered that the only way such a diverse group of Christian ministers could function as a team was to focus on the two things that everyone had in common – patriotism and Jesus Christ.[26] These two loyalties provided the boundaries of my career. Did the latter resolve all religious issues? No, but it provided a true foundation for me to ensure that my faith was grounded in Jesus Christ while at the same time allowing me the freedom to facilitate everyone's right to their own religious expression. My self-imposed motto was, "Apart from Christ, nothing really matters." This truth served as my singular "line in the sand" and was non-negotiable. Defending this single *credo* with "gentleness and reverence"[27] enabled me to safely navigate the waters of pluralism.

To be candid, I did experience some discord among colleagues, but to be equally honest, this was the exception, not the rule. Working within religious diversity (even among Christians) demands that the chaplains work together to facilitate religious freedom and is as much a matter of tenor and timing as it is with the words we use. When Hans Küng, emeritus professor at the

---

25 I am not suggesting a "demythologizing" process that strips away the incarnation, virgin birth, and miracles to arrive at the *kerygma* of the Gospel (e.g. as in Rudolf Bultmann's writings); rather a willingness to forego one's denominational customs to arrive at a common belief that is core to all Christian traditions.

26 Concisely conveyed in the ancient Christian symbol of the *Ichthys* (Greek: fish). The Greek word served as an acrostic with each letter representing Ἰησοῦς Χριστός, Θεοῦ Υἱός, Σωτήρ (Jesus Christ, God's Son, Savior). A simple drawing of this symbol in the dirt was enough for the underground church to identify a Christian in the first three centuries.

27 *Cf.* 1 Pt. 3:15

University of Tübingen, rhetorically asked, "Is Christ divided?"[28] he was considering the existing state of the universal church. Willing to forego one's ecclesiastical traditions and focus exclusively on Jesus Christ, the Protestant chapel, at any given military installation, answers that question every Sunday with a resounding, "Christ is not divided."

Of course, there are always exceptions to a unified chaplain team, and the most notable in my career occurred while I was the Senior Staff Chaplain for the United States Air Force Academy.

Chapter Three – Censoring Military Chaplains – A Case Study

Conducting ministry within military boundaries is the chaplain's challenge. Sometimes it is hard to visualize how the evangelical chaplain can remain true to Jesus Christ while following military regulation, but in fact, these government guidelines also serve to protect the religious rights of the chaplain. Demonstrating one facet of this dynamic (protecting the chaplain's freedom of speech in the pulpit) is a case study taken directly from the church/state debacle at the Air Force Academy (AFA) in 2004-2005.

Written from the perspective of the Senior Staff Chaplain (Colonel Whittington), the study begins with an accusation levied against a conservative chaplain for preaching in a "stridently evangelical tone." As his supervisor, Chaplain Whittington was encouraged to "reconsider the worship dynamics" and order his subordinate to soften his rhetoric or be removed from the pulpit. The suggestion was not only naïve but unconstitutional; an interpretation corroborated in the writings of Jay Sekulow and Robert Ash from the American Center of Law and Justice.

> As the court in *Rigdon v. Perry* aptly noted, "While military chaplains may be employed by the military to perform religious duties, it does not follow that every word they utter bears the imprimatur of official military authority; if anything, the content of their services and

---

28 Hans Küng, "Is Christ's Table Divided"? *International Christian Digest* (ICD) 1:7 (Sep 1987), 37.

counseling bears the imprimatur of the religious ministries to which they belong." From that, the *Rigdon* court concluded that there was "no need for heavy-handed censorship, and any attempt to impinge on the [chaplain's] constitutional and legal rights [wa]s not acceptable."[29]

The incident went into crisis mode when (at the same time) complaints from religious minorities surfaced among the cadets, followed by a frenzied media attack against evangelical Christians.

Serving as a segue to *Part Two*, the AFA case study revealed that in order for the chaplain to attend to the religious needs of the troops – inside and outside the chapel walls – he must know his boundaries and share the message of Christ with the utmost courtesy.

Part Two – MINISTRY "INSIDE" THE WALLS

In chaplain parlance, "ministry inside the walls" describes the day-to-day work of the chapel team – chaplains, chaplain assistants, paid civilian staff, and volunteers. The typical chapel serves the military family community in much the same way a local church supports a civilian community – by providing inspirational worship on Sunday and meaningful religious programs during the week. Both require the presence of strong pastoral leadership.

Chapter Four – Servant Leadership

Unlike his civilian counterpart, the military chaplain cannot visit his community (the size of a small American town), without those to whom he ministers knowing that he outranks eighty-eight percent of them.[30] Yes,

---

29 *Rigdon v. Perry*, 962 F. Supp. 150 (D.D.C. 1997) cited in Jay Alan Sekulow and Robert W. Ash, "The Religious Rights of Those in Uniform," *Journal of Faith & War* (July 10, 2011), http://faithandwar.org/index.php?option=com_content&view=article&id=126%3%20Athe-religious-rights-of-those-in-uniform&catid=44%3Astrategic-leadership&Itemid=55&showall=1(accessed Jan. 5, 2012). Jay Sekulow is Chief Counsel for the American Center of Law and Justice; Robert W. Ash is the ACLJ's Senior Litigation Counsel for National Security Law.

30 Upon entering the Armed Forces, chaplains are commissioned as First Lieutenants (O-2). O-2 and above comprise approximately 12% of all military personnel. See United States Office of the Under Secretary of Defense for Acquisition, Technology, and Logistics, September 2011, at http://siadapp.dmdc.osd.mil/personnel/MILITARY/ms0.pdf.

it is true that the chaplain carries "rank without command authority" but his commissioning affords him all protocol commensurate to the rank he wears – and every soldier, sailor, marine, airman, or coastguardsman knows as much. If the chaplain fails to understand this reality, he will either be perceived as abdicating his responsibilities or abusing his position, and both are unconscionable as God's servant.

There is no single difference between the civilian pastor and the military chaplain that is more conspicuous than their daily dress. Other than a clerical collar, there is nothing that separates the civilian minister from the community wherein he serves; and even if there is a noticeable *collar* identifying one as clergy, the clothing immediately conveys the office of a servant, one whose presence is there to help. The military uniform is an altogether different visual and the chaplain who understands this will see it as a ministry asset, not a detriment.

While serving at the Air Force Chaplain School I (Whittington) had the privilege of introducing every incoming class to the Chief of Chaplains. The Chief would then share a few thoughts and open the discussion up for questions. During my first year at the school, Chaplain, Major General Sam Thomas was scheduled to speak to a group of Second Lieutenant Chaplain Candidates. As a Catholic priest, who also held the honorary designation of Monsignor, Chaplain Thomas wore several titles: Chaplain, General, Monsignor, Father, Pastor, and Reverend. During *Questions and Answers* one of the young candidates asked him, "Sir, which title do you go by?" Chaplain Thomas, with a bit of a gleam in his eye said, "Whichever works." To a Catholic parishioner he was Father Thomas, to the base community he was Chaplain Thomas, and when asked to intervene when an airman was being mistreated he was General Thomas. Whichever worked!

On the first day of duty, the military chaplain, by virtue of rank, will be looked upon as a leader. Leadership models are abundant – transformational, transactional, participative, situational, charismatic, servant – and there are advocates of each who vigorously defend their position. In our experience at practically every echelon of Air Force leadership – from the local squadron to a major command – the most successful commanders embraced the model of "servant leadership." They may not have labeled it as such but they practiced its biblical principles. Though the model has strong historical ties, from Lao Tzu to Robert Greenleaf,[31] the military chaplain will find its divine origin within Holy Scripture the most compelling source.

Unlike leadership approaches with a top-down hierarchical style, servant leadership emphasizes consensus building, teamwork, empowerment, mutual respect, and the moral use of power. Every branch of the armed forces has at its core, ethical values the Department of Defense considers to be essential to mission success. These values, grounded in our Judeo-Christian heritage, are easily memorized but challenging to live.

Our divine calling demands that we not only understand these biblical virtues, but, by the grace of God, model them by emulating the life of Christ in worship, counseling, bible study, and prayer. All of these ministries occur at all places and at all times – on base, aboard ship, and in the field – but it is the Sunday worship service that defines the chaplain's ministry "inside" the walls.

Chapter Five – A Practical Theology of Worship

Working within diversity is a daunting task, especially for the newly appointed chaplain coming from the civilian community where the most challenging worship issue for many pastors and their congregations is whether or not to sing traditional hymns or contemporary songs during the Sunday service. In a typical military setting, the effective chaplain must develop an appreciation for all kinds of Protestant worship styles: General Protestant, Contemporary, Gospel, and Liturgical. In the broadest context, even the most junior ranking chaplain would do well to familiarize himself with all worship services that regularly occur in the military chapel, which include Protestant, Catholic, Orthodox, Ecumenical, Jewish, Interfaith, and those special worship services exclusive to those in the Profession of Arms. Still, however important it is for

---

31 Robert Greenleaf (1904-1990) is generally considered to have coined the phrase "servant leadership" and founded the Greenleaf Center for Servant Leadership in 1964.

the evangelical chaplain to be familiar with all the worship services the chapel provides, his primary calling from God and country is to excel in that which he controls; his own pastoral leadership. To that end, he must encourage a Christ-centered celebration reminding America's warriors that they are never alone. In calm and crisis, the Lord is their shepherd.

Chapter Six – Building a Protestant Program

Religious diversity is commonplace within the military, but few civilian pastors entering the chaplaincy understand the challenges of building an overall religious program for a diversified Protestant community. Even with a *field manual* it is a daunting task. The challenge is exacerbated when the chaplain realizes, "there is no *field manual.*"

Considering that no two installations have exactly the same mission parameters, spiritual needs, and religious demographics, one can easily understand why such a resource is non-existent. Every installation within a single military branch is unique, and the problem is exponentially more challenging when attempting to provide specific guidelines for all of the military chaplaincies. Still, the uniqueness of each military installation should not preclude one from developing a general template for building a Protestant program, one that could be flexible enough to adapt itself to most peacetime military communities. This chapter provides such a template.

Written from Chaplain Davidson's personal experiences, this practical model describes a fifteen-step process to guide the chaplain tasked with building a Protestant program. Knowing that every installation is unique, the reader is encouraged to be flexible, adapting the various steps as needed.

As Sunday is given to providing inspirational worship services for the soldiers, the rest of the week is dedicated to meeting all other spiritual needs, best accessed through a ministry of presence – an expression understood by all chaplains to designate every venue of ministry outside of the chapel walls.

Part Three – MINISTRY "OUTSIDE" THE WALLS

Alex Montoya argued that a biblical philosophy of the church must be rooted in biblical ecclesiology, "the role of the church."[32] Asserting that the Christian has two grand purposes: to worship and witness, he defined the church as a "redeemed community of sinners set apart to worship God in Christ."[33] The chaplain is called to do both in worship and "ministry of presence." Remember, the Christian shares the message of God not only by the words one speaks, but by how he or she lives.[34]

Taking ministry outside the walls of the chapel is not only sound, biblical theology, but lies at the heart of the military chaplaincy. The ministry of Christ himself was characterized by his taking the "chapel to the people," no matter where they were located – hillsides, plains, sea, wilderness. As Chaplain (LTC) John D. Laing, reminded the reader in his well-written book, *In Jesus' Name,* "[Jesus] went 'into the trenches' with his ministry."[35] In chaplain parlance, ministry "outside" the walls is best described as a "ministry of presence." If successful, it must be predicated on a clear understanding of the dual role of the chaplain as "commissioned officer and ordained minister." Once understood, the evangelical chaplain is equipped to address matters of faith and reflect the light of Jesus Christ in foxholes, at home, and overseas.

Chapter Seven – The Enigmatic Role of the Chaplain – Officer or Clergy?

In the course of our Air Force careers, we were asked hundreds of times, "Are you an *officer* first or a *chaplain* first"? The question is at best, moot; at worst, irrelevant, as retired Navy Chaplain Gary R. Pollitt argued,

> On the one hand [a chaplain is] ... a qualified clergy-person of a religious faith group who has been fully authorized to minister within that faith group's tradition. On the other hand, the military chaplain is

---

32 Alex D. Montoya, "Approaching Pastoral Ministry Scripturally," *Pastoral Ministry: How to Shepherd Biblically,* ed. John MacArthur (Nashville: Thomas Nelson, 2005), 50.

33 *Ibid.,* 51.

34 *Cf.* I Jn. 3:18

35 John D. Laing, *In Jesus' Name* (Eugene, Oregon: Resource Publications, 2010), 3. *Cf.* Mt. 5:1f; Lk. 5:1f, 6:17f

a commissioned officer who has come under military jurisdiction for the purpose of assisting in command responsibility to provide for the religious free exercise of all eligible personnel.[36]

Chaplains are ordained civilian clergy appointed as commissioned officers to serve in the armed forces. It is considered one of three "professional" appointments within the military, the other two being medical doctors and judge advocates (theology, medicine and law). If a chaplain's denomination withdraws his clerical ordination, the commissioned officer is *de facto* no longer a chaplain. If the military revokes a chaplain's commission, the clergyman is, in effect, no longer a commissioned officer. Ordination and rank are inseparable. The challenge for the chaplain, then, is balancing the two.[37] Without the proper balance between the cross and the rank, the Christian chaplain's ministry will be ineffective and short-lived; but when the two roles are complementary, the servant of God is well-equipped to address biblical issues with political consequences.

Chapter Eight – Controversial Matters of Faith

Whether one realizes it or not, everyone has a worldview – the lens through which we observe life and act accordingly. Typically nations, races, religions, and organizations of all milieus (e.g. military) share a collective lens, complete with organizational presuppositions and biases. The individual is no different, just alone. Formed by surrounding influences (family, religion, education, culture, and information) one's worldview is generally absorbed by osmosis. To borrow the common pop culture expression, "It is what it is."

Others, however, have put serious thought into what they believe and can provide a rationale defense. It is in this category where one would hope to

---

36 Gary R. Pollitt, "Synopsis of Issues and Problems," *House Resolution 5122, Title V, Section 590 – Military Chaplains* (June 28, 2006), http://hc.pcr.cap.gov/downloads/hr5122.pdf (accessed Jan. 6, 2012). HR 5122 was the House of Representatives version of the FY2007 National Defense Authorization Act. The final bill, signed by President George W. Bush on Oct. 17, 2006, did not include Title V, Section 590 "Military Chaplains."

37 Interestingly, the Air Force investigation into the tragic crash of the Thunderbirds in 1982 concluded that the lead jet had a jammed stabilizer on the tail of Thunderbird "1" – a component that steadies the plane in flight. In flight, as in ministry, balance is essential to life.

find Christian chaplains, men and women who have dedicated their lives to a vocation knowing full well that its future is neither lucrative nor celebrated. Honestly, who in his right mind would pursue Christian ministry in the 21st century unless he felt called by God? Your authors could possibly envision a scurrilous clergyman in the High Middle Ages when theology was considered the "Queen of the Sciences" but not in today's secular world where Christianity is largely relegated to myth and its ministers, unenlightened.

Called by God! There it is. That's the lens through which the conservative Christian chaplain sees the world, the nation, the military, and the soldier. According to a group of prominent Flemish philosophers, every worldview must address certain key questions.[38]

- What is the nature of our world?

- What future is open to us?

- How are we to act in this world?

It is virtually impossible for any two people, including Christians, to view the world through the exact same lens; but if we believe the Bible to be the Word of God, it is possible to agree on certain biblical premises. In response to the questions above, the Scriptures teach:

- **What is the nature of our world?** God exists (Heb. 11:6) and created us *imago Dei* (Gen. 1:27). Tempted by lust and pride (I Jn. 2:16), humanity rebelled against God in the Garden of Eden and as a result of that rebellion, sin and death entered the world (Rom.5:12-14).

- **What future is open to us?** God sent His son to redeem humanity (Jn. 3:16) and "to all who received Him, who believed in His name, He gave power to become children of God" (Jn. 1:12).

- **How are we to act in this world?** As Jesus treated others with dignity and respect, so we should follow in His footsteps (Mt. 7:12, 1 Pt. 2:21).

---

38 The authors listed seven components, each with its own specific questions. These three questions are central to interpreting one's worldview. For a complete list, see Diederik Aerts, *et al. World Views – From Fragmentation to Integration* (Brussels: VUB Press, 1994), 25.

One's worldview cannot be overemphasized as it serves as the foundation for all thought, word, and action (within the local pastorate as well as the military chaplaincy). As a Christian minister you must be true to Scripture and conscience, but unlike a local pastor, there is an additional responsibility for the military chaplain to facilitate every soldier's First Amendment rights. If the situation requires the chaplain to compromise his Christian faith and ministry, a man-of-faith may have no option other than to resign his commission and return to civilian ministry.[39] Never, in any circumstance, allow yourself to be caught up in the deceitful distractions of rank, promotion, and power. If you do, you will serve neither God nor country.

Within this chapter the evangelical chaplain will be encouraged to synchronize his actions with his Christian worldview, determining one's approach to controversial matters of biblical faith – from the repeal of Don't Ask, Don't Tell (DADT), to the issues surrounding public prayer in the "name of Jesus," and evangelism *versus* proselytism. Though these are important issues, the greater principle is being true to one's faith and conscience. As the reader will discover in the closing chapter, foxholes are everywhere and the chaplain's ministry in the trench is the heart and soul of his Christian witness.

Chapter Nine – Ministry in the Foxhole

"There are no atheists in foxholes." The precise origin of the aphorism may be uncertain but its veracity is unchallenged, at least by America's warriors.[40] Regardless of its derivation, its popularity speaks volumes of the spiritual need of the soldier in the battlefield and its truth has been demonstrated in every American battle from Bunker Hill to the Afghan mountains. From those earliest years, chaplains accompanied American troops in battle. Why? Well, perhaps because "there are no atheists in foxholes." Whenever our armed forces go into battle the chaplain goes with his troops. As a noncombatant, his very presence is a reminder of the Holy. The soldier's right to religious freedom is more

---

39   *Cf.* Jas. 4:17

40   There is no single source one can credit for the origin of the phrase. It remains in obscurity. Though most historians attribute the maxim to the World War II journalist Ernie Pyle, others have been mentioned as well, even Army Chaplain William T. Cummings during the Battle of Bataan in 1942.

pronounced on the battlefield than anywhere. And the chaplain's ministry of presence – providing spiritual care and advice to field commanders – cannot be overstated.

Broadly speaking, "foxhole" is a metaphor. The chaplain will find himself in a foxhole even during peace-time and training. Praying with a young jet mechanic at midnight in the middle of February just south of the Arctic Circle, the hangar becomes a foxhole. Listening to a sailor's marital problems while underway on the USS Harry S. Truman, the ship becomes a foxhole. Comforting a soldier at the graveside of his battle-buddy, the cemetery becomes a foxhole. Accompanying a First Sergeant en route to the local correctional facility to visit one of his troops caught in a bar room brawl, the jail cell becomes a foxhole. Ministry of presence is pronounced, not only on the battlefield, but in foxholes all over the world – every time the chaplain and the soldier share a word.

Enjoy the Read

Matters of Conscience closes with "Ministry in the Foxhole" because that sums up the whole of the chaplain's life. No less than the Apostle Paul becoming "all things to all men" in order to save some,[41] so the chaplain becomes "a soldier, in order to minister to soldiers" that some might believe in Christ and be saved. The military chaplain has also promised to "support and defend the Constitution of the United States," and borrowing a poetic verse from the great Robert Service, "A promise made is a debt unpaid."[42] We are indebted to God and America, and though the latter is temporal, the conscientious chaplain takes both commitments seriously.

It is our fervent prayer that *Matters of Conscience* will help the evangelical chaplain balance his allegiance to Christ and the Constitution – facilitating every soldier's religious freedom while remaining true to his faith. Trusting you have enjoyed reading the expanded overview, we now invite you to dig deeper.

---

41 *Cf.* 1 Cor. 9:22

42 Robert Service, "The Cremation of Sam McGee," *The Best of Robert Service: Illustrated Edition* (Philadelphia: Running Press, 1990, c. 1983), 160.

- PART ONE -
THE BOUNDARIES

The historical and constitutional boundaries of the chaplaincy and the policy directives that govern the day-to-day activities of its chaplains

CHAPTER ONE

WAS AMERICA FOUNDED AS A CHRISTIAN NATION?

I have lived, Sir, a long time, and the longer I live, the more convincing proofs I see of this truth – that God Governs in the affairs of men. And if a sparrow cannot fall to the ground without his notice, is it probable that an empire can rise without his aid?[1]

– Benjamin Franklin, July 28, 1787

The Christian Church – An Historical Enigma (Chaplain Whittington)

On my first day of active duty, I heard my first religious joke. From that day until I retired decades later I would enjoy hearing hundreds of other humorous anecdotes, generally beginning with "a minister, priest, and rabbi walked into a bar...." Interestingly, I have forgotten all but one – the first one. Following a rather heated chaplains meeting, I was leaving the conference room with a Catholic priest when he stopped and asked, "Do you know the most powerful argument that proves God's existence?" Thinking this was a test for the rookie I frantically tried to remember the philosophical arguments for God from seminary (cosmological, teleological, ontological, etc.). Feeling somewhat mentally disheveled, I just said, "No sir, what is the greatest argument for God's existence?" The priest, now visibly frustrated from the previous meeting, said, "The surest proof that God exists is that the Church has survived for two thousand years ... in spite of the clergy." Though I enjoyed a good laugh, I must confess, there were moments in the following thirty years that left me wondering how much truth was guised in the humor.

---

1 Benjamin Franklin (July 28, 1787). Franklin's request for prayer at the Continental Confederation Congress is preserved in the Library of Congress; http://www.loc.gov/exhibits/religion/vc006642.jpg (accessed May 17, 2013).

The Christian Church has impacted humanity in remarkably good ways – establishing universities, hospitals, welfare agencies, charities, and orphanages – but it also has a dark side. Church history is stained with the blood of Christian martyrs but only in the first few centuries was the perpetrator pagan Rome. From medieval Europe to the colonization of North America, Christian blood was more-often-than-not shed by Christians. And religious persecution – as any elementary school student knows – was the predominant reason that those early settlers arrived at Plymouth Rock in 1620. In *Religion and the Founding of the American Republic*, the distinguished scholar James Hutson, reminded his reader:

> Many who settled British North America were driven to the New World by religious persecution, conducted by European states seeking to secure religious uniformity in their dominions. Uniformity was sought by Catholic and Protestant countries alike ... with the result that the faith that controlled political power persecuted dissenters. In the name of Jesus Christ, Catholics killed Protestants and Protestants killed Catholics; both groups harassed and killed dissenting coreligionists. Religious persecution, as observers in every century have noted, has a fearful tendency to be sanguinary and implacable.[2]

So it began; a European immigration for freedom. True, the settlers were in search of greater wealth, land, and the freedom to start over and build what many perceived as a utopia; but it was their faith that served as the core of what would be known as the American spirit. Colonial America's decision to be free of the entanglement of government and religion began 150 years before the colonies declared their independence. And though the Founders clearly wanted to establish a government free of political and religious oppression, they did so as theists infusing their Judeo-Christian worldview into all of their actions.

---

2 James H. Hutson, *Religion and the Founding of the American Republic* (Washington: Library of Congress, 1998), 2. This is a very informative read. Prepared as a companion piece for the Library of Congress exhibition, the research is impeccable and very well written. Dr. Hutson is the Chief of the Manuscript Division at the Library of Congress and a noted expert on the Founding Era.

The Context of Religious Freedom

In recent years there has been a resurgence of authors – historians, professors, politicians, and clerics – engaging in the "America as a Christian Nation" debate. It appears that some from both sides of the issue want to score a victory regardless of the evidence; liberal scholars and fundamental preachers forfeiting their integrity in a blatant disregard of the historical facts. Though not intending to diminish the need for historical scholarship, researching the evidence does not require an advanced degree complete with an impressive list of language skills; after all, the vast majority of all the Founding Era writings were in English. It does, however, demand a tenacity to exert the energy and time needed to read the formal documents and private writings of the Founders, and provide an honest assessment.

Perhaps the greater problem rests with the question itself. There is a difference between asking "Was America 'founded' as a Christian nation?" and asking "Was America predominantly 'Christian' at its founding?" A comprehensive study of the historical evidence is far beyond the scope of this book, but considering the mandate of the United States military chaplaincy – to facilitate the religious freedom of all military personnel – it seems only natural to provide an historical context for the First Amendment by considering five foci: (1) the formal documents – Declaration of Independence, Constitution, *Federalist Papers;* (2) the First Amendment; (3) the Founders' religious faith; (4) the religious demographics of eighteenth-century America; and, (5) the establishment of the Congressional chaplaincy.

(1) Three Formal Documents

Proponents who argue that Christianity played a minor role in America's quest for independence point to the eighteenth-century colonial papers where there is a much greater focus on Enlightenment political theory than on biblical reason. However, noted historian John Fea cautioned that one should not "dismiss this lack of religious language too quickly." He continued,

Though references to God seldom found their way into the formal documents produced by those challenging British tyranny, the Bible and Christian themes were often used in their private writings and by members of the clergy as a justification for the Revolution ... and ... the Continental Congress did not hesitate to invoke the Almighty on behalf of its cause.[3]

Declaration of Independence

Fea was right in his assessment of the original intent of the Declaration of Independence; that it is what it claimed to be, "a 'declaration' of 'independence' from England and an assertion of American sovereignty in the world."[4] However, the document's four references to God cannot be overlooked and at the very least, lend themselves to the conclusion that the five delegates appointed to draft the document – its chief architect Thomas Jefferson, John Adams, Benjamin Franklin, Robert R. Livingston, and Roger Sherman – were theists. Moreover, the same must be true for the other fifty-one signatories, or one is forced to indict the integrity of the Congress. The four references to God stand on their own merit:

(1) When in the Course of human events, it becomes necessary for one people to dissolve the political bands which have connected them with another, and to assume among the powers of the earth, the separate and equal station to which the Laws of Nature and of **Nature's God** entitle them, a decent respect to the opinions of mankind requires that they should declare the causes which impel them to the separation.

(2) We hold these truths to be self-evident, that all men are created equal, that they are endowed by their **Creator** with certain unalienable Rights; that among these are Life, Liberty and the pursuit of Happiness.

(3) We, therefore, the Representatives of the united States of America, in General Congress, Assembled, appealing to the **Supreme Judge** of the world for the rectitude of our intentions, do, in the Name, and by Authority of the good People of these Colonies, solemnly publish and declare, That these United Colonies are, and of Right ought to be Free and Independent States.

---

3 John Fea, *Was America Founded as a Christian Nation?* (Louisville, KY: John Knox Press, 2011), 107.

4 *Ibid.*, 128.

(4) And for the support of this Declaration, with a firm reliance on the protection of ***divine Providence,*** we mutually pledge to each other our Lives, our Fortunes and our sacred Honor.[5]

Constitution

Similarly, the Constitution "was never meant to be a religious document, nor did its framers set out to use the document to establish a Christian nation,"[6] though, the wisdom of its authors did allow for amendments – as in the case of the Thirteenth Amendment – which Fea recognized as an opportunity "to atone for past sins."[7]

There were two influential groups vying for their particular version of the government; the Federalists were in support of the newly drafted Constitution, the Antifederalists in opposition to it. Important figures astutely argued both sides. For our study, it needs to be noted that some of the strongest eighteenth-century advocates of a Christian America were the Antifederalists who opposed several clauses within the draft.

Interestingly, the First Amendment served as the political compromise to ensure Virginia's ratification of the Constitution without the need for a second convention. With nine states required for ratification, every vote was critical. Fearing "a second convention would dissolve into chaos, making ratification even more difficult,"[8] James Madison approached the influential Baptist preacher, John Leland of Virginia, who had challenged ratification because the Constitution contained no guarantee of religious freedom. A deal was struck between the two – Madison would support an amendment to ensure religious freedom if Leland would defend the secular nature of the Constitution. The vote was taken and ratification was secured by a slim margin. Though New Hampshire became

---

5 The text can be viewed at "The Charters of Freedom" government archival website. See http://www.archives.gov/exhibits/charters/declaration.html (accessed Jan. 22, 2012). Bold and italics are included for emphasis.

6 Fea, 150.

7 *Ibid.,* 154.

8 Mark G. Toulouse, *God in Public: Four Ways American Christianity and Public Life Relate* (Louisville: Westminster John Knox Press, 2006), 9.

the pivotal ninth state to ratify the Constitution four days earlier, Virginia's compromise led the way for establishing the Bill of Rights – in the eyes of the Christian faithful, a political trade covered with God's fingerprints.

In view of the deal between Madison and Leland, Professor Toulouse of Texas Christian University, reached an interesting conclusion. He argued that Christians cannot have it both ways. If they defend the Constitution as a Christian document they have to part ways with some of the staunchest defenders of the faith in the Founding Era – the Antifederalists. If however they want to continue to make the argument that America was a Christian nation, they are forced to agree with the Antifederalists who were "skeptical and critical of the framers of the Constitution."[9] Still Toulouse's syllogism may be faulty. Making the connection that the Constitution is not a Christian document; therefore, America is not a Christian nation, is missing the point.

Several authors in recent years have argued that America was not a Christian nation during the formative years of the Republic – an assertion that seemed as ludicrous to us as it did to the renowned historian, James Hutson, who thought the claim seemed "as absurd as a declaration that grass is not green."[10] In *Forgotten Features of the Founding*, Hutson challenged the assertions of several well-credentialed scholars who have asserted that America was not a Christian nation; not the least of which, were Isaac Kramnick and R. Laurence Moore – co-authors of *The Godless Constitution* – and Professor Jon Butler of Yale.[11] In a scholarly rebuttal, Hutson provided the reader with a partial critique of their assertions; most notably challenging their lack of attention to historical evidence.

Professors Kramnick and Moore claimed that the Constitution was a godless document because "God and Christianity are nowhere to be found in the

---

9   *Ibid.*, 160-161.

10   James Hutson, *Forgotten Features of the Founding: The Rediscovery of Religious Themes in the Early American Republic* (New York: Lexington Books, 2003), 111.

11   See Isaac Kramnick and R. Laurence Moore, *The Godless Constitution: The Case Against Religious Correctness* (New York: W.W. Norton Publishers, 1996) and Jon Butler, "Why Revolutionary America Wasn't a 'Christian Nation,'" in James H. Hutston, ed., *Religion and the New Republic* (Lanham, Md., Rowman & Littlefield, 2000), 187-202.

American Constitution."[12] Hutson counters with "Kramnick and Moore must have read the Constitution with as little attention as they did the *Federalist*."[13] Then he proceeded to draw the reader's attention to Article 7 where "In the year of our Lord" was used for the date 1787, and Article 1, section 7, where the "...language does nothing less than write the Christian Sabbath into the Constitution by presuming that the president will not work on Sunday."[14] Hutson reserved more credence for Professor Butler's work recognizing that it flowed directly from "two decades of stimulating scholarship" but argued that Butler repeatedly cited "misleading application[s]" and "unreliable figures."[15]

Federalist Papers

Published from 1787-1788, the *Federalist Papers* were written to persuade New Yorkers to ratify the proposed Constitution. Originally written under the pseudonym "Publius," the authors are "under dispute, but the general consensus is that Alexander Hamilton wrote 52, James Madison wrote 28, and John Jay contributed the remaining five."[16] As in the Declaration of Independence and the Constitution, the authors' intent was not religious, but political. Though the *Federalist Papers* were written to inform the public on the merits of the Constitution, not the virtue of Christianity, it is misleading to conclude that "These essays fail to mention God anywhere," as asserted in Kramnick and

---

12 Kramnick and Moore, 27.

13 Hutson, *Forgotten*, 113-114.

14 *Ibid.*, 114. The portion of Article 1, section 7, that Hutson alluded to is as follows: "If any Bill shall not be returned by the president within ten days (Sundays excepted) after it shall have been presented to him, the same shall be a Law, in like manner as if he had signed it ..."

15 *Ibid.*, 120. The "misleading application" is in reference to the word "indifference" in Hector St. John de Crèvecoeur's *Letters from an American Farmer* (1782) where he claimed that "religious indifference is imperceptibly disseminated from one end of the continent to the other." Hutson asserted that Butler stressed the "indifference to Christian practice" by "repeatedly citing with approval Crèvecoeur's misleading application of this term to the citizens of the new republic." See Hutson, *Forgotten*, 114, 120. The "unreliable figures" is in reference to the conclusion of two sociologists, Rodney Stark and Roger Finke, from an article published in 1988 concluding that church membership in the Founding Era was in the 10-20 % range. Hutson writes, "Confidence in Stark and Finke is shaken by their casual regard for facts." *Ibid.*, 116.

16 For a complete archive of all 85 essays, see FoundingFathers.info at http://www.foundingfathers.info/federalistpapers/.

Moore's *The Godless Constitution*.[17] When one takes the time to read the collection, the claim is false.

In *Federalist 2*, John Jay alluded to "Providence" in three successive paragraphs crediting the "design of Providence" for protecting our fledgling nation "throughout a long and bloody war."[18] If the reader is tempted to interpret "Providence" as a reference to nature and not God (an argument that loses sight of the context), then *Federalist 37* removes all doubt. James Madison "ascribes the success of the Philadelphia Convention to God's power"[19] with unmistakable clarity, "When the Almighty himself condescends to address mankind in their own language, his meaning, luminous as it must be, is rendered dim and doubtful by the cloudy medium through which it is communicated."[20] In *Federalist 43*, Madison once again invokes the name of God; by arguing that the Constitution should indeed supersede the *Articles of Confederation*, he appeals to the "transcendent law of nature and of nature's God, which declares that the safety and happiness of society are the objects at which all political institutions aim, and to which all such institutions must be sacrificed."[21]

Returning to the question "Was America predominantly 'Christian' at its founding?" one could argue that it depends upon semantics. If the sole criterion is the number of times Christian language is used in the formal documents of the American Revolution – specifically, the Declaration of Independence, the Constitution, and the *Federalist Papers* – then the answer is arguably, "no." Yet who defines a people with the legal rhetoric of formal documents? Even if one looks exclusively at the formal documents the case could be made that, though the language has few direct references to the Judeo-Christian God, the whole of the revolutionary movement was infused with Christian vernacular and values.

---

17 Kramnick and Moore, 31.

18 *Federalist 2*, paragraphs 4-6.

19 Hutson, *Forgotten*, 113.

20 Note the eleventh paragraph of *Federalist 37*.

21 *Federalist 43*, section 9, paragraph 3.

That the Founders believed America's exceptional status in the world was due, in no small part, to God's providential care is without challenge. As Jon Meacham argued, "...even the most single-minded advocates of religious freedom were personally motivated and inspired by religious convictions." Referencing *Federalist 37*, Meacham reminded his readers that James Madison attributed America's "relief in the critical stages of the revolution" to the "finger of that Almighty hand,"[22] but it was the "elusive, shape-shifting Franklin [who] was even more sentimental than Madison about God's hand in the framing of the new government."[23] Borrowing from Scripture and history, Franklin cajoled:

> I have lived, sir, a long time; and the longer I live, the more convincing proofs I see of this truth, *that God governs in the affairs of men!* And if a sparrow cannot fall to the ground without his notice, is it probable that an empire can rise without his aid? We have been assured, sir, in the sacred writings, that except the lord build the house, they labor in vain that build it. I firmly believe this; and I also believe that without his concurring aid, we shall succeed in this political building no better than the builders of Babel: we shall be divided by our little partial local interests, our projects will be confounded and we ourselves shall become a reproach and a byword down to future ages. And what is worse, mankind may hereafter, from this unfortunate instance, despair of establishing government by human wisdom, and leave it to chance, war and conquest.[24]

Benjamin Franklin was not alone in his conviction that the God of the Bible was providentially engaged in the founding of America. Hutson described the representatives of the Continental Confederation Congress (1774-1789), as "deeply religious men." He then added,

> With little official power, a small and often absentee membership, and no permanent home, [these deeply religious men] defeated the world's greatest military power, concluded the most successful peace treaty in

---

22 Meacham, 87-88.

23 *Ibid.,* 88.

24 Benjamin Franklin, request for prayer at the Continental Confederation Congress (July 28, 1787); cited in Meacham, 89.

American history, survived severe economic turbulence, and devised a brilliant plan for settling the American West. Equally remarkable was the energy Congress invested in encouraging the practice of religion throughout the new nation, energy that far exceeded the amount expended by any subsequent American national government."[25]

If ever there were a Davidic-type covenant between God and government, it was the founding era of this Republic. Not a theocracy, but a clear understanding that both God and government had a role to play, and if either one chose to dissociate from the other, failure was imminent. Because of this tension – the struggle to understand the relationship between God and government – religion became the first subject of the Bill of Rights.

(2) The First Amendment of the Constitution

The deliberations that led to the ratification of the newly drafted Constitution – though long and arduous – were not without merit. Without a centralized power to stabilize the currency, regulate commerce, levy taxes, pay off war debts, and guarantee balance among the three branches of government, proponents of the new Constitution believed the nation could not survive. The Antifederalists conceded that the Articles of Confederation did not provide adequate centralized authority for the new Republic but were suspicious that too much political power in the hands of a few could evolve into a new kind of tyranny. To garner support for ratification a compromise was reached between the two parties that guaranteed the rights of the individuals and states. Of the twelve amendments proposed on September 25, 1789 by the First Congress of the United States; ten were ratified in December of 1791. Known as the Bill of Rights these ten amendments formulated our basic liberties, not the least of which was our freedom of religion.

"Congress shall make no law respecting an establishment of religion, or prohibiting the free exercise thereof...." So begins the First Amendment, which guaranteed our religious freedom, the "most inalienable and sacred of

---

25   *Ibid.*

all human rights" according to Thomas Jefferson.[26] Every American should take note that religion is the first subject of the First Amendment, suggesting a perceived need even greater than the revered freedoms of speech, press, assembly, and petition. That may be surprising in today's secular climate, but in the Founding Era, one's freedom to live, work, and worship without the entanglement of the government was at the forefront of the revolutionary movement. The First Amendment consists of only sixteen words in two brief clauses, but volumes have been needed to explain its application.

The Establishment Clause – Protecting the Church

Defending the first clause in today's political climate, one might argue that the Framers wanted to protect the state from over-zealous Christians. Yet students of American history know otherwise, as Yale Professor Stephen Carter explained:

> ...we actually know a great deal about the history of the Establishment Clause and about the development of the ideal of a separated church and state ... In particular, we know that for most members of the Founding Generation the idea of separating church from state meant protecting the church from the state – not the state from the church.[27]

With full knowledge of their own history, the Founders were adamant about protecting religious organizations from the overreaching hand of the state. Even in James *Madison's Memorial and Remonstrance,* a document often cited to advocate a clear separation of church and state, Madison "frames the argument principally as a protection of the church, not as a protection of the state."[28]

It is a misconception that Jefferson advocated a secular government with no role for religion; on the contrary, he "shared the general view that government

---

26 Thomas Jefferson, "Freedom of Religion at the University of Virginia" (October 7, 1822) in *The Complete Jefferson,* ed. Saul K. Padover, (New York: Duell, Sloan & Pierce, 1943), 958.

27 Carter, 115.

28 *Ibid.,* 116. Madison's document (1785) was written "to defeat Patrick Henry's bill to support all churches in Virginia by assessments from the population at large," and is often taken out of its original context by those wanting to remove all semblance of religion from the public square.

support for religion was not in itself an evil, but that the state had to be prevented from exercising coercive authority over the religions...."[29] In sum, the Founders believed the government should not be entangled in the affairs of the church, but their initial intent was to protect the church, not the state. To ensure such protection, there needed to be a "wall of separation" between the two.

Though the metaphor of a "wall of separation" was first used by Roger Williams defending the Christian's right "to worship without the interference of the state,"[30] the familiar phrase is generally attributed to Thomas Jefferson, from a letter to the Danbury Baptist Association in Connecticut.

As a religious minority, the Connecticut Baptists were upset that the state government considered their religious liberties as privileges awarded by the good graces of the government, not the inalienable rights that Jefferson championed. To their delight, President Jefferson's reply on January 1, 1802 supported their position with these celebrated words:

> I contemplate with sovereign reverence that act of the whole American people which declared that their legislature should make no law respecting an establishment of religion, or prohibiting the free exercise thereof, thus building a *wall of separation between church and state.*[31]

The reader would do well to note that the "wall of separation" was not built by the government but by the "whole American people." Ironically, Jefferson's intent was to support the citizen's right to express his or her faith in public; and yet, these famous words have now become the mantra of those who want to remove all symbols of religion from town squares to state capitols to the halls of Congress. To argue that his words have been misrepresented is an understatement.

Two days after Thomas Jefferson penned those immortal words, "...thus building a wall of separation between church and state," he attended a Christian worship

---

29 *Ibid.,* 117.

30 *Ibid.,* 116.

31 Emphasis is ours; excerpt taken from a photocopy of Jefferson's original letter in Hutson, *Religion,* 85.

service conducted in, of all places, the House of Representatives.[32] According to press reports, President Jefferson even participated in the congregational singing of Psalm 100.[33] Dr. Hutson believed that Jefferson's attendance in the worship service "must be considered a form of symbolic speech that completes the meaning of that [Danbury Baptist] letter."[34] Further study of the historical evidence would indicate that Christian worship services were being conducted in several government buildings in those early days; including the Supreme Court Chamber.[35] Hutson concluded, "It is no exaggeration to say that, on Sundays in Washington during Thomas Jefferson's presidency, the state became the church."[36] To argue that Jefferson believed that religion and government were antithetically opposed to one another is unfounded and a flagrant disregard for the historical context.

The Free Exercise Clause – Protecting the Individual

As the Establishment Clause protects organized religion, so the Free Exercise Clause protects the individual. They are not only complementary, they are mutually essential. This is especially recognized within the military with both soldiers and chaplains. If the government has the power to favor one religion over another, by necessity, it usurps the religious freedom of all soldiers. If, on the other hand, the government stifles the religious freedom of the chaplain – thereby creating its own clergy – it treads dangerously close to a state-sponsored church. Both clauses work in tandem and underpin the military chaplaincy.

Securing the religious rights of the soldier is no different than the constitutional protection afforded to any other citizen. And these rights extend to the posts

---

32 The first services in the Capitol, held when the government moved to Washington in the fall of 1800, were conducted in the 'hall' of the House in the north wing of the building. In 1801 the House moved to temporary quarters in the south wing, called the 'Oven,' which it vacated in 1804, returning to the north wing for three years. Services were conducted in the House until after the Civil War." Hutson, *Religion*, 88.

33 Cited in Fea, 166.

34 James H. Hutson, "Thomas Jefferson's Letter to the Danbury Baptists: A Controversy Rejoined," *William and Mary Quarterly*, 3rd series, 61 (October 1999), 788-790.

35 See Manasseh Cutler, diary, Dec. 23, 1804 and John Quincy Adams, diary, Feb. 2, 1806. Cited in Hutson, *Religion*, 90.

36 *Ibid.*, 91.

and bases where they live, work, and worship. By adding the Free Exercise clause, it is obvious that the Founders intended to protect the citizen's right to public displays of religion. Mark Toulouse's *God in Public* provided this succinct explanation:

> The one thing the free exercise clause does not do is push religion underground. Religion in America does not have to be merely private. It is public as well. Religious practices often gain public notice. For that reason, the second portion of the First Amendment guaranteed individuals the right to practice their religion ... [and] ... the right to assume a public place in American life. In other words, though the institutions of church and state are separated, there is no constitutional separation between religious values and public life in America. Some religions may choose to separate their practices and beliefs from public life. That is their choice ... but the Constitution does not require it.[37]

The Constitution guarantees freedom *of* religion; not *from* religion. Without the *first* amendment, all subsequent freedoms are suspect and the Founder's America ceases to exist.

Continuing with our proposal that America was predominantly "Christian" at its founding, we invite the reader to consider the religious faith of the four most recognized leaders in early America.

(3) The Founders' Faith

In the preface of historian John Fea's informative book *(Was America Founded as a Christian Nation?)* the author proposed that the answer depended upon semantics – how one defines a "Christian." Do we define a "Christian" by a "collection of theological truths that the church through the ages has described as Christian 'orthodoxy,'" or by orthopraxy, "the behavior, practice, and decisions of the founders ... [as they] conform to the spiritual and moral teachings of Christianity as taught in the Bible"?[38]

---

37 Toulouse, 38.

38 Fea, xvi.

Though historians and theologians may differ on Fea's tenets of orthodoxy, it is an interesting test. Of the fifty-five delegates to the 1787 Constitutional Convention, seven Christian denominations were represented: Roman Catholic, Church of England (Episcopalian, after American Independence), Presbyterian, Congregationalist, Lutheran, Dutch Reformed, and Methodism.[39] Though Calvinism provided the foundational theology for the Congregational, Dutch Reformed, and Presbyterian churches in early America, more than one-half of the delegates claimed to be under the confessional of the Church of England – a denomination whose theological roots are steeped in Catholicism, not the Protestant theology of Calvin. Yet, if defining the general tenets of orthodoxy as Trinitarian and a firm belief in the divinity of Jesus Christ, one could label each Founder as orthodox or unorthodox.

Having already noted that the formal documents revealed a measure of orthopraxy (an infusion of Judeo-Christian values with a scarcity of religious language), we now turn to four of the most prominent figures in the Founding era – George Washington, John Adams, Thomas Jefferson, and Benjamin Franklin. Many of the Founders were far more orthodox in their religious beliefs than these four (such as John Witherspoon, John Jay, and Samuel Adams) but none are more widely recognized.

George Washington

Unlike Adams, Jefferson, and Franklin, we have little historical evidence revealing the specifics of George Washington's faith. Regardless, Washington remains the most religiously visual of all the Founders, due in no small part to Henry Brueckner's iconic painting, *The Prayer at Valley Forge* (1866).[40]

What we do know about our first President is that he kept his faith very private. He was christened in the Anglican Church in April 1732, married the devoutly religious, Martha Dandridge Custis in 1759, and attended monthly worship at

---

39   Frank Lambert. *The Founding Fathers and the Place of Religion in America*. (Princeton, NJ: Princeton University Press, 2003), 236-264.

40   Though the chronology of the historical evidence casts doubts on the accuracy of the painting. Fea, 171-172.

one of two Anglican churches within the boundary of Virginia's Fairfax Parish,[41] though as President (1788-1796), Washington attended church nearly every Sunday; St. Paul's Church in New York and while in Philadelphia, Christ Church.[42]

Professor Fea noted that Washington "used the term 'Providence' 270 times in his writings, usually employing it as a synonym for the Judeo-Christian God."[43] Though mistakenly identified as a deist, General Washington undoubtedly believed that God intervened in the affairs of humanity. As Fea argued, "Eighteenth-century deists believed in a 'watchmaker God' – a deity who created the world as we know it and then drew back and let it run on the natural laws that he set in place."[44] The content of Washington's writings, prayers, and speeches reflect one who deeply believed in "the great Author of the Universe whose divine interposition was so frequently manifested in our behalf."[45] The history of the chaplaincy in the United States' armed forces predated the Continental Army, and General Washington's use of Christian chaplains demonstrated his fervent belief that the presence of a Christian clergyman was "a vital and necessary part of the military structure both for morale and morality of the soldiers, as well as the soul of the nation."[46]

When inaugurated as the first President of the United States on April 30, 1789, the general stood on the balcony of Federal Hall in New York City, improvised "So help me, God" at the conclusion of the presidential oath, knelt and kissed the Bible.[47] Repairing to the Senate Chamber, he delivered the first inaugural address where he invoked God's blessings at both the beginning and the end of his remarks.

---

41 *Ibid.*, 177-178.

42 Paul K. Longmore, *The Invention of George Washington* (Berkeley University of California Press, 1988), 115, 118, 130.

43 Fea, 175.

44 *Ibid.*

45 George Washington, "Letter to Reverend Samuel Langdon, September 28, 1789," in *The Writings of George Washington from the Original Manuscript Sources 1745-1799*, ed. John C. Fitzpatrick, vol. 30 (Washington Resources: University of Virginia Library, electronic version). See http://etext.virginia.edu/washington/fitzpatrick/ (accessed Feb. 10, 2012).

46 Laing, 32.

47 Meacham, 15.

Such being the impressions under which I have, in obedience to the public summons, repaired to the present station, it would be peculiarly improper to omit in this first official act my fervent supplications to that *Almighty Being* who rules over the universe, who presides in the councils of nations, and whose providential aids can supply every human defect, that His benediction may consecrate to the liberties and happiness of the people of the United States a Government instituted by themselves for these essential purposes, and may enable every instrument employed in its administration to execute with success the functions allotted to his charge ... Having thus imparted to you my sentiments as they have been awakened by the occasion which brings us together, I shall take my present leave; but not without resorting once more to the benign *Parent of the Human Race* in humble supplication that, since He has been pleased to favor the American people with opportunities for deliberating in perfect tranquility, and dispositions for deciding with unparalleled unanimity on a form of government for the security of their union and the advancement of their happiness, so His divine blessing may be equally conspicuous in the enlarged views, the temperate consultations, and the wise measures on which the success of this Government must depend.[48]

Following the inaugural address, President Washington led the Vice-President, the Senate and House of Representatives in a processional to St. Paul's Chapel to hear the prayers of the newly appointed Chaplain of the Senate, the Right Reverend Samuel Provoost.[49]

With what little historical information we have, it is clear that Washington was a devout believer in the God of Scripture. He regularly attended a Christian church, employed the first chaplains in the Continental Army, and publicly demonstrated his faith at his first inauguration. Whether he was a Christian or not, only God knows, but there is little doubt that he believed that the new

---

48 Transcript copy found at http://www.bartleby.com/124/pres13.html (accessed Feb. 9, 2012). Emphasis is ours. The reader should also note that all inaugural addresses (except Washington's second inaugural consisting of only 135 words) have cited God's providential blessing in some form. See Toulouse, 54.

49 *The Debates and Proceedings in the Congress of the United States,* ed. Joseph Gales, Vol. I (Washington: Gales & Seaton, 1834), 25.

Republic was indebted to God's providential care and intervening power and lived his life accordingly.

John Adams

As ambiguous as the historical documents are in referencing the specifics of Washington's religious beliefs, the writings of John Adams[50] leave no doubt. A prolific writer, Adams' devoutly believed he was a Christian. In David McCullough's novel, *John Adams,* the Pulitzer prize-winning author described the second President as "… a great-hearted, persevering man of uncommon ability and force … [and] as his family and friends knew … a devout Christian."[51]

Granted, his Christian beliefs were not orthodox. As a graduate of Harvard in the eighteenth century, his Christianity was partially influenced by deism and humanism[52] resulting in what most scholars proposed as devout Unitarianism, denying the divinity of Jesus Christ.[53] Still, one would be hard-pressed to consider Adams' lifestyle anything but Christian in practice. Returning to Professor Fea's distinction of "orthodoxy" versus "orthopraxy" to distinguish one who believed in the deity of Jesus Christ and one who lived according to His teachings, one could surmise that Adams "passes the 'orthopraxy' test, but fails … the 'orthodoxy' test."[54]

And pass the orthopraxy test, Adams did! He believed that attending church on a regular basis was extremely beneficial, referred to Jesus as "the most benevolent Being that ever appeared on Earth,"[55] and considered the Sermon

---

50 John and Abigail Adams exchanged over 1,100 letters from 1762-1801. He also kept a series of small diaries written between 1753 and 1804, and completed his autobiography in 1807. See *Adams Family Papers* in The Massachusetts Historical Society, An Electronic Archive: http://www.masshist.org/digitaladams/aea/index.html (accessed Feb. 5, 2012).

51 David McCullough, *John Adams* (New York: Simon & Schuster Paperbacks, 2001), 18-19.

52 See Howard Fielding, "John Adams: Puritan, Deist, Humanist," *Journal of Religion,* Vol. 20, No. 1 (January 1940), 33-46.

53 Fea, 193.

54 *Ibid.,* 192.

55 John Adams letter to Thomas Jefferson, February 2, 1816, *The Adams-Jefferson Letters,* vol. 2, ed. Lester J. Cappon (Chapel Hill: University of North Carolina Press, 1959), 462.

on the Mount[56] as the epitome of his religion.[57] In a letter to Benjamin Rush, Adams wrote:

> The Christian religion, as I understand it, is the brightness of the glory and the express portrait of the character of the eternal, self-existent, independent, benevolent, all powerful and all merciful creator, preserver, and father of the universe, the first good, first perfect, and first fair. It will last as long as the world. Neither savage nor civilized man, without a revelation, could ever have discovered or invented it. Ask me not, then, whether I am a Catholic or Protestant, Calvinist or Arminian. As far as they are Christians, I wish to be a fellow disciple with them all.[58]

Writing to his beloved Abigail in 1775, Adams attributed New England's moral fiber to regular worship attendance.

> New England has in many Respects the Advantage of every other Colony in America, and indeed of every other Part of the World, that I know any Thing of ... The Institutions in New England for the Support of Religion, Morals and Decency, exceed any other, obliging every Parish to have a Minister, and every Person to go to Meeting ....[59]

James Hutson reminded his reader "[In the aftermath of the Revolutionary War] the religious proclamations, enjoining fasts and thanksgiving" saturated the political landscape "petitioning God that national sins might be forgiven 'through the merits and mediation of Jesus Christ.'" He further noted that John Adams implored "the Redeemer of the World freely to remit all our offences."[60] However unorthodox Adams' specific beliefs, his life reflected a devout faith in God and a moral life based upon the teachings of Jesus Christ.

---

56 Mt. 5-7

57 Fea, 193.

58 John Adams letter to Benjamin Rush, January 21, 1810, in *The Works of John Adams, Second President of the United States,* IX, with notes and illustrations by Charles Francis Adams (Boston: Little, Brown and Company, 1854), 627.

59 John Adams letter to Abigail, Oct. 29, 1775, in *Adams Family Papers* in The Massachusetts Historical Society, An Electronic Archive: http://www.masshist.org/digitaladams/aea/index.html (accessed Feb. 5, 2012).

60 Hutson, *Forgotten,* 127.

Thomas Jefferson

Perhaps the most religiously-complex of all of the Founders, Thomas Jefferson was a spiritual enigma. His early life was inundated with orthodox Christianity. He was born into an Anglican home, schooled by Anglican ministers at the College of William and Mary, married by the Anglican Church, and had his five children christened as Anglicans.

He was a believer in Jesus as "the most innocent, the most benevolent, the most eloquent and sublime character that ever has been exhibited to man"[61] but not as the Incarnate Word. Yet he considered himself a "real Christian" (using Jefferson's own words) because he was committed to the moral teachings of Jesus, and believed the purity of these doctrines (if preached to the whole civilized world) would convert the human race to Christianity.[62] John Fea goes as far as imagining Jefferson as sounding like an evangelist.[63] Though he elevated the teachings of Jesus above all other human systems, he did not believe the Bible to be the inspired Word of God. The contradictions continue. He prided himself a man of the Enlightenment, but when observing the universe in all of its glory, he was moved to heavenly praise – best expressed he believed, in the 148th Psalm.[64]

> Praise the LORD!
> Praise the LORD from the heavens,
> Praise him in the heights! Praise him, all his angels,
> Praise him, all his host! Praise him, sun and moon,
> Praise him, all you shining stars!
> Praise him, you highest heavens, and you waters above the heavens!
> Let them praise the name of the LORD![65]

61 Thomas Jefferson's letter to Dr. Joseph Priestley, April 9, 1803. See *Thomas Jefferson, 1743-1826. Letters*, Electronic Text Center, University of Virginia Library, http://etext.virginia.edu/toc/modeng/public/JefLett.html (accessed Feb. 10, 2012).

62 See Jefferson's letter to Benjamin Waterhouse, June 26, 1822. *Ibid.*

63 Fea, 206.

64 Thomas Jefferson's letter to John Adams, April 11, 1823, in *Adams-Jefferson Letters*, ed. Cappon, 592.

65 Ps. 148:1-5 (RSV)

He inherited 135 slaves in 1773 when his father-in-law died and relied on slavery to support his family's lifestyle his entire life, yet somehow separated the individual sin of slavery from its national blight. Jefferson lamented,

> There must doubtless be an unhappy influence on the manners of our people produced by the existence of slavery among us. The whole commerce between master and slave is a perpetual exercise of the most boisterous passions, the most unremitting despotism on the one part, and degrading submissions on the other ... Indeed I tremble for my country when I reflect that God is just: that his justice cannot sleep for ever: that considering numbers, nature and natural means only, a revolution of the wheel of fortune, an exchange of situation, is among possible events: that it may become probable by supernatural interference! The Almighty has no attribute which can take side with us in such a contest ... The spirit of the master is abating, that of the slave rising from the dust, his condition mollifying, the way I hope preparing, under the auspices of heaven, for a total emancipation, and that this is disposed, in the order of events, to be with the consent of the masters, rather than by their extirpation.[66]

Was Jefferson a Christian? Using Fea's label of orthopraxy or orthodoxy, "Jefferson devoted his life to the teachings of Jesus, but failed virtually every test of Christian orthodoxy."[67] Perhaps Jon Meacham, in his insightful account of religion and politics in the Founding Era, said it best.

> Nothing was simple about Jefferson, and nothing is simple about the debates over religion and public life nearly two centuries after him. Neither conventionally devout nor wholly unbelieving, Jefferson surveyed and staked out an American middle ground between the ferocity of evangelizing Christians on one side and the contempt for religion of secular *philosophes* on the other. The right would like Jefferson to be a soldier of faith, the left an American Voltaire. He was,

---

66 Thomas Jefferson, *Notes on the State of Virginia, Query XVIII: Manners*, 1781. See electronic transcript at *Teaching American History*, http://teachingamericanhistory.org/library/index.asp?document=529 (accessed Feb. 10, 2012).

67 Fea, 215.

depending on the moment, both and neither; he was, in other words, a lot like many of us.[68]

Benjamin Franklin

Just prior to Franklin's death, Ezra Stiles, the Calvinist president of Yale College, asked Franklin to clarify his religious beliefs. To the thousands of readers over the centuries who have enjoyed Franklin's wit in *Poor Richard's Almanack,*[69] his clever reply to Reverend Stiles is not surprising.

> You desire to know something of my Religion. It is the first time I have been questioned upon it: But I do not take your Curiosity amiss, and shall endeavour in a few Words to gratify it. Here is my Creed: I believe in one God, Creator of the Universe. That He governs it by his Providence. That he ought to be worshipped. That the most acceptable Service we can render to him, is doing Good to his other Children. That the Soul of Man is immortal, and will be treated with Justice in another Life respecting its Conduct in this. These I take to be the fundamental Principles of all sound Religion, and I regard them as you do, in whatever Sect I meet with them. As to Jesus of Nazareth, my Opinion of whom you particularly desire, I think the System of Morals and his Religion as he left them to us, the best the World ever saw, or is likely to see; but I apprehend it has received various corrupting Changes, and I have with most of the present Dissenters in England, some Doubts as to his Divinity: tho' it is a Question I do not dogmatise upon, having never studied it, and think it needless to busy myself with it now, when I expect soon an Opportunity of knowing the Truth with less Trouble.[70]

His parents were pious Puritans, attending the old South Church in Boston where Benjamin was baptized in 1706.[71] Though reared on a heavy religious diet of New England Calvinism, he rejected the notion of grace and believed

---

68 Meacham, 4.

69 Franklin edited the *Poor Richard's Almanack* from 1733 to 1758.

70 Benjamin Franklin's letter to Ezra Stiles, March 9, 1790. See *The Founding Faith Archive* for the full transcript at www.beliefnet.com/resourcelib/docs/44/Letter_from_Benjamin_Franklin_to_Ezra_Stiles_1.html (accessed Feb. 11, 2012).

71 Walter Isaacson, *Benjamin Franklin: An American Life* (New York: Simon & Schuster, 2003), 5-15.

that man's immortal soul will be judged in proportion to his virtuous conduct on this side of eternity. In the risk of negating the enormous good that this great statesman did for his country and its citizens, his "virtuous conduct" did not extend to his family, at least from an orthodox perspective. His common-law marriage to Deborah Read in 1730, subsequent absence from her life (even choosing to remain in London upon her death), and his estrangement in later life from his illegitimate son, William, tell another story.

It is unmistakably clear from Franklin's writings, that he believed (as did Washington) "God governs in the affairs of men."[72] Once again, the reader is left with an unsettling truth – Franklin was a devout believer in God's providential care for those whose cause was just and whose religion was lived virtuously, but one who dismissed a salvation of "grace through faith in Jesus Christ" apart from works. Or, in Franklin's words, "A virtuous Heretick shall be saved before a wicked Christian."[73] "In the end," Fea concluded, "he fails the orthodoxy test and would receive a below average grade on the orthopraxy test."[74]

The Other Founders

The Founding Fathers are generally assigned to one of two subsets: the fifty-six Signers of the Declaration of Independence and the fifty-five Framers to the 1787 Constitutional Convention. Though the religious beliefs of the more obscure Founders are scarce, there is hardly a doubt that they all believed in God; from the very orthodox John Witherspoon – a devout Presbyterian and the only active minister to sign the Declaration of Independence – to the more ambiguous George Washington. Say what you will about the specific Christian tenets of their faith, the facts reveal an unmistakable belief in God's providential interaction in the founding of America.

---

72 Franklin (July 28, 1787).

73 Benjamin Franklin, "Proposals Relating to the Education of Youth in Pennsylvania," 1749, in *The Papers of Benjamin Franklin,* ed. Leonard W. Labaree, 37 vols. (New Haven: Yale University Press, 1959-2003), 1:265-266, cited in *The Founders on Religion,* ed. James H. Hutson (Princeton: Princeton University Press, 2005), 57.

74 Fea, 226.

In addition to the formal documents and the religious beliefs of the Founders, answering the question, "Was America predominantly 'Christian' at its founding" demands that we consider the religious demographics of the Founding Era.

(4) Founding Era Religious Demographics

James Hutson devoted a full chapter to "The Christian Nation Question" in the well documented *Forgotten Features of the Founding*.[75] In his critique of "well-credentialed scholars [who] have asserted that the United States during the Founding Period was not a Christian nation," Hutson challenged their claim on two counts: the contents of the formal documents and the religious demographics of early America. Of the latter, he explained that since the vast majority of America's 3,173,000 citizens in 1790 described themselves as Christians, "how can sober scholars claim that the new American republic was not a Christian nation?"[76] He began his critique with an article introduced into the scholarly material in 1935 by William Warren Sweet which asserted (without evidence according to Hutson) that church membership in 1760 was one in fourteen – less than ten percent. As often is the case, subsequent authors have cited these statistics "which have been bandied about for some time in scholarly circles"[77] without providing any reliable evidence.

Moreover, historians who purport that America was not founded as a Christian nation also tend to separate those who attended worship service on a regular basis and those who did not – a distinction between the "churched" and the "unchurched," including the latter in their number of non-Christians. In a very poignant script, Hutson argued:

> In recent years some scholars have suddenly converted the Founding Period's putative mass of unchurched Americans into a godless host whose existence demonstrates that the new republic was not a Christian nation. This radical revision of accepted wisdom has been

75 Hutson, *Forgotten*, 111-132.

76 *Ibid.*, 111.

77 *Ibid.*

motivated by a desire to cripple a political campaign mounted by the so-called religious right which is accused of using the notion of a "Christian nation" as a weapon to roll back political gains by advocates of abortion, homosexual rights, and secularized public education. Reactionaries on the right are depicted as scheming to stamp out such initiatives by branding them as illegitimate on the grounds that they are incompatible with the Christian principles on which the nation was founded ... Those making the case against the Christian nation candidly acknowledge that they are employing scholarship for partisan purposes.[78]

To argue that a person must regularly attend the plenary worship of a recognized denomination to be considered "Christian" is not only unscholarly, but illogical. Though there are many reasons that one may choose to be a non-participant in Sunday worship, Hutson provided the most obvious reason for eighteenth-century America – logistics. Local ministers would often visit "those 'unchurched' by distances and inaccessible locations in the American backcountry" and instead of finding skeptics and unbelievers, "they often found them organized into makeshift Christian congregations ... 'hungry after the Word.'"[79]

The same is true today. In the most recent religious poll, statistics revealed that though seventy-seven percent of all Americans considered themselves Christian, only sixty-four percent attended church at least once a month and thirty-five percent seldom or never attended.[80] The historical evidence supports a similar dichotomy in the early Republic, as Hutson concluded, "Though precise numbers are unobtainable, most Americans in 1776 were members/ adherents of a Christian church," and the vast majority of those remaining would have considered themselves devout Christians.[81]

---

78 *Ibid.*, 112-113.

79 *Ibid.*, 126.

80 "In U.S., 77% Identify as Christian," *Gallup Politics* (Dec. 24, 2012) at http://www.gallup.com/ poll/159548/identify-christian.aspx (accessed Apr. 29, 2013).

81 Hutson, *Forgotten*, 126.

(5) The Establishment of the Congressional Chaplaincy

With the unambiguous references to the Judeo-Christian God within the formal documents, the undisputed faith of the Founders, and the overwhelming majority of early America devoutly Christian, it is no surprise that one of the first duties of the Continental Congress was to appoint the first Congressional Chaplain.

On September 5, 1774, as the delegates from the American colonies gathered in Philadelphia to discuss a proper response to Britain's Coercive Acts[82] the first Continental Congress was officially in session. During this arduous time, many of the delegates felt the need to invoke God's presence on their deliberations; therefore, on the opening day of the first Congress, Thomas Cushing of Massachusetts motioned that "the daily sessions be opened with prayer."[83] In a letter to his wife, Abigail, John Adams implied that the delegates were divided on whether or not prayer should be a part of the daily proceedings; not that they were opposed to prayer being a part of the congressional assembly but – belonging to different denominations – were unsure if they could worship together. However, Samuel Adams, siding with Cushing, eloquently persuaded the delegates to reconsider. Adams continued,

> Mr. S.[amuel] Adams arose and said he was no bigot, and could hear a prayer from a gentleman of piety and virtue, who was at the same time a friend to his country. He was a stranger in Phyladelphia, but had heard that Mr. Duché ... deserved that character, and therefore he moved that Mr. Duché, an episcopal clergyman, might be desired, to read prayers to the Congress, tomorrow morning.[84]

With such inspirational words, the Reverend Jacob Duché (1737-1798), the

---

82   The Coercive Acts (known by the Americans as the Intolerable Acts) were a series of laws passed by the British Parliament in 1774. The laws were written to punish the city of Boston for its participation in the Boston Tea Party. It outraged colonists not only in Boston but throughout the thirteen colonies and served as the impetus for the first Continental Congress.

83   Fea, 122. To view the original source, see Letter from John Adams to Abigail Adams, Sep. 16, 1774 [electronic edition], *Adams Family Papers: An Electronic Archive*, Massachusetts Historical Society, http://www.masshist.org/digitaladams (accessed Feb. 5, 2012).

84   *Ibid.*

Rector of Christ Church in Philadelphia, was appointed as the first chaplain to the Continental Congress. On the following day, Duché appeared and read several prayers and the daily Collect concluding with the prescribed thirty-fifth Psalm. Adams again wrote Abigail,

> ...this was the next morning after we heard the horrible rumour of the cannonade of Boston. I never saw a greater effect upon an audience. It seemed as if Heaven had ordained that Psalm to be read on that morning ... [Then Duché] struck out into an extemporary prayer, which filled the bosom of every man present. I must confess I never heard a better prayer or one, so well pronounced ... with such fervour, such ardor, such earnestness and pathos, and in language so elegant and sublime ... It has had an excellent effect upon everybody here.[85]

Reverend Duché continued in an unofficial role until elected as the first chaplain for the Continental Confederation Congress on July 9, 1776. His office was short-lived, however, as he defected to the British in 1777.[86] Congress moved quickly to appoint joint chaplains to succeed Duché – Anglican William White (1748-1836) and Presbyterian George Duffield (1732-1790).[87] On April 15, 1789, a joint resolution was passed by the First Congress establishing the practice of appointing two chaplains. The tradition of the Congressional chaplaincy had begun.

When the Senate first convened in New York City on April 6, 1789, it appointed the Reverend Samuel Provoost, Episcopal Bishop of New York, as its first

---

85 *Ibid.* It is interesting to note that according to John Adams, the reading of this Psalm immediately followed the news of the British bombardment of Boston. As a reminder to the reader, note how the first *pericope* of the 35th Psalm reads in the King James Version. One can only imagine how the delegates must have felt as the Psalm was being read – that God was clearly on their side in the fight against tyranny. These were the words they heard, "Let them be confounded and put to shame that seek after my soul: let them be turned back and brought to confusion that devise my hurt. Let them be as chaff before the wind: and let the angel of the LORD chase *them*. Let their way be dark and slippery: and let the angel of the LORD persecute them. For without cause have they hid for me their net *in* a pit, *which* without cause they have digged for my soul. Let destruction come upon him at unawares; and let his net that he hath hid catch himself: into that very destruction let him fall. And my soul shall be joyful in the LORD: it shall rejoice in his salvation. All my bones shall say, LORD, who *is* like unto thee, which deliverest the poor from him that is too strong for him, yea, the poor and the needy from him that spoileth him?" (Psalm 35:1-10, KJV)

86 Hutson, *Religion*, 51.

87 *Ibid*, 56.

chaplain. Soon after, on May 1, 1789 the House of Representatives named Reverend William Lynn, a Presbyterian from Pennsylvania, as the first official chaplain of the House. Since those early days, both houses have elected a chaplain at the beginning of each Congress.[88]

Why the perceived need for an officially appointed chaplain in both houses of Congress? Religious skeptics have argued that it was an already established political tradition with no real spiritual substance, but given the brevity of the tradition (1776-1789) set against the recurring theme of "God's providential care" in the Founders' writings, the latter is far more plausible. President Washington explained it best in his first inaugural speech – delivered on April 30, 1789 – interestingly inserted between the appointments of the Chaplain of the Senate and the Chaplain of the House.

> It would be peculiarly improper to omit in this first official act my fervent supplications to that Almighty Being ... who presides in the councils of nations ... that His benediction may consecrate ... the liberties and happiness of the people of the United States.[89]

Conclusion

Within the formal documents – Declaration of Independence, Constitution, and the *Federalist Papers* – there are twelve religious references.[90] Christian references are far more numerous in the private writings of the Founders than the formal papers; not surprising however, as the latter were never intended to be religious documents. Nonetheless, of the twelve, two are unmistakably

---

88 Between 1855 and 1861, the House called upon local clergy to serve as chaplains without any official appointment. The 35ᵗʰ Congress discontinued the tradition of electing a Senate chaplain, and invited local clergy to alternate in opening the daily sessions with prayer; however, the 36ᵗʰ Congress reinstated the former custom. For a complete history of both the House and Senate chaplaincy, see *The Office of the Chaplain,* United States House of Representatives at http://chaplain.house.gov/chaplaincy/history.html (accessed Feb. 12, 2012).

89 Transcript copy found at http://www.bartleby.com/124/pres13.html (accessed Feb. 9, 2012).

90 The twelve references are as follows: Declaration of Independence ("nature's God," "Creator," "Supreme Judge," and "divine Providence"); Constitution ("Year of our Lord" in Article 7 and in Article 1, Section 7, an exemption for Sunday not to be counted against the president's 10 day requirement to return a bill once presented by Congress, which presumes Sunday as a day of Christian worship for the president); *Federalist Papers* ("Providence" used three times in *Federalist 2,* "Almighty" used twice in *Federalist 37,* and "nature's God" used once in *Federalist 43*).

Christian and the remaining ten are biblical synonyms for the Judeo-Christian God. Granted, compared to the body of work represented by the formal documents, these religious allusions are minimal, but undeniably present.

When compared to the private writings of the Founders and the public officials saturating the land with "religious proclamations, enjoining fasts, and thanksgiving,"[91] it becomes abundantly clear that the omission of such language in the formal documents said more about the Founders' vision of religious freedom than it did about the religious demographics of the early Republic.

To argue that the populace at large was predominantly irreligious while the written evidence of their elected representatives revealed a deeply religious congressional body is irrational. Of the estimated three million people living in eighteenth-century America, scholars estimate the number of Jews at about 1,000 with "Muslims, Hindus and Buddhists ... counted on the fingers of one hand."[92] Given the challenges of traveling even short distances – impassable roads during inclement weather, family illness, and the daily needs of farm life – regular Sunday worship attendance was virtually impossible for rural America. Still, some plausible estimates reveal a seventy percent attendance rate.[93]

With virtually all of early America adhering to the Christian faith, it is not surprising that the Continental Army understood the value of the military chaplain. Years before the Continental Congress appointed Jacob Duché as its first chaplain, the state militias had established the precedent of inviting the clergy to minister to the spiritual needs of the troops. Just as the politicians felt the need for a Christian chaplain, so did the military officers in the field, offering to pay the chaplains' salaries "at their private expense."[94]

---

91 Hutson, *Forgotten*, 127.

92 *Ibid*, 111.

93 This figure is proposed by Patricia Bonomi and Peter R. Eisenstadt, "Church Attendance in the Eighteenth-Century British American Colonies," *William and Mary Quarterly* 39, no. 2 (April 1982), 247, cited in Hutson, *Forgotten*, 126.

94 Letter written by George Washington to Robert Dinwiddie of Mount Vernon, September 23, 1756, at Electronic Text Center, University of Virginia Library, etext.virginia.edu/toc/modeng/public/WasFi01.html (accessed Apr. 4, 2012).

Was America predominantly 'Christian' at its founding? In view of the undisputed references to God in the formal documents, the unmistakable belief in the Christian God embraced by the populace, and the official appointment of Christian clergy by Congress, the answer is a resounding "yes."

If, however, one is asking the question, "Was America 'founded' as a Christian nation?" suggesting that Christianity deserved special recognition over other religions, the same historical evidence would reveal an emphatic "no." The clear predominance of Christianity in the early Republic contrasted with the minimal use of religious language in the formal documents and the protection of religious freedom as the first constitutional right afforded the people, spoke volumes of the Founders' intent.

Were the Founders believers in God? Yes! Did they envision a government removed from God? Absolutely not! The overwhelming majority of our Founders agreed with Thomas Jefferson, that religious liberty was "the most inalienable and sacred of all human rights."[95] And from this most sacred right, a nation evolved.

As the Pacific Air Forces Command Chaplain, Col. Whittington traveled to Hawaii, Guam, South Korea, Alaska, Okinawa, and Japan reminding the troops of America's Judeo-Christian heritage (Yokota AB, Japan, National Prayer Luncheon, 2003).

---

95 Carter, 106.

CHAPTER TWO

PLURALISTIC QUAGMIRES

So Paul, standing in the middle of the Areopagus, said: Men of Athens, I perceive that in every way you are very religious. For as I passed along, and observed the objects of your worship, I found also an altar with this inscription, 'To an unknown god.' What therefore you worship as unknown, this I proclaim to you.

Apostle Paul – Acts 17:22-23

What's a Christian to do? How can the Church fulfill its purpose within such pluralism – a dizzying array of conflicting subcultures, languages, and religions? To many geo-political leaders within the Middle East, Christianity seems indistinguishable from its parent and is simplistically grouped with Judaism – both religions considered a nuisance, at best; at worst, arch-enemies of the state.[1] Eastern religions are flourishing and Nature religions are resurfacing from the past (polytheism, pantheism, animism) to such a point that a European political writer traveling through the country has satirically remarked "it is easier to find a god than a man."[2] Nonetheless, there seems to be plenty of room for the atheist as well – astrology, philosophy, humanism – from those who believe their fate rests with the alignment of the planets, to the atheistic materialist whose god is pleasure and the chief end of human existence, and those who deny the metaphysical world altogether.

Where is this pluralistic quagmire? Arguably the answer could be twenty-first century America but the previous description was from the Greco-Roman world

---

1 Robert Jamieson, A.R. Fausset, David Brown, *A Commentary, Critical and Explanatory, on the Old and New Testaments* (Oak Harbor, WA: Logos Research Systems, Inc., 1997); S. Acts 17:16-17.

2 *Ibid.*

of the first century – the early years of the Christian church.[3] Living within a pluralistic culture is nothing new to the Christian community.

The Early Church and Religious Pluralism

Jesus of Nazareth lived and died at the crossroads of humanity. When He was crucified on Golgotha, Pontius Pilate ordered the inscription, "The King of the Jews"[4] to be written in Hebrew, Latin, and Greek – the languages of the three major cultures living on that crossroad. He was buried in a local tomb, only to be resurrected three days later "in accordance with the Scripture."[5] Following his resurrection, Jesus "... presented himself alive after his passion by many proofs, appearing to [the disciples] during forty days, and speaking of the kingdom of God."[6] After promising the indwelling of the Holy Spirit, Jesus "was lifted up, and a cloud took him out of their sight."[7] Ten days later, on the Jewish holy day of *Pentecost*,[8] Jesus' promise was fulfilled and the Holy Spirit descended on the faithful[9] and "the Lord added to their number day by day those who were being saved."[10] The Christian church was born.

Though the first decade was not without suffering, the persecution of Jesus' disciples was minor and limited to Jerusalem and its environs. This changed, however, with the stoning of the disciple Stephen.[11] According to Luke's account in Acts, "On that day a great persecution arose against the church in Jerusalem; and they were all scattered throughout the region of Judea and Samaria."[12]

---

3 It was Petronius, a contemporary writer at Nero's court, who said it was "easier to find a god in Athens than a man." *Ibid.*

4 *Cf.* Mk. 15:26, Mt. 27:37, Lk. 23:38, Jn. 19:19.

5 1 Cor. 15:4 (RSV)

6 Acts 1:3 (RSV)

7 Acts 1:9 (RSV)

8 *Cf.* Acts 2:1. *Pentecost* was a holy day in ancient Israel commemorating the giving of the Law on Mount Sinai. Though referred in modern Judaism as *Shavuot* (the Festival of Weeks), the reason for the celebration has not changed.

9 Acts 2:37-47 (RSV)

10 Acts 2:47 (RSV)

11 Acts 7:58 (RSV)

12 Acts 8:1 (RSV)

Corroborated by Scripture[13] and modern scholarship,[14] the Jerusalem church affirmed every tenet of contemporary Judaism, with the significant exception of its core *didachē* – the belief that Jesus was the Messiah. Prior to Stephen's execution, the early Church was exclusively Jewish – in culture, language, and religion – but this would soon change.

The scattered disciples traveled as far as Antioch of Syria, nearly 400 miles to the north of Jerusalem. What a cultural shock they must have experienced! Though Jerusalem was situated at the crossroads of three cultures, it remained an exclusively Jewish community of about 25,000; conversely, Antioch was the third largest metropolis in the Roman Empire (only Rome and Alexandria were larger) and anything but Jewish! The city boasted a multi-ethnic, multi-cultural, multi-lingual, cosmopolitan populace of over one-half million. Though in those early months, the scattered church spoke to no one except Jews, in a city of 500,000 Gentiles,[15] it wasn't long before the Roman world was introduced to Christianity.

> Now those who were scattered because of the persecution that arose over Stephen traveled as far as Phoenicia and Cyprus and Antioch, speaking the word to none except Jews. But there were some of them, men of Cyprus and Cyrene, who on coming to Antioch spoke to the Greeks also, preaching the Lord Jesus. And the hand of the Lord was with them, and a great number that believed turned to the Lord ... and in Antioch the disciples were for the first time called Christians.[16]

---

13 There is absolutely no doubt that the early church continued to worship in the Temple. "And day by day, attending the temple together and breaking bread in their homes, they partook of food with glad and generous hearts" (Acts 2:46; also note the many references in Acts 1-7).

14 Alister McGrath of Oxford University (in affirming the Scriptural account) wrote, "In effect, they [early Christians] seemed to regard Christianity as an affirmation of every aspect of contemporary Judaism, with the addition of one extra belief — that Jesus was the Messiah..." See Alister E. McGrath, *Christianity: An Introduction* (Malden, MA: Blackwell Publishing, 2006), 174.

15 The term *gentile* basically includes everyone other than the Jew. In the Greek/Hebrew Scripture, the word referred to all of the "nations" other than Israel.

16 Acts 11: 19-21, 26b. "Christian" was an appropriate designation for a Greek-speaking community to introduce. Χριστός *(Christ)* is the Greek equivalent of the Hebrew מָשִׁיחַ *(Messiah)*; literally, "anointed one." Χριστιανός (Christian) was the Greek description for those "belonging to the party of Christ" – a description the Jews would have never used.

From Syrian Antioch, the Christian message spread throughout the Greco-Roman empire – a world filled with pagan religions, mystery cults, mythology, and atheistic philosophies.[17] Though persecuted, Christianity flourished.

The Roman Empire showed toleration to any religion which could satisfy three conditions: (1) exhibit high moral character; (2) be subordinate to the political and social structure; and (3) tolerate the religions of the Empire. According to the Roman authorities, Christianity failed on all three counts.[18] The Early Church was considered by the Roman state as a sect within Judaism, which stood under legal protection.[19] As the separation became more obvious and as the majority of converts were drawn from Gentiles, Christian persecution shifted from Judaism to the pagan population. It is a common fact that Christianity grew in spite of persistent and often severe persecution in the first three centuries, persecution that rose to a crescendo early in the fourth century.[20]

To avoid unnecessary notice of the Roman authorities, Christians began holding their worship services under the veil of secrecy, which most certainly contributed to the gross misunderstanding of the content of Christian morality by the pagans. The accusations varied. The Christians refused to participate in pagan ceremonies and were consequently considered atheists.[21] Their lack of participation in community affairs, which were inundated with pagan ritual beliefs, caused them to be known as "haters of the human race."[22] They were

---

17 *Cf.* Acts 22:28. Scripture is replete with such encounters. Perhaps the most well-known passage is Paul's entry into Athens (Acts 17:16-34). The glory of Athens as the proud city of Hellenism was fading but it still remained a vital cultural center. Paul's message to the Stoic and Epicurean philosophers (pantheists and atheists, respectively) provides valuable insight into how a Christian can engage pagan philosophers. The whole of 1 Peter was written to the churches scattered throughout Asia Minor (present day Turkey), reminding the Christian to "Always be prepared to make a defense to anyone who calls you to account for the hope that is in you, yet do it with gentleness and reverence" (1 Pt. 3:15).

18 H.B. Workman, *Persecution in the Early Church* (Cincinnati: Jennings and Graham, 1906), 382.

19 *Cf.* Acts 18:14-16

20 Kenneth Scott Latourette, *A History of Christianity* (New York: Harper & Row, 1953), 81-93.

21 Henry Bettenson, *The Early Christian Fathers* (New York: Oxford University Press, 1958), 9. Bettenson, commenting on the use of the term "atheist" in *The Martyrdom of Saint Polycarp*, chapter 3, explains that the term was commonly applied to Christians because they refused to worship heathen idols and had no images or shrines of their own.

22 Tacitus, in *Annales*, XV.44, explained that Nero had used the Christians for scapegoats after a fire

charged with gross immoralities. It was said that both sexes met together at night, that a dog was used to extinguish the lights, and that promiscuous intercourse followed.[23] Garbled reports circulated about their worship practices that infants were regularly sacrificed and consumed. Misunderstandings of the terms "brother and sister," the constant referral to "love," and the exchange of the "holy kiss" all contributed to the incredible confusion that surrounded Christian fellowship.

Christians not only replied to the attacks on their faith, but did more. They counter-attacked. Pointing out the weaknesses of the pagan religions and giving positive reasons for believing in Christianity, they began to win converts from all levels of society – the illiterate and the educated. Emulating Christ, they took seriously the central message of "loving one's neighbor," and "treating others as you want to be treated."[24] The whole of 1 Peter – written during the Christian persecution by the emperor Nero (A.D. 37-68) – is an admonition by the Apostle to the Christian churches in Asia Minor to live exemplary lives in spite of the tyranny.

> For what credit is it, if when you do wrong and are beaten for it you take it patiently? But if when you do right and suffer for it you take it patiently, you have God's approval. For to this you have been called, because Christ also suffered for you, leaving you an example that you should follow in his steps. He committed no sin; no guile was found on his lips. When he was reviled, he did not revile in return; when he suffered, he did not threaten; but he trusted to him who judges justly ... [and when conversing with those outside the faith] Always be prepared to make a defense to anyone who calls you to account for the hope that is in you, yet do it with gentleness and reverence."[25]

---

had consumed Rome in A.D. 64. An "immense multitude" of confessed Christians were then arrested and convicted, "not so much on the charge of arson as because of hatred of the human race."

23   Latourette, 82.

24   *Cf.* Mt. 22:34-40; 7:12

25   1 Pt. 2:20-23; 3:15 (RSV)

The Military Chaplain and Religious Pluralism

From the apostolic era to eighteenth-century America to the present day, Christianity is familiar with religious and cultural diversity. We live and work within pluralism. This is not a new dynamic for the twenty-first century military chaplain; ministering to those of different faith traditions has been the hallmark of the American chaplaincy from the Founding era.

The reader will recall the unofficial appointment in 1774 of the Anglican clergyman, Jacob Duché, as the first chaplain for the Continental Confederation Congress (chapter 1). In a letter written by John Adams to his wife Abigail, the Massachusetts delegate explained that the motion was initially opposed because "we were so divided in religious Sentiments, some Quakers, some Anabaptists, some Presbyterians and some Congregationalists, so that We could not join in the same Act of Worship."[26] The American chaplaincy – congressional and military – is rooted in religious diversity.[27]

Arguably, the greater challenge for the Christian chaplain will be working within ecumenism – chaplains from different Christian denominations – not necessarily interfaith (such as Jewish, Islam, Hindu). Sectarian Christianity predated America's declaration for independence but in a free republic whose invitation to the world welcomed the "tired, poor, huddled masses yearning to breathe free," continued growth of religious diversity was a certainty. With a prophetic flare, Lieutenant Commander Nickols described today's chaplaincy twenty-five years ago.

> As one travels the nation's highways, one can see not only the familiar synagogues and churches, but also the new signs of religious pluralism: the architecture of Islamic mosques and Buddhist temples.

---

26 Letter from John Adams to Abigail Adams, September 16, 1774 [electronic edition], *Adams Family Papers: An Electronic Archive*, Massachusetts Historical Society, http://www.masshist.org/digitaladams (accessed Feb. 5, 2012).

27 A 1790 census revealed that 83.5% of the population was English, that only one-twentieth of one percent of the population was Jewish, and that there were only 20,000 Roman Catholics. Martin E. Marty, *Righteous Empire: The Protestant Experience in America* (New York: Dial, 1970), 16. Cited in LCDR James P. Nickols, "Religious Pluralism: A Challenge to the Chaplain Corps," *Military Chaplains' Review* (Fall 1986), 86.

It is no longer possible to think only in terms of Protestant, Catholic, or Jew; we must think in terms of a plurality of religious groups, each group having a constitutional right to express its faith in American society. *Pluralism* is a word no longer foreign to the American tongue. Pluralism changes the fabric of American society and challenges the American military chaplaincies ... How soon the day will come when the military chaplaincy will commission a Moslem or Buddhist as a chaplain no one can say with certainty. But the day will come.[28]

Religious Demographics

That day has arrived, though determining the specific religious demographics of the 313 million citizens of the United States is virtually impossible as religious affiliation is no longer a part of the official American census. Still, 2012 statistical polling has generalized the citizenry as follows: 77 percent Christian, 1.7 percent Jewish, 0.6 percent Muslim, 2.6 percent "Other non-Christian," 15 percent "No religious identity," and 2.2 percent as "No response given."[29] Military personnel typically reflect the national demographics (other than gender), and religious affiliation is no exception.

Though the military chaplaincy has historically sought to equitably represent its service members, there are a disproportionate number of Christian chaplains in the Department of Defense, and an even greater disparity among the Christian chaplains, with clergy from evangelical denominations outnumbering other Christian churches.[30] Yet if not for the evangelical Christian, with a heart-felt calling *Pro Deo et Patria*[31] in this time of need, there would be a devastating shortage of military chaplains and the collateral damage would unmistakably be the soldier's right to religious freedom; for even though the biblically conservative chaplain firmly believes that every soldier, sailor, marine, airman,

---

28 Nickols, 92.

29 "In U.S., 77% Identify as Christian," *Gallup Politics* (Dec. 24, 2012) at http://www.gallup.com/poll/159548/identify-christian.aspx (accessed Apr. 29, 2013).

30 Conspiracy theories alleging a unified effort of the evangelical churches are rampant and without merit. Frankly, such opponents give far too much credit to the evangelical denominations which have neither the hierarchical structure nor the inclination to exert the energy to consolidate their efforts.

31 Latin motto of the Army Chaplaincy: *Pro Deo et Patria* [for God and Country].

and coastguardsman needs Jesus Christ, he also understands the constitutional mandate to facilitate every person's religious freedom.

A Working Definition

And therein rests the distinction between the chaplain's working definition of pluralism within the military community and the technical definition so often bandied about in American society. Christian and secular scholars tend to agree on the technical meaning of pluralism, as reflected in the following brief litany provided by Michael A. Milton, President and Professor of Practical Theology at Reformed Theological Seminary, Charlotte, North Carolina.[32]

- Reverend John Stott – an Anglican cleric and distinguished evangelical Christian scholar – defined pluralism as "an affirmation of the validity of every religion."

- Episcopalian Professor M. Basye Holland-Shuey, said, "Pluralism ... holds to one's own faith, and at the same time, engages other faiths in learning about their path and how they want to be understood ... Pluralism and dialogue are the means for building bridges and relationships that create harmony and peace on our planet home."

- Susan Laemmle, Rabbi and Dean of Religious Life at USC, described the tenets of the ideology of religious pluralism as "... all spiritual paths are finally leading to the same sacred ground."

Diana L. Eck of *The Pluralism Project at Harvard University* expanded the definition with four points:

- Pluralism is not diversity alone, but t*he energetic engagement with diversity.*

- Pluralism is not just tolerance, but *the active seeking of understanding across lines of difference.*

- Pluralism is not relativism, but *the encounter of commitments.*

- Pluralism is *based on dialogue.*[33]

---

32 Cited in Michael A. Milton, "Biblical Preaching in a Pluralistic Culture," *Christianity.com,* at http://www.christianity.com/11569909/ (accessed Jan. 15, 2012).

33 Diana L. Eck, "What is Pluralism?" *The Pluralism Project at Harvard University,* at http://pluralism.org/ (accessed Dec. 15, 2011). Emphasis is in original.

Such a universalistic view of humanity (e.g. all persons are saved regardless of their beliefs) led Milton to distinguish between *pluralistic* and *pluralism*. One, he clarified, "is a matter of numbers" while "the other is a matter of ideology."[34] The Christian lives within a pluralistic society but must not participate in pluralism.

Scripture corroborates Milton's warning. If one believes in the preeminent authority of Holy Scripture, there is no way for the Christian to conclude that all religious roads lead to God. The New Testament is too straightforward for even the casual Bible student to believe that one can be saved apart from Jesus Christ. It may be considered passé to use the Bible as one's guide, but truth is not driven by the generational whims of society; it transcends time and culture. Paul's exclamation "All scripture is inspired of God"[35] is as true today as it was when the Apostle wrote to his protégé Timothy. And this God-breathed scripture is unmistakably clear – Jesus is the Son of God and the world's Savior.

- In the beginning was the Word, and the Word was with God, and the Word was God ... And the Word became flesh and dwelt among us, full of grace and truth; we have beheld his glory, glory as of the only Son from the Father (John 1:1, 14. RSV).

- Jesus said to him, "I am the way, and the truth, and the life; no one comes to the Father, but by me (John 14:6. RSV).[36]

- Then Peter, filled with the Holy Spirit, said to them, "Rulers of the people and elders, if we are being examined today concerning a good deed done to a cripple, by what means this man has been healed, be it known to you all, and to all the people of Israel, that by the name of Jesus Christ of Nazareth, whom you crucified, whom God raised from the dead, by him this man is standing before you well. This is the stone which was rejected by you builders, but which has become the head of

---

34 Milton.

35 2 Tim. 3:16a (RSV)

36 Some scholars interpret the phrase "no one comes to the Father except through me" as "no one comes to the Father except in the aforementioned 'way, truth, and life,'" which could be found in several of the world's religions. The text, however, simply does not support this interpretation. This is the sixth of Jesus' seven "I am" statements in the Gospel of John (6:48; 8:12; 10:9, 11; 11:25; 14:6; 15:1). The text is emphatic – salvation is not obtainable through many ways; only through Jesus – the embodiment of the way, truth, and life.

the corner. And there is salvation in no one else, for there is no other name under heaven given among men by which we must be saved" (Acts 4:8-12. RSV).

- If you confess with your lips that Jesus is Lord and believe in your heart that God raised him from the dead, you will be saved. For man believes with his heart and so is justified, and he confesses with his lips and so is saved (Romans 10:9-10. RSV).

- I do not nullify the grace of God; for if justification were through the law [of Moses or any religious law], then Christ died to no purpose (Galatians 2:21. RSV).

It is an absolute fact that the Christian chaplain ministers to a community as diverse as America itself. Unlike his civilian counterpart, the chaplain is at the beck and call of the entire community; not to affirm the validity of their religion, but to facilitate their freedom to believe it. Your authors appreciated the nuance of Milton's distinction between serving within a pluralistic culture and participating in pluralism as understood by the academic, but in fact, the chaplain doesn't live in the ivory tower of academia; he serves the soldier on the front lines – figuratively and literally. Perhaps Chaplain (MAJ) Scott M. Bullock, serving at the United States Army Chaplain Center and School, provided the best working definition for the military chaplain.

Religious pluralism [Bullock reasoned] is simply the reality of a constitutionally mandated, interfaith body of spiritual leaders providing for the free expression of religion for all servicemen and their families. This expresses the collective effort to uphold the First Amendment rights for all our citizen-servicemen.[37]

Pluralism "Inside the Walls" – The Protestant Problem

All three policy directives (Army, Navy, and Air Force) provide their respective chaplaincies with specific roles and responsibilities. Though imbued

37 Scott M. Bullock, "Faithful Ministry within the US Military Chaplaincy's Pluralistic Environment," *Fundamental Baptist International Fellowship,* n.d. at http://fbfi.org/flm-articles/121-faithful-ministry-within-the-us-military-chaplaincys-pluralistic-environment (accessed Oct. 20, 2011).

with service-specific vernacular, the general responsibilities are very similar, expressed in Army Regulation 165-1.

3–2. Chaplain as professional military religious leader

a. General – All Chaplains provide for the nurture and practice of religious beliefs, traditions, and customs in a pluralistic environment to strengthen the spiritual lives of Soldiers and their Families. Chaplains conduct the religious programs and activities for the Command and provide professional advice and counsel on religious, moral, and ethical issues.

3–3. Chaplain as principle military religious advisor

a. General – (1) Chaplains serve on the special or personal staff of a command with direct access to the commander. (2) Chaplains, in performing their duties, are expected to speak with a prophetic voice and must confront the issues of religious accommodation, the obstruction of free exercise of religion, and moral turpitude in conflict with the Army values.[38]

Chaplains are pragmatic. They generally know the nomenclature of their respective policy directives but certainly don't memorize the regulation (rewritten, by the way, every few years). For decades, chaplains from all services have expressed their constitutional responsibilities in simple terms – providing spiritual care and moral advice to all troops – in worship, counseling, and ministry of presence. There are pluralistic hurdles for the Christian chaplain to negotiate when dealing with the troops in counseling and field ministry, but the greater challenge clearly rests with one's colleagues "inside the walls" of the chapel.

With the constitutional protection of the First Amendment, worship on U.S. military bases is by its very nature, a pluralistic phenomenon.

The impetus for the military chaplaincies and basic shape and structure are implied in the "non-establishment" and "free exercise" provisions of the Bill of Rights. The latter provision implies the responsibility

---

38 3-2 and 3-3 in Army Regulation 165-1 (Dec. 3, 2009).

of the government to provide for access to religious life impeded by the special circumstance of military service. The former requires that the government's exercise of that responsibility stop short of direct sponsorship of religion. The result is a unique and pluralistic system.[39]

This phenomenon begins with the appointment of chaplains on the basis of denominational (and faith-group) availability and the needs of the military as determined by the respective Chief of Chaplains office. Though the system of denominational quotas based upon church membership is no longer used, appointments to the chaplaincy are still designed to reflect faithfully the religious complexion of the American populace. With over a hundred Christian denominations represented, the military chaplaincy not only attempts to mirror American religious society but creates a unique pluralistic dilemma where cooperation is paramount for ministry but denominational identity is demanded in worship, as military historian Richard G. Hutcheson explained:

> Organizationally, the American military chaplaincies are fully integrated. In contrast to the chaplaincies of certain other nations, where there are parallel Protestant and Roman Catholic chaplaincies, each with its own Chief of Chaplains and organizational structure, our chaplaincies are administratively unified. A Roman Catholic senior chaplain may, and frequently does, supervise the work of a group of chaplains made up not only of other Roman Catholics but also Protestants of a variety of denominations, and perhaps Jewish, Latter-Day Saints, and Orthodox chaplains as well. The same title, "chaplain," is used to address priests, rabbis and ministers alike. The Chief of Chaplains may be of any religion. Administratively, there is no distinction ... Religiously, however, each chaplain's ministry is determined by his own church. The right of the chaplain to conduct public worship – and by implication his entire ministry – in accordance with the rites, rules and practices of his own church is carefully detailed in the official regulations of all the services. This clear distinction between the administrative area, which is completely integrated and

---

39 Paul Otterstein, "Theological Pluralism in the Air Force Chaplaincy," *Military Chaplains' Review* (Fall 1987), 89.

completely uncoerced is the working basis of the chaplain's ministry to a pluralistic society.[40]

In today's military chaplaincy pluralism is a spoken way of life, considered by most to be a largely realized goal, but that is far from the practical truth. It is at best a journey, with the travelers being replaced every generation; and in effect, starting over. Though the better part of the chaplain's time will be with the troops, the greater pluralistic challenge will be collegial, working with one's fellow chaplains.

Since differences of opinion are most disruptive when "congregated," the Christian's interpretation of plurality becomes a problem most noticeable during corporate worship. Ironically, this is the crucial moment the Christian church should experience oneness of spirit – celebrating our unity with God and each other in true *koinōnía*.[41] Such diversity has created what some refer to as the "Protestant Problem." While some chaplains define the problem in broad terms,[42] the heart of the issue remains clear; how do chaplains from different ecclesiastical traditions facilitate true fellowship among worshippers (from an even broader religious spectrum) in a single worship service?

This concern was addressed as far back as the 1970s within military communities and from this discussion a greater variety of Protestant services emerged, and are still being used in the twenty-first century military; specifically, a contemporary, gospel, and liturgical liturgy in addition to a general Protestant worship. While this may address the issue of ecclesiology[43] as it pertains to

---

40   Richard G. Hutcheson, Jr., *The Churches and the Chaplaincy* (Atlanta: John Knox Press, 1975), 119. Though published in 1975, Hutcheson's excerpt is as current today as it was when written. However true Hutcheson's assertion, "...each chaplain's ministry is determined by his own church," it is equally true that the chaplain's roles and responsibilities are governed exclusively by the Department of Defense.

41   *Koinōnía*, translated "fellowship" as in 1 Jn. 1:1-4; or "participation" as in 1 Cor. 10:17-18 where the context is the celebration of the Lord's Supper in the plenary worship.

42   S. David Chambers' description of the problem as a theological problem (identity), a pragmatic problem (worship), and a logistical problem (financial) is accurate when the Protestant chaplains are called upon to work together in a single worship service. See S. David Chambers, "The Protestant Problem," *Military Chaplains' Review* (Fall 1987), 81-88.

43   Though the word "ecclesiology" was coined in the 19th century the meaning is as ancient as the New Testament. The word comes from two Greek words *ekklēsía* (church) and *logía* (words) and generally refers

different cultural styles of worship, it does not solve the problem of disunity among believers. Or does it?

Though New Testament Christians were united in their central message – expressed in the single *credo* "Jesus is Lord"[44] – their unity was certainly not based on ecclesiological agreement. There is scanty evidence in the New Testament for a precise pattern of worship, but one cannot read about the churches in Antioch, Jerusalem, Corinth, or Rome without surmising that the liturgy of the New Testament church was influenced by its particular milieu.[45]

For example, the differences between the Jerusalem and Antioch churches are profound. Acts 15 informs us that the Christians in Antioch did not keep the Jewish dietary laws. It can be safely assumed that they did not meet in the local synagogue at the designated hours of prayer, recite the *Shema*[46] or sing the Ascent Psalms during worship as did the apostolic church in Jerusalem.

Christian scholars of the last two centuries have cited Scripture and the writings of the Early Church, suggesting cultural differences in the celebration of the Lord's Supper.[47] The great German scholar Joachim Jeremias argued that the Upper Room meal was a *Paschal* meal.[48] With the textual confusion between the Synoptics[49] and John, some scholars suggest that the Last Supper was another meal which would also furnish a certain religious solemnity and consecration, namely, the *Sabbath* meal (*Chaburah*).[50] And what of the

---

to the practices of the church (e.g. the way the church celebrates the sacraments, its liturgy, polity, method for choosing its clergy, bishops, elders, deacons, etc.).

44 *Cf.* Rom. 10:9, I Cor. 12:3

45 *Cf.* Acts 15, 1 Cor. 10-14, Rom. 12

46 Dt. 6:4-9 (RSV)

47 See *Didache* 9,10, 14; Ignatius, *Philadelphians* 4, *Smyrnaeans* 8; Justin, *Apology I*, 65; Tertullian, *Prescription Against Heretics* xxxvi; *Acts of John* 86, 110; *Acts of Peter* 2; Hippolytus, *Apostolic Tradition* iv, x.

48 Joachim Jeremias, *The Eucharistic Words of Jesus* (Philadelphia: Fortress Press, 1966), 79-83. The term *paschal* is believed to have originated from the Latin (passing over) and refers to the Passover meal.

49 The word "synoptic" refers to the gospels of Matthew, Mark, and Luke. The term comes from the Greek *syn* (together) and *optic* (seen) and it means to give an account from a similar point of view. The first three gospels have many similarities (miracles, parables, etc.) and as such are called the Synoptics.

50 Josef A. Jungmann, *The Early Liturgy to the Time of Gregory the Great*, translated by Francis A. Brunner (London: Darton, Longman & Todd, 1960), 31ff. See also Gregory Dix, *Shape of the Liturgy* (London:

Pauline meal celebrated in the midst of the Corinthian love feast (*Agapē*)? Additionally, F. F. Bruce (one of the leading conservative biblical scholars of the twentieth century) argued that the New Testament evidence suggested "Episcopalian, Presbyterian, and Congregational church orders" in the early church. Moreover,

> The one uniform pattern [Bruce claimed] which can indeed be discerned in the New Testament is the pattern of flexibility which facilitates instead of impeding the free movement of the Spirit as he makes provision for the churches and their members as and when the need arises.[51]

Optional observance of Jewish dietary laws, non-compulsory formal liturgical prayers, different cultural settings for the Lord's Supper, and a mixture of church polity all reinforce the probability that the worship pattern of the early church changed according to its cultural milieus. What did not change from culture to culture, however, was the theological core that imbued every aspect of the church's worship; the *kérygma*[52] of Scripture – Jesus is the Christ, the Son of God. This is important for the evangelical chaplain to appreciate when collegial differences surface.

Pluralism "Outside the Walls"

Discussed in greater detail in *Part Three*, the bulk of the chaplain's ministry is experienced "outside the walls" of the chapel, described in the policy directives as "ministry of presence." Within this ministry of presence – praying with a deployed soldier, encouraging a young airman working on an F-16 at midnight, comforting a distraught sailor on ship in the Persian Gulf whose family is in crisis – the chaplain shares the love of God, regardless of the troop's religious preference. The chaplain's constitutional mandate is perfectly in line with his

---

Dacre Press, 1970), 103. The *chaburah* was the Hebrew practice of male friends sharing a common meal together at regular intervals, generally on the evening before Sabbath.

51 F.F. Bruce, "Lessons from the Early Church," *In God's Community*, eds. David J. Ellis and W. Ward Gasque (Wheaton, IL: Harold Shaw Publishers, 1978), 159.

52 In biblical scholarship κήρυγμα (related to the Greek verb κηρύσσω – "to preach" as used in Lk. 4:18-19) has come to mean the whole of the Christian message, "Jesus is Lord."

calling as a Christian minister. As a reminder to the reader, the Christian is to give an account of the hope that is within him *when called upon* by others.[53] Coercion and a misuse of power have no place in the Christian's life – military or otherwise. Even when asked by the soldier to share one's faith, the chaplain should always respond with the utmost respect.

In Hebrew, the word "meditate" means to "mumble to oneself" (as in Joshua 1:8; Psalm 1:2b).[54] When we meditate on Scripture, we simply recite the Word of the Lord as we go about our daily life, whether walking the tarmac on a remote air base, visiting with a sailor underway, or entrenched in the desert sands of Fallujah. Sharing your faith by "living" a Christian life – the biblical meaning of meditation – is who you are as a Christian, and your fellow soldier will take note of your actions, giving credence to your words. People who live their lives by applying Scripture will be noticed and respected, and that is evangelism.[55]

Common Ground

Several years ago, researchers at the University of Illinois tested twenty pilots possessing only a Visual Flight Rules (VFR) rating. They were each put in a flight simulator with exactly the same conditions – fair weather followed by a storm. The pilots were skilled aviators, but were not certified under Instrument Flight Rules (IFR). As long as the weather was pleasant, everything went well, but the moment the simulator operator rolled in a storm, the pilots began to lose control. And within an average of 178 seconds, they went into a "graveyard spiral" and crashed; twenty pilots who were very

---

53 *Cf.* 1 Pt. 3:15

54 In Hebrew (הָגָה), *hāgâ* literally means "to murmur, to mutter; to make sound with the mouth." It implies "talking to oneself." William Wilson, *Wilson's Old Testament Word Studies* (McLean, VA: MacDonald Publishing Co., n.d.), 271. See also Herbert Wolf, *Theological Wordbook of the Old Testament* edited by R. Laird Harris, Gleason L. Archer, Jr., Bruce K. Waltke (Chicago: Moody Press, 1980), 205.

55 There is a lot of confusion among military and congressional leaders as to what constitutes proselytism by chaplains, primarily fueled by extremists from both sides of the issue. The Christian chaplain must recognize the difference between *evangelism* and *proselytism* (chapter eight) in order to fulfill his divine calling to "do the work of an evangelist" and his constitutional mandate to facilitate religious freedom.

capable of keeping a plane aloft in good weather, but could not survive more than three minutes in a storm.[56]

The Christian chaplain works within a pluralistic community, a religious storm if you will, complete with gale-force winds of doctrine and egos to match. Chaplains need to be IFR rated to survive; to be familiar with the one instrument – the Word of God – that can help one safely navigate any storm. While society may see our pluralistic culture as a detriment, the evangelical chaplain sees it as an incredible opportunity to reflect the love of Christ – to share the greatest story ever told – but without finding common ground with one's colleagues and respecting their individual journey of faith, the chaplain's ministry will be limited, at best.

The division addressed by the Apostle Paul in 1 Corinthians is somewhat analogous to the denominational diversity among Christian chaplains. Paul's solution to division was to remind the church that Paul, Peter, and Apollos were all messengers of Christ. After a lengthy appeal (chapters 1-14), the great Apostle concluded with these words:

> Now I would remind you, brethren, in what terms I preached to you the gospel, which you received, in which you stand, by which you are saved, if you hold it fast—unless you believed in vain. For I delivered to you as of *first* importance what I also received, that Christ died for our sins in accordance with the scriptures, that he was buried, that he was raised on the third day in accordance with the scriptures ... [so] thanks be go God, who gives us the victory through our Lord Jesus Christ.[57]

Note the adjective *first* (*prōtos*) in the above passage. In the Greek text it is an adjective indicating "first in time, number, or sequence."[58] Other issues may be worthy of discussion, but the Gospel – Jesus death, burial, and resurrection

---

56 "178 Seconds to Live" (DOT pamphlet) at http://www.faa.gov/about/office_org/field_offices/fsdo/fai/local_more/alaskan_articles/media/178%20Seconds%20to%20Live.pdf (accessed May 18, 2013).

57 1 Cor. 15:1-4, 57 (RSV); emphasis is ours.

58 Wilheim Michaelis, *"Protōs,"* ed. Geoffrey W. Bromiley, in *Theological Dictionary of the New Testament: Abridged in One Volume* (Grand Rapids, Michigan: William B. Eerdmans Publishing Company, 1985), 966.

– surpasses them all. The early church experienced unity through a common loyalty proclaimed in the confession, "Jesus is Lord,"[59] – the sole creedal test of fellowship and the substance of its faith. The Christian chaplain is commissioned by the President of the United States to facilitate the soldier's religious freedom. He is also called by Almighty God to share that which is of "first importance" to the soldier – the redemptive message of Jesus Christ. Yet if one insists on impressing his own brand of Christianity upon his colleagues, troops, and commanders, he will fail on both counts.

Remember "Who" You Are ... And To "Whom" You Belong

It is important for the Christian chaplain to never forget that one's ordination comes not from the government, but the church; and to be more precise, Jesus Christ! The Christian chaplain must understand that his ultimate allegiance is to God.

Cognizant of the establishment clause that ensures the American people that Congress will not establish a national church, all three of the military services have made it clear that chaplains will minister "in accordance with the tenets ... of the religious organization that certifies and endorses them."[60] In other words, in matters of faith the chaplain's loyalty is to his church; and ultimately, to Jesus Christ. We have seen some chaplains over the course of a career forget *who* they are and to *whom* they belong. And when the military chaplain replaces his theological center with his own vainglorious drive for promotion and political correctness, he mocks the very motto he purports to live by – *Pro Deo Et Patria.*[61]

Several years ago Colonel Whittington was assigned to the Air Force Chaplain Service Institute (CSI) as chief, Education division; responsible for all education and training at the AF Chaplain School. Though CSI taught over 1,900 students a year in residence and distance learning, its primary tasking from the Air Force

59   Phil. 2:11 (RSV)

60   AR 165-1, Section 3-2, *b.* (3). The same protection is found in AFI 52-1, Section 3.4.2 and SECNAVINST 1730.7D, Section 6.e.

61   Latin: For God and Country.

Chief of Chaplains was to instruct the 550 chaplains who annually attended the Orientation, Intermediate, and Senior Chaplain Courses. Within weeks of his arrival, the new team began to notice a common pattern emerging within the Intermediate and Senior course. The students, especially the more senior chaplains, were physically, emotionally, and spiritually tired upon arrival; not surprising, considering their leadership responsibilities. Physical fatigue is easy to treat with a good night's rest, but emotional and spiritual fatigue; well, that's more challenging.

After each class the faculty would gather to scrub the course – similar to a flight debriefing following a training sortie. What the team noticed was not only the fact that many of the chaplains were physically exhausted, but more importantly, some of them seemed to have forgotten their calling as ministers. The staff agreed that though rank, position, and assignments are important to all military personnel, if it is the only thing that is discussed in the corridors, something is awry.

With that in mind, the schedule was rewritten to include a spiritual retreat on the first day of each class – no uniform, no wearing of rank, no electronics of any kind, and no discussion of anything remotely resembling promotions or career-advancing assignments. The retreat was held in a peaceful country setting about an hour's drive from CSI. The early morning consisted of three messages (fifteen minutes each) and a brief time of collective prayer. What the students did the rest of the day was up to them; they could find a stretch of grass and sleep, or take a walk in the woods, spend time in prayer, or read. Conversation was discouraged.

Wayne Oates (1917-1999), former Professor of Psychiatry and Behavioral Sciences at the University of Louisville's School of Medicine, wrote a little volume called *Nurturing Silence in a Noisy Heart.* We recommend it to every reader who covets a quiet moment in a noisy world.

> Silence is something you hunt for. You rarely find it in a pure state. For example, where would you find the most silence in your everyday life?

Simply being alone in total solitude during a day, a week, a month, and/or a year is a luxury [especially for the military chaplain]. Yet, in order to grow silence in a noisy heart, such solitude ... is necessary to our very being, our survival. We can't wait for a cloistered cathedral, a dearly-paid-for-room by the seaside, a yearned for walk in an ancient forest, an untouched wilderness. We need silence now.[62]

Conclusion

The retreat quietly closed with these words: "Remember your calling. You were ministers before you were chaplains, and you were Christians before you were ministers. Never forget *who* and *whose* you are! The Air Force Chief of Chaplains, Major General Charles Baldwin (2004-2008) was fond of reminding his Christian chaplains, "Keep the main thing, the main thing." As long as the chaplain "keeps the main thing, the main thing," treats all soldiers with the religious respect they deserve, and shares Jesus Christ with the utmost courtesy, working within a pluralistic military community will be a joy.

---

62 Wayne E. Oates, *Nurturing Silence in a Noisy Heart* (Garden City, New York: Doubleday & Company, Inc., 1979), 6.

CHAPTER THREE

CENSORING MILITARY CHAPLAINS
A CASE STUDY BY CHAPLAIN, COLONEL WHITTINGTON

Chaplains will conduct services that are within the scope of their personal faith tenets and religious convictions.

– *Air Force Instruction 52-101 (3.2.2.1.)*

"Check Your Faith at the North Gate"

As a member of the senior staff, I was standing at attention as the Superintendent of the Air Force Academy (AFA) entered the conference room in the spring of 2005.[1] Generally the boss would have everyone take their seats, then turning to the Senior Staff Chaplain, would ask him to share a spiritual thought-for-the-day, but at this particular staff meeting, no such request was made. In its place, the lieutenant general exclaimed to all present, "Check your faith at the North Gate." Though I empathized with the Superintendent's frustration, I uncharacteristically blurted out "No sir, we can't do that." To his credit, the Academy's senior leader agreed, "I know Whit" and then motioning to his senior officers to take their seats, the weekly staff meeting began without further comment.

With the United States Air Force Academy (USAFA) reeling from the sexual assault scandal in 2003[2] the USAFA leadership was in no mood for its weekly staff discussion on what had become a full-blown investigation of the alleged "religious intolerant" climate of the Academy – the second crisis in less than one year.

---

1 This case study is written in the first person by your co-author, Colonel Whittington, who served as the Senior Staff Chaplain for the Air Force Academy in 2004-2005.

2 As a result of the scandal the Air Force assigned a new leadership team; issues were addressed and a new climate was fostered to include greater attention given to the "spiritual" dimension.

My involvement began on July 30, 2004 when I received an After-Action Report from a team of visiting divinity students from a prominent university. My predecessor had agreed to allow the students to observe all aspects of USAFA Basic Cadet Training (BCT) at Jack's Valley.[3] Consisting of six graduate students, their faculty advisor, and a chaplain sponsor from the AFA chapel staff, the student team concluded its unsolicited report with a litany of criticisms of one particular evangelical Protestant chaplain.

The chaplain was accused of encouraging the cadets (during a voluntarily attended Sunday worship service) to "pray for the salvation of fellow BCT members" and "witness to fellow Basic Cadets."[4] The students surmised that such "stridently Evangelical themes challenged the necessarily pluralistic environment of BCT" and "expressed a concern that the overwhelmingly Evangelical tone" was divisive.[5] They strongly suggested that my office "reconsider the worship dynamics."[6] The discussion that continued on the heels of the written report was unmistakably clear – counsel the evangelical to soften his sermon rhetoric or assign a different chaplain to preach to the cadets.

Removing a chaplain from the pulpit for preaching within the scope of his personal faith tenants would have been a clear violation of Air Force Instruction 52-101. Moreover, silencing a chaplain's free speech in a voluntarily-attended worship setting would come dangerously close to a breach of the First Amendment. After all, the chaplain's speech, according to Jay Sekulow, Chief Counsel for the American Center of Law and Justice, is not "government speech which must be squelched to avoid violating the establishment clause."[7] Reminding a chaplain of the scriptural admonition to preach with "the utmost

---

3 Jack's Valley is a 3,300 acre training complex located in the wilderness surrounding USAFA in Colorado's Rocky Mountains. It is used for general military training for all cadets but is primarily used during the second half of Basic Cadet Training (BCT) each summer by the new cadets. It is an arduous training environment designed to get the cadets to work together as a team – obstacle course, leadership reaction course, confidence course, assault course, and small arms training. During this training period in 2004, cadets were invited to participate in outdoor worship services (Christian, Jewish, and Muslim).

4 MEMORANDUM FOR CH COL MICHAEL WHITTINGTON (30 July 2004), paragraph 5.4.

5 *Ibid.*, paragraph 5.4.1.

6 *Ibid.*, 5.4.1.

7 Sekulow and Ash (July 10, 2011).

courtesy"[8] is always appropriate; but removing one from a Sunday pulpit for adhering to his denominational doctrine is inexcusable for an experienced senior chaplain.

"Extremes beget Extremes"

The recommendation of the divinity students to "reconsider the worship dynamics" due to an "overwhelmingly Evangelical tone" is indicative of the naivety of the American public when imagining the role of a military chaplain. Restricting a chaplain's message during a worship service would set a most dangerous precedent.

Ironically, many civilian church members (influenced by a largely misinformed clergy) tend to believe that the military chaplain is nothing more than a clerical pawn of the government, directed to preach a watered-down message that serves no purpose other than to appease Washington bureaucrats. Conversely, those organizations touting a complete separation of religion from all government activities believe just the opposite; namely, that the biblically-conservative Christian chaplain needs to cease and desist from all evangelical themes such as prayer and witnessing for Jesus Christ. The chaplain can preach on Sunday, providing he is sensitive to the religious diversity of his congregation and follows a politically correct script.

Both accusations are misguided: (1) The evangelical chaplain is *not* a pawn of the state and (2) is *protected* by the Constitution and Department of Defense policy directives to proclaim the denominational tenets of his Christian faith in the pulpit.

It may be difficult for those advocating the separation of the church from the state to understand that the Christian chaplain's ability to facilitate the religious freedom of the soldier is in direct proportion to his biblical commitment to "live a life worthy of the calling to which [he has] been called" (Eph. 4:1). His willingness to "support and defend the Constitution against all enemies" and the

---

8   1 Pt. 3:15 (*The Message*)

energy he expends to accommodate the soldier's First Amendment rights must be balanced by his ultimate allegiance to Jesus Christ. For the Christian chaplain, the two are interdependent; clearly illustrated in the fact that he is deemed "out of uniform" if the cross is missing.

Professor Toulouse of Brite Divinity School (Texas Christian University) also sees the Christian's role in the public square as an extension of one's ultimate loyalty to Jesus Christ. Drawing from a sermon by Martin Luther King, Jr. – the *Parable of the Good Samaritan* (Luke 15) – the Reverend King reasoned, "I must not ignore the wounded man on life's Jericho Road, because he is a part of me and I am a part of him. His agony diminishes me, and his salvation enlarges me."[9] Toulouse then inferred that Jericho's Road is analogous to the Christian's life in the public arena and concluded, "For Christians, loyalty is never given to the nation only, or first, but rather to God ... Christian commitment comes before patriotism."[10]

My point exactly; though I would add the caveat, Christian commitment, in the eyes of the military chaplain, is patriotism at its best. The connection has been lost on the misinformed American who wants to remove God from the public square. The famous French historian, Alexis de Tocqueville (1805-1859), was on-target when he exclaimed "Despotism can do without faith, but freedom cannot."[11]

"My Religion is Patriotism"

Though the purpose of this case study is to focus the reader's attention on the constitutional rights of the military chaplain in the pulpit, the broader context at the Academy involved serious allegations of a religiously intolerant culture being fostered by Air Force leadership. However, the 2004 "culture and climate" survey revealed less than one percent of the 4,353 cadets had "experienced or observed a person being subjected to adverse discrimination

9   Martin Luther King Jr., *Strength to Love* (New York: Harper & Row, 1963), 31; cited in Toulouse, 43.

10   *Ibid.*

11   Alexis de Tocqueville, *Democracy in America,* translated and edited by Harvey C. Mansfield and Delba Winthrop (Chicago: University of Chicago Press, 2000); cited in Toulouse, 44.

due to their religious belief."[12] Still, any religiously intolerant behavior needed to be addressed; so, in typical military fashion, a team was assembled and a strategic plan ensued. The proposal was a four-phased plan developed by the Chaplains' Office and the Culture and Climate division of the AFA Training Wing culminating in a presentation called "Respecting the Spiritual Values of Persons" – an aggressive strategy designed to reach every person at the AFA by August 2005.[13]

What began as a legitimate effort to remind all personnel of mutual respect, quickly escalated into a frenzied media attack against evangelical Christians! As the media continued its onslaught, serious accusations were levied against individual leaders and the Academy as a whole. Investigations ensued. The media was quick to alert the public to the Inspector General (IG) inquiries at the AFA but strangely silent on their findings – a total exoneration of the institution and its leadership by the Air Force and the Department of Defense.

During the crisis, meetings were convened with all parties – cadets, faculty, staff, base personnel, and leadership. During one of the meetings I happened to be chairing, a professor shouted, "My religion is patriotism." To my unpleasant surprise, I noticed a few heads in the audience nod with approval as I was thinking, "I guess that means the Constitution is the Bible and the government, the head of the Church." And this remark was from a respected professor, and I might add, a friend. The moment saddened me but spoke volumes of America's disconnect from the Founders' intent, for the few heads nodding in agreement were the very ones alleging that religion was too intertwined in Academy life.

---

12 The USAFA Culture and Climate survey of spring 2004 revealed that 98.6% of all personnel believed it to be "desirable to respect those with different faiths" and when asked if they had "experienced or witnessed religious discrimination," the metrics showed a "1.3" on a scale of 1-5 with 1 being "never," and 5 being "frequently."

13 The four phases were (1) Defining the challenge; (2) Looking in the mirror; (3) Turning the tide; and (4) Embedding culture – to "impact a positive cultural change in the shortest amount of time."

"The Unthinkable becomes Thinkable"

Odd, isn't it? If these self-proclaimed champions of the First Amendment have their way, the government would provide the doctrinal construct for the chaplain's message and ministry, and in effect, contravene the establishment clause of the First Amendment. As the reader, it is your prerogative to dismiss this syllogism as unrealistic, but I encourage you to stop for just a moment to seriously consider the "unrealistic" becoming "real," or in the words of Francis Schaeffer (1912-1984), the "unthinkable" becoming "thinkable."[14] Proposed in the 1970s, Dr. Schaeffer explained:

> The thinkables of the eighties and nineties will certainly include things which most people today find unthinkable and immoral, even unimaginable and too extreme to suggest. Yet – since they do not have some overriding principle that takes them beyond relativistic thinking – when these become thinkable and acceptable in the eighties and nineties, most people will not even remember that they were unthinkable in the seventies. They will slide into each thinkable without a jolt.[15]

That which was morally unacceptable in one generation may, in the next generation, be unquestioned. Originally published in 1979, Schaeffer's *Whatever Happened to the Human Race?* is an interesting read for twenty-first century America. With even a quick perusal of the writings of this renowned Christian philosopher, one cannot help but relate our present society's abject indifference to illicit sexual behavior once considered immoral (unthinkable) but glamorized in today's society.

In a similar manner, the Founders understood these certainties of human nature: life's experiences are not hereditary; there is no guarantee that what one generation is willing to die for, the next generation will even deem

---

14 Francis A. Schaeffer and C. Everett Koop, *Whatever Happened to the Human Race?* Volume Five of *The Complete Works of Francis A. Schaeffer: A Christian Worldview* (Westchester, Illinois: Crossway Books, 1982), 282. Dr. Schaeffer was a prolific author and one of the most influential Christian philosophers of the twentieth century.

15 *Ibid.,* 283.

worthy to defend; and that which was unthinkable in one generation, may be thinkable in the next. Knowing this, they provided certain boundaries within the Constitution to ensure that the power exercised by the government – even in the most subtle of ways – could not be used to unduly influence its citizenry. In other words, the church is not the mouthpiece of the government, even if the clergy dons a military uniform and is paid from the federal coffer.

United States Air Force Academy basic cadets take the Oath of Office before participating in the demanding Basic Cadet Training in Jack's Valley. In the background is the Cadet Chapel.

Lessons Learned

As in all crises, several important lessons were learned by all conscientious leaders at the Air Force Academy. For the chaplain staff, there were three important take-a-ways – facilitate the religious freedom of all airmen, know the regulation, and when preaching, reflect Christ – reminders for the more experienced chaplains and valuable lessons for others wanting to learn.

(1) Facilitate the Religious Freedom of All Airmen

To begin with, denying the religious freedoms of one group in order to facilitate the First Amendment rights of another group is not only unconstitutional, but in fact, counterproductive. What began as an effort to address the legitimate concerns of a few cadets, ended by inhibiting the religious expression of the whole student body! As a result, religious discussions all over the campus were discouraged. Several faculty and staff were told to remove their Bibles from their desks, and all expressions about God and "to" God (i.e. prayer) were cautioned, or as in the case of Falcon stadium, outright forbidden. United States Representative Joel Hefley of Colorado called it an attempt to "scrub religion from public life ... at the Academy."[16] Religious freedom must be extended to all, including the evangelical Christian.

(2) Know The Regulation

The authority that underpins the military chaplaincy is recorded in Title 10 of the United States Code,[17] but it is the policy directives of each respective service that govern the day-to-day activity of the chaplain. These directives were not haphazardly prepared; they were judiciously researched, debated, worded, and given the full signatory status of a military regulation for two very important reasons: (1) to protect the First Amendment rights of the individual chaplain, and (2) to enable the chaplain to facilitate those same rights for every soldier, sailor, marine, and airman. Supported by Air Force Instruction 52-101, the evangelical chaplain has the legal right to persuasively proclaim his Christian faith from the chapel pulpit.

---

16 Walter Jones (R-NC), a senior member of the House Armed Services Committee, was even more dramatic when he exclaimed, "There's going to come a time, if we don't draw the line in the sand now, that we will lose the right to practice what we believe." Both references were taken from Stephen Adams, "The Architecture of a Smear: the campaign to end public prayers at the Air Force Academy," *Citizen Magazine* (October 2005). www.freerepublic.com/focus/f-news/1501437/posts (accessed 20 Nov 2011).

17 See sections 3073, 3547, 3581, 5142, and 8067.

(3) When Preaching, Reflect Christ

Just because something is legal, doesn't make it right in the eyes of God. The effective chaplain not only knows his legal boundaries, he knows how to communicate the message of grace. The choice and tenor of the words we use will either welcome or repel the listener; after all, as ambassadors for Christ, God makes His appeal through us.[18] As conservative Christian chaplains, we have the constitutional right to boldly preach Christ from the military pulpit, but we also a biblical charge to do so with "gentleness and reverence."[19]

18 *Cf.* 2 Cor. 5:20

19 *Cf.* 1 Pt. 3:15

- PART TWO -
MINISTRY "INSIDE" THE WALLS

Working within the Chapel:
Leadership, Worship, and
Building a Protestant Program

CHAPTER FOUR

SERVANT LEADERSHIP

Jesus ... rose from supper, laid aside his garments, and girded himself with a towel. Then he poured water into a basin, and began to wash the disciples' feet, and to wipe them with the towel with which he was girded.

Apostle John – John 13:3-5

Rank and Leadership – A Personal Reflection by Chaplain Whittington

In 2004, I was invited to Bolling Air Force Base, Washington D. C. – headquarters of the Chief of Chaplains (HQUSAF/HC) – as a member of the Command Chaplains' Leadership Council. The summons came from the newly promoted Chaplain, Major General Charles Baldwin - the fifteenth Air Force Chief of Chaplains.

We were a small group – eight Major Command (MAJCOM) Chaplains, the Senior Staff Chaplain of the Air Force Academy, senior staff members from HQUSAF/HC, and a few other key players. It was not unusual for the new Chief to summon his (or her) Command Chaplains and other senior leaders to Washington where he would unfold his strategic plan – his vision for the future of the Air Force chaplaincy. It was also an opportune time for the global chaplain leadership and the new boss to get better acquainted, though it wasn't as if the council didn't know Chaplain Baldwin. We had worked together for years when he served as the Deputy Chief of Chaplains (brigadier general). Still everyone present understood how leadership styles could change when moving from the "right" to the "left" seat – from co-pilot to pilot, if you will. Every chaplain on the council understood that they worked directly for their local Air Force commander but they also understood that their success in the field was indelibly tied to their relationship with Washington. What kind of leader would the new Chief be? What changes would he make? As the well-known Christian author, John Maxwell quipped, "Anyone can steer the ship, but it takes a leader to chart the course."[1] What change-in-vector would General Baldwin implement? More importantly "how" would he implement the changes?

Were we going to be forced to endure a top-down hierarchical style for the next several years with every communiqué and visit from headquarters requiring high-maintenance with little, if any, spiritual purpose? Or, as Robert Greenleaf suggested, would the top-chaplain be a servant-leader who "by acting with integrity and spirit, builds trust and lifts people and helps them grow"?[2] Would he ask for our opinion? Build consensus? Emphasize mutual respect and teamwork? In effect, would he be Christ-like? I didn't envisage having the answer by the week's end but I was hoping for a glimpse of the future. To my pleasant surprise ("shock" would be a more adequate descriptive), I would have my answer before evening taps of the first day.

As an aside (but pertinent to this context) everyone in this select group understood that the next promotion to brigadier general would more than likely come from someone gathered at that meeting. It was not a pervasive thought, but for anyone present to pretend it didn't exist would be disingenuous at best; at worst, a lie. To be equally fair, however, the thought in-and-of itself, was not ungodly; it was a fact. Every experienced military officer (chaplain or otherwise) understands the promotion system. One's record must be above reproach and there are several stellar records vying for a single promotion to the general officer rank. One's record is important but one's position (such as Command Chaplain for a Unified Combatant Command or Air Force Major Command) and the Promotion Recommendation Form (PRF), hand-written by a four-star general, would be the deciding factor for most promotion boards.

---

1 John C. Maxwell, *The 21 Irrefutable Laws of Leadership* (Nashville: Thomas Nelson Publishers, 1998), 33.

2 Robert K. Greenleaf, *The Servant Within: The Transformative Path*, ed. Hamilton Beazley, Julie Begs, and Larry C. Spears (Mahwah, NJ: Paulist Press, 2003), 32. Cited in Dan R. Ebener, *Servant Leadership Models for your Parish* (Mahwah, NJ: Paulist Press, 2010), 11.

To this day, I deeply respect my colleagues attending this particular council meeting but all would agree there was no shortage of ego present.

The day's agenda called for an evening meeting, but before the first word was shared we were asked to congregate in a small, unfamiliar conference room. As we stood about the room waiting for Chaplain Baldwin, the conversation was pleasant but not always transparent. As suggested above, some *tête-à-tête* was a polite feint to get the latest word in upcoming assignments and positioning for promotion, while other chats were exactly as they appeared – renewing old acquaintances and making new friends. Regardless of the motive, the gathering was a stir with boisterous conversation, and no one seemed to notice the small basin of water and towel positioned at the edge of the raised platform at the front of the room.

Like conditioned dogs in Ivan Pavlov's classic experiment, within a minute of the assigned time (without a word being spoken) everyone quietly took their seat; waiting for the familiar announcement, "Ladies and gentlemen, the Chief of Chaplains." At that signal we would all stand at attention until the next familiar words, "Please take your seats" were heard, but the words were never spoken. In its place, Chaplain Baldwin (accompanied by the Deputy Chief of Chaplains, Cecil Richardson) casually walked up to the platform and sat down next to the basin of water. There, the Chief of Chaplains briefly shared his vision for the next few years; in his words, "Keeping the main thing, the main thing." Borrowing from Holy Scripture,[3] he talked about Jesus' concept of leadership – servant leadership – and then asked if we would remove our shoes and socks to allow him the honor of washing our feet. One by one, we walked up to the platform and sat down, extending our smelly, sweaty feet to a major general. He washed. Chaplain Richardson dried. And not a word was spoken the entire time.

When all were seated, he briefly appealed to the Bible – not comparing himself to Jesus but encouraging us to hear, see, and (figuratively) apply the words of the Master, "If I ... have washed your feet, you also ought to wash one another's

3   *Cf.* Jn. 13:3-15; Mk. 9:33-35; Lk. 22:24-27

feet."[4] In that brief moment, with my foot extended, I felt very uncomfortable – but for the right reason. And I do not believe I was alone in my discomfort. In a room full of chaplains "at the top of their game," every man present would have traded places with the new two-star – believing they could do as well or better leading the chaplaincy. And then, he washed my feet. Unbelievable! After lifting a silent prayer of confession, I promised the Lord, "I will follow your chosen servant, anyplace, anytime."

The meeting was over and nothing more was said. Words were not needed. Everyone was familiar with the biblical context of John 13 – the disciples arguing over who was the greatest – and how Jesus' actions (without a word spoken) rebuked their selfishness and pride.[5] The metaphor was understood by all. If we were to be an effective "visible reminder of the holy" we must know "who" we are in God's sight. And when you know who you are, you can wash feet! As I returned to my quarters, the words of Jesus were dancing about in my head, "If anyone would be first, he must be last of all and servant of all."[6]

Three Leadership Styles – Authoritarian, Participatory, Relational

To what style of leadership should the Christian chaplain aspire? There has been no shortage of emerging leadership theories in the past few decades but practically all of them can be reduced to three broad types: authoritarian, participatory, and relational.

Generally referred to as the "Great Man" leadership theory, authoritarian leaders are those who lead from the top down. Assuming that all great leaders are born, not made, they dismiss the need to build consensus once the facts are known; simply telling their subordinates what they want done and how to do it. As a positive descriptive, the term "charismatic" could equally describe the authoritarian leader; many mega-church pastors, politicians, and military commanders are charismatic leaders. If accompanied with charm and

---

4 Jn. 13:14 (RSV)

5 *Cf.* Lk. 24:24-30

6 Mk. 9:35 (RSV)

grace, arrogance is perceived as confidence and a non-participatory style as decisiveness – both leadership qualities to be admired.

The participatory leader is one who is willing to exert enormous energy, encouraging his or her staff to participate in open discussion. Even when the leader believes all the facts are known, he continues to build consensus in an attempt to move forward as a unified team – each member "owning" the decision as if it were his idea. This "participatory" leadership style was best expressed by Brigadier General Ken Hess after assuming command of the 374th Airlift Wing, Yokota Air Base, Japan, in 1994. At the time, Chaplain Whittington was serving as the Wing Chaplain and was in attendance at General Hess' first staff meeting. Before seating his senior staff, the commander exclaimed, "I covet consensus, but make no mistake; in lieu of consensus, I will make a decision." And he was true to his word – a leader who built consensus.

Relational leaders aspire to nothing less than a transformation of the organization – a pursuit of excellence from the team as a whole and a notable change for the better in every follower. Perhaps the most prevalent leadership style in transformational and servant leadership theories, relational leaders have high ethical and moral standards; believing the needs of the individual and the success of the organization are interdependent. In this brief study, "relational," "transformational," and "servant-leader" are used interchangeably. They inspire followers by helping them fulfill their potential. Going beyond the participatory-leader, the servant-leader claims that the organization can accomplish its mission only insofar as the followers' needs are met – enhancing their growth and increasing teamwork.

At a hurried glance, one might think that each subsequent leadership style in the above listing is sequential; that the next-mentioned style is progressively better than the one it preceded. Perhaps that is true if the reader only considers the amount of energy the leader would need to exert in a particular style; but in fact, all three are corroborated by Scripture and should be used as needed.

Four Determining Factors – Situational Leadership

Depending on the situation, successful leaders find themselves using one of the three styles interchangeably, the choice determined by the circumstances – an approach referred to as *Situational Leadership.* The acclaimed leadership theory was developed by Paul Hersey and Ken Blanchard over forty years ago and described in the first edition of *Management of Organizational Behavior.*[7] The theory claimed that the best leadership style (designated S1-S4) could only be determined once the leader understood the readiness level of the follower (designated R1-R4). A combination of two "readiness" factors (capability + willingness) determined the appropriate style the leader should employ (described in the model as "telling," "selling," "participating," or "delegating").

S1 – "Telling" style for the "Unable and Unwilling"

The R1 follower is "unable and unwilling." If the leader identifies the follower as unskilled and lacking confidence to accomplish the task at hand, he has no choice but to be very directive (S1) "telling" the subordinate what, when, where, and how to do the job. Building rapport with the employee may divert the follower's attention from the mission; a style that would work if the follower was willing, but will not work with the insecure employee. According to Hersey and Blanchard, the leader needs to employ a "high task – low relationship" style. Skills can be learned; the greater challenge for the leader is determining why the follower is insecure.

Far too many senior chaplains fail in leadership because they presume that every ordained minister is prepared to function in a military setting. In truth the military chaplaincy and the civilian parish are very different ministries, requiring related but different skills. One may be an excellent preacher but have no concept of what it takes to be the officer-of-primary-responsibility (OPR) for the Commander's National Prayer Breakfast. The new chaplain may have an advanced degree in Christian theology, but be totally unfamiliar working within a religiously diverse community. With few exceptions, the

---

7 Published by Prentice Hall, the book is now in its tenth *edition.*

inexperienced military chaplain needs a hands-on supervisor with the stated goal of helping the young chaplain pursue excellence.

S2 – "Selling" style for the "Unable but Willing"

Readiness level two (R2) is characterized by a follower who continues to be "unable" to perform the task at hand but is "willing." The failure to do the job well may not be due to incompetence, just inexperience. The successful leader will understand this and correlate his leadership style to accommodate the lack of experience. This calls for the leader to be task-focused and relationship-focused. The subordinate is motivated, just unfamiliar with the mission. Without insulting the member's ability to perform the mission, the leader must persuade the employee to consider another way to accomplish the task; in effect, he must exert energy relating to the employee, "selling" (S2) him on the right way to accomplish the job.

Many exceptional chaplains may be "unable but willing." Everyone in the military is transient. It is not uncommon for military personnel to move every eighteen months – permanent changes of station (PCS), temporary duty assignments (TDY), and deployments. And with every move, comes a new responsibility. Even when the job is similar, the new position demands a learning curve due to unfamiliarity with the location, mission, leadership, and staff. One may be willing and capable, but until the job is familiar, the leader will need to be attentive to the follower – listening, offering suggestions; in a word, coaching.

S3 – "Participating" style for the "Able but Unwilling"

The first two quadrants in the Hersey-Blanchard model (S1 and S2) are leader-driven, but the R3 follower needs more than direction from the boss, he needs motivation. When the follower is "able but unwilling" to accomplish the task, the leader must discover why the member is insecure and somehow inspire the person to pursue excellence. This calls for the leader to partner with the subordinate and "participate" (S3) in the task at hand.

S4 – "Delegating" style for the "Able and Willing"

When the person is both "able and willing" the leader can delegate – the type of follower every supervisor wants and every military commander demands. An R4 follower is highly competent, committed, and motivated. The leader appreciates what this person brings to the table – a leader in his own right – and trusts that whatever he does, will be done well.

Some version of *Situational Leadership* has been aptly used by military leaders for decades. There is continued debate, however, on Hersey and Blanchard's dismissal of the importance of building relationships at the "telling" and "delegating" level, which leads us to the *modus operandi*[8] of leadership – the heart of the leader.

The Leader's Motive – Servant Leadership

Jesus was on His way to the cross when the mother of James and John Zebedee asked for two thrones. With an immaturity that belied her age, she had no concept of the kingdom Jesus was in route to claim – a realm purchased with sacrificial love, suffering, and service.

> Then the mother of the sons of Zebedee came up to him, with her sons, and kneeling before him she asked him for something. And he said to her, "What do you want?" She said to him, "Command that these two sons of mine may sit, one at your right hand and one at your left, in your kingdom." But Jesus answered, "You do not know what you are asking."[9]

The request angered the other ten apostles, though they too struggled with pride and envy and had no concept of godly leadership. Then the Lord called the twelve together and shared the real meaning of greatness – the heart of a godly leader.

> You know that the rulers of the Gentiles lord it over them, and their great men exercise authority over them. It shall not be so among you;

8 Latin: mode of operation

9 Mt. 20:20-22a (RSV)

but whoever would be great among you must be your servant, and whoever would be first among you must be your slave; even as the Son of man came not to be served but to serve, and to give his life as a ransom for many.[10]

Disappointed by their self-centeredness, Jesus gently reshaped their concept of a leader, "Whoever would be great among you must be your servant." Out of respect for the Teacher, they listened in silence, but more than likely, their heads were cocked as if to say, "What on earth is he talking about?" The ancient world would have never equated "leader" with "servant." Then again, the Roman leaders were motivated by power and pride. Jesus was motivated by love. The question for today's leader is simple, "Which of the two *modi operandi*[11] will get the best results?"

Over the centuries, the Christian church is one of the few organizations that have identified the role of the leader as a servant. In truth, until we understand our roles as "servants" we will never experience God's vision for the church. Why? Because the body cannot be healthy unless all the parts are functioning as God ordained them to function.[12] The same is true of any organization wanting to accomplish a particular mission – each individual must be trained and motivated to pursue excellence. Synergy is the key, and the team is successful only insofar as the members excel. "Servant" leadership centers on the needs of others but begins within the heart of the leader.

There can be no serious discussion about *Servant Leadership* without mentioning Robert Greenleaf's body of work. The oft-used phrase *servant leadership* was coined by Greenleaf in his essay, *The Servant as Leader,* published in 1970. As noted in the *Greenleaf Center for Servant Leadership,*

> [*Servant Leadership*] begins with the natural feeling that one wants to serve, to serve first. Then conscious choice brings one to aspire to lead. That person is sharply different from one who is *leader* first, perhaps

---

10 Mt. 20:25b-28 (RSV)

11 Latin: modes of operation

12 *Cf.* 1 Cor.12:14-26

because of the need to assuage an unusual power drive or to acquire material possessions....The leader-first and the servant-first are two extreme types. Between them there are shadings and blends that are part of the infinite variety of human nature....The difference manifests itself in the care taken by the servant-first to make sure that other people's highest priority needs are being served. The best test, and difficult to administer, is: Do those served grow as persons? Do they, *while being served,* become healthier, wiser, freer, more autonomous, more likely themselves to become servants?[13]

No one familiar with Scripture could read the above excerpt without having many biblical passages come to mind; not the least of which, are John 13:5-17, Matthew 22:34-40, and Philippians 2:1-11.

In John's Gospel, Jesus humbly washes the disciples feet; the same followers who moments before were arguing which of them was the greatest.[14] In the Matthean text, Jesus equated loving one's neighbor with loving God.[15] While in a Roman prison, the Apostle Paul encouraged all Christians to emulate Jesus Christ and "do nothing from selfishness or conceit, but in humility count others better than yourselves."[16] And then, as if the great apostle were speaking directly to the world's leaders, he added, "Let each of you look not only to his own interests, but also to the interests of others."[17] Without a doubt, Christian scripture corroborates Greenleaf's thesis – if the leader's motive is to serve *first,* success is eminent. The challenge for all military leaders is to ensure that their motive is genuine.

Modus operandi is everything. Better to do the wrong thing for the right reason, than the right thing with an ulterior motive! There is no greater condemnation in all of Scripture than to be described by God as a hypocrite – one who

13 "What is Servant Leadership?" in *Greenleaf Center for Servant Leadership,* http://www.greenleaf.org/what-is-servant-leadership/ (accessed July 24, 2012); italics in original.

14 *Cf.* Jn. 13:5-17 and Lk. 22:24ff

15 *Cf.* Mt. 22:34-40

16 Phil. 2:3 (RSV)

17 Phil. 2:4 (RSV)

pretends to be someone he is not.[18] In classical Greek, the word *hypokritēs* meant "actor." As the scholar, U. Wilckens explained, "Human life comes to be compared to the stage ... [where] actors are deceivers."[19] The military leader whose motive is promotion, position, and power is doomed to fail. Granted, he may be able to "act the part" for a season, but the mask will eventually come off and those who follow will see him for what he is – one who only pretends to care about his people.

For a team to excel the leader's title and position are superfluous; especially for the military leader whose rank is obvious. In fact, Greenleaf argued that an organization could be successful without one even designated "leader." In a compilation of unpublished essays, he quoted Lord Acton, Professor of History at Cambridge University, "Power tends to corrupt and absolute power corrupts absolutely." And then he added, "In my book, *Servant Leadership,* I argue the case for shared power with colleagues who are equals as a preferable alternative to the concept of single chief."[20]

Just as military doctrine drives the commander's strategic plan, so leadership doctrine shapes the leader's strategic plan; but what exactly is *doctrine?* Etymologically, the word comes from the biblical Greek *didaskalía*, which in the first century, meant "teaching." Within a few years, however, the early church would define *didaskalía* as the sum of all apostolic teaching, hence *dogma* – the *doctrine* of the church.[21] In its most simple form, therefore,

---

18 The 23rd chapter of Matthew – commonly referred to as the chapter of the seven woes – provides the reader with unmistakable proof that God abhors those who (hypocritcally) mistreat others. Each pericope begins with the words, "Woe to you ... hypocrites!" Cf. Mt. 23:13ff

19 U. Wilckens, "Hypokritēs," ed. Geoffrey W. Bromiley, *Theological Dictionary of the New Testament: Abridged in One Volume* (Grand Rapids, Michigan: William B. Eerdmans Publishing Company, 1985), 1235-1236.

20 Robert Greenleaf, *Seeker and Servant: Essays by Robert Greenleaf,* eds. Anne T. Fraker and Larry C. Spears (San Francisco: Jossey-Bass Publishers, 1996), 58. This sounds very similar to the fictitious story that Greenleaf credited as one of the five ideas that shaped his life's work (*Ibid,* 43). The story, written by Herman Hesse, chronicled the joys and trials of a band of men on a fabled journey to the East searching for the "ultimate Truth." The central figure in the story is Leo – a man of extraordinary presence – who lifted the men's spirits with song and verse as he humbly performed menial chores along the road. Suddenly, the servant, Leo, disappeared and the group fell into chaos. Years later, the narrator of the story and one of its travelers, is taken into the religious order that sponsored the journey only to discover that the simple servant, Leo, was in fact the noble leader of the sect. See Herman Hesse, *Journey to the East,* trans. Hilda Rosner (New York: The Noonday Press, 1957).

21 K H. Rengstorf, "διδασκαλία," *Theological Dictionary of the New Testament, Abridged In One*

doctrine is the *teaching* behind the blueprint– the body of principles that validate the strategic plan.

The Leader's Strategic Plan – What, Where, How?

As all military leaders, chaplains are responsible to apply the same leadership guidelines as those at every level of command: providing a clear picture of what the leader sees (vision), developing the plan to get there (strategy), and implementing the plan with character (core values). All three components are necessary – vision, strategy, core values. If this were a journey, *vision* asks, "What is our destination?" *Strategy* asks, "Where is the road that will get us there?" And *character* asks, "How do we conduct ourselves on the journey?"

(1) Vision – What is our destination?

As a father of three sons – all of whom enjoyed learning to play baseball as soon as they could hold a bat – Chaplain Whittington vividly remembers telling his boys, "You can only 'hit' what you see" as he would gently toss the ball toward them. Our natural reflex is to close our eyes and move out of the way when a baseball is thrown our way; but in fact, the safest posture to take is an alert stance with eyes wide open. This is especially true if you want to actually "hit" the ball! "Hitting" the ball is precisely the metaphor the leader needs to remember. It serves no purpose for the batter to know the proper stance and have mastered the perfect swing only to close his eyes before impact.

Without a vision, it is impossible to lead. The best one could expect to do is maintain the *status quo,* but (borrowing a second sports metaphor) even treading water takes energy and the swimmer will eventually sink, having never moved. The greater tragedy with a visionless leader, however, is that he takes the whole team down with him.

King Solomon lamented, "Where there is no vision, the people perish."[22] Maxwell

---

Volume, ed. Geoffrey W. Bromiley (Grand Rapids, MI: William B. Eerdmans Publishing Company, 1985), 166. *Cf.* Tit. 2:1 and 1 Tim.1:10.

22 Proverbs 29:18 (KJV).

argued that the leader's vision is "indispensable."[23] This well-known Christian author is not alone in his assessment; most experts in the field of leadership assert that "Vision is the spirit behind the organization" and the sole energizing principle of the strategic plan.[24] While some leadership theorists separate the organization's *vision* from their stated *goal*, this study will use the two words interchangeably. Not to be confused with the strategy itself or the core values that imbue the organization with purpose, the servant-leader (in dialogue with his team) asks, "What is our destination?" "Where do we need to go?" or "What exactly do we need to accomplish?" Once agreed upon, goals are set – clear, measurable, realistic, and mission oriented.

Unlike civilian clerics, chaplains work within the framework of the local military mission; an organization inherently burdened with limited time constraints, personnel that pack-up and move on a moment's notice, and frequently modified objectives. The Army, Navy, and Air Force Chiefs of Chaplains may have the luxury of implementing a strategic plan to accomplish a three, five, or ten-year vision for their respective service, but the senior chaplain in the field operates within a much smaller timeframe. Asking the question, "Where do we want to go?" is tempered with the follow-up question, "How much time do we have?" These are challenging questions and absolutely prerequisite to developing a successful strategy for implementing ministry in a military setting; but the more challenging the task, the greater the need for the *servant-leader* to exert the energy to build consensus and empower the team to accomplish the mission. Though a shared vision empowers the team, Maxwell noted the inspiration is nonetheless attributed to the one who made it happen.

> My observation over the last twenty years has been that all effective leaders have a vision of what they must accomplish. That vision becomes the energy behind every effort and the force that pushes through all the problems. With vision the leader is on a mission and a contagious spirit is felt among the crowd until others begin to rise alongside the leader. Unity is essential for the dream to be realized.

23   John C. Maxwell, *Developing the Leader Within You* (Nashville: Thomas Nelson Publishers, 1993), 125.

24   Loughlan Sofield and Donald H. Kuhn, *The Collaborative Leader – Listening to the Wisdom of God's People* (Notre Dame, Indiana: Ave Marie Press, 1995), 56.

Long hours of labor are given gladly to accomplish the goal. Individual rights are set aside because the whole is much more important than the part. Time flies, morale soars upward, heroic stories are told, and commitment is the watchword. Why? Because the leader has a vision![25]

This is the starting point – the leader's vision – but it is only the beginning. However essential it is to mission success, it serves no purpose without a plan!

(2) Strategy – Where is the road that will get us there?

Regardless of rank or position, everyone understands the value of a plan. We execute them every day – the cook in the dining hall carefully follows a proven recipe in order to feed a thousand soldiers, the jet mechanic working on the F-22 Raptor proceeds in accordance with the maintenance schedule provided by Lockheed Martin/Boeing, the Catholic chaplain follows a prescribed liturgical order for Sunday Mass. Why? To achieve the desired goal!

Once the servant-leader and his team have decided on the destination, the next logical step is determining which road will get us there. What is the plan to reach the goal and realize the vision? Unfortunately, there is no prescribed strategy that one could replicate that would fit every situation; no cookie-cutter template that will work in every setting. Every vision is unique and demands its own specific plan to reach the desired goal; however, based upon certain leadership presuppositions – *Relational* style, *Situational Leadership* process, and certain core values that are commensurate to the *Servant Leader* – there are logical sequential steps for the leader to follow.

(a) Brainstorm

There is a synergistic energy in every group, regardless of size. Jesus emphasized that His disciples were to travel "two by two," not individually.[26] Without going into a full *exegetical* study of the biblical text, it is clear that our Lord believed "two" traveling together could accomplish more than each individual traveling

---

25 Maxwell, *Developing*, 125.

26 *Cf.* Mk. 6:7 and Lk. 10:1

alone. *Synergy* argues that the combined effort of the team is greater than its individual members – the sum is greater than the parts.

All successful leaders would echo a resounding "amen" to that truth. It's as if there is an additional entity present when two or more are gathered. If two are gathered to work on a problem, there is the brain-power of three; if three, then the brain-power of four; and so on. In fact, many leaders would argue that the synergy of a group (up to about twelve people) exponentially grows in proportion to the number within the group. The effective leader takes advantage of this phenomenon.

Once the vision has been articulated, the first step is to gather the team and brainstorm. What exactly do we need to *do* to accomplish our goal; to realize our vision? As early as 1953 management expert Alex Osborn suggested four general rules to follow when brainstorming, and recommended these guidelines be posted throughout the panel session: criticism is ruled out, free-wheeling is welcomed, quantity is wanted, and combination and improvement are sought.[27] Brainstorming is a challenge for both the leader and the team as a whole; especially in the military structure where certain rank-protocols are culturally engrained.

Frankly, this cultural fear is inescapable but there are certain things the senior chaplain can do to minimize its effect; such as setting the ground rules (above), and highlighting the guideline: "withholding criticism." Operating within an announced timeframe, the leader could also relocate the team to an offsite venue where the staff would be comfortable wearing civilian clothes. If deployed, the senior chaplain may invite a smaller team of chaplains, chaplain assistants, and key lay leaders for a similar session; for no matter where the chaplain may find himself, successful ministry begs the question, "What must be done to accomplish the goal"? And this question can best be addressed within the framework of a team – putting certain ideas on the table that, if acted on, would accomplish the prescribed goal.

---

27 Alex F. Osborn, *Applied Imagination* (New York: Charles Scribner's Sons, 1963), 156.

(b) Identify the Steps

Once all of the ideas have surfaced, the leader should facilitate a second discussion encouraging the team to identify those ideas that would realistically reach the desired goal. This is an appropriate time to introduce a different set of guidelines. No longer should the team focus on quantity or withhold criticism; rather, this is the time for quality and candor. Every idea needs to be carefully scrutinized to ensure that it meets certain criteria, best applied in the form of a question:

- Will it have an achievable impact on the ministry's vision?

- Is it measurable?

- Can we do it within the mission's time-constraint?

- Do we have the resources to accomplish it – personnel, technology, and money?

Again, consensus is critical and unfortunately, there are no shortcuts. Anyone who has been through this arduous process will admit that it is exhausting. The greatest challenge for the leader is keeping the team focused on the task at hand, vectoring every conversation toward the stated vision, measuring every proposal with the same repetitive words, "If this step becomes part of our strategic plan, will it help us realize our vision?"

(c) Prioritize the Steps and Assign the Officer of Primary Responsibility (OPR)

Other than the actual implementation, this is the most important step within the strategic plan. John Maxwell considered prioritizing as "the key to leadership"[28] and exclaimed, "Leaders never grow to a point where they no longer need to prioritize."[29]

Putting "first things first" is not only a secular truth but a biblical imperative.

---

28 Maxwell, *Developing*, 17.

29 Maxwell, *Irrefutable*, 175.

Jesus said, "*First* be reconciled to your brother," before you offer your gift at the altar of God.[30] He scolded the religious leaders whose priorities were backwards, calling them "hypocrites," who should *first* take the log out of their own eye, before they take the speck out of their brother's eye.[31] There is a sequential order to creation. Light was created on the first day, the firmament (air) and water on the second day, and dry land and plant life on the third day.[32] Then the Lord God created all living creatures to include the ones made in his own image – man and woman – on the sixth day.[33]

Not only is there a natural order to creation, but even God's plan to spread His word is prioritized – the first step leading to the second, and so forth. The Apostle Paul reminded the Corinthian church,

> How are men to call upon him in whom they have not believed? And how are they to believe in him of whom they have never heard? And how are they to hear without a preacher? And how can men preach unless they are sent?[34]

God even prioritizes His own Word! All Scripture is equally inspired but it is not equally important. Again, the great Apostle addressing the Corinthian church set the priority when he exclaimed, "For I delivered to you as of *first* importance what I also received, that Christ died for our sins in accordance with the scriptures, that he was buried, [and] that he was raised on the third day in accordance with the scriptures."[35] Paul was adamant in prioritizing what he preached! Apart from God's plan of redemption, everything else is secondary. Discerning what needs to be done *first* is important for one's journey toward heaven *and* on earth.

Not only should the leader ensure that the steps are prioritized, but he

---

30   Mt. 5:24 (RSV)

31   Mt. 7:32 (RSV)

32   *Cf.* Gen. 1:3-5 (light), 1:6-8 (firmament and water), and 1:9-13 (dry land and vegetation).

33   *Cf.* Gen. 1:20-27

34   Rom. 10:14-15a (RSV)

35   1 Cor. 15: 3-4 (RSV)

should work towards getting the right people to implement them. Maxwell recommended that the leader "understand the Pareto Principle in the area of people oversight and leadership."[36] The Pareto Principle (commonly called the 20/80 principle) claims that "20 percent of your priorities will give you 80 percent of your production, IF you spend your time, energy, money, and personnel on the top 20 percent of your priorities."[37] The successful chaplain leader will take every opportunity to assign the most challenging steps to his most mature colleagues, affording him the time to ensure the success of those less experienced.

(d) Implement the Plan!

In the final analysis, the "proof" as they say, "is in the pudding." An unimplemented plan indicts both leader and team, yet there are some chaplains (and leaders from all professions) who seem to believe that the process of building the plan is the end-goal! Once they exert the energy to discuss the issues, the vision is miraculously realized. Perhaps it is the pastoral side of the chaplain that enables the lie. It is analogous to a counseling session where a soldier confesses to a particular problem. After an hour of cathartic dialogue (but no recommended plan for the soldier to change his behavior) the chaplain considers the counseling a success; after all, he did his part by listening. The epistle of *James* addresses this delusion, "If a brother or sister is ill-clad and in lack of daily food, and one of you says to them, 'Go in peace, be warmed and filled,' without giving them the things needed for the body, what does it profit?"[38] The Lord is unyielding in His praise of those who do not love "in word or speech" but demonstrate their love "in truth and action."[39] As James admonished, "Be doers of the word and not hearers only."[40] So it is with the strategic plan. Measure your success by the *doing* not the process.

---

36 Maxwell, *Developing,* 19.

37 *Ibid.,* 17. The word "IF" is capitalized for emphasis in the original source.

38 Jas. 2:15-16 (RSV)

39 1 Jn. 3:18 (RSV)

40 Jas. 1:22 (RSV)

(3) Character – How do we conduct ourselves on the journey? (A Personal Reflection by Chaplain Whittington)

As a child of seven, I stole a piece of bubblegum from the local grocer. It was a small neighborhood food market of the type that has just about disappeared from the American landscape; nicknamed *Gene's* after the man who owned the little store. Everyone in the community knew Gene as their friend and neighbor. As I grew older, I discovered that the man who wielded the large butcher's knife was actually a nice man, but to a seven-year old boy, he looked like a mean giant – an uncommonly tall, bald-headed, stocky, burly-looking guy. While my father was paying for the handful of groceries he set on the countertop, I secretly picked up a piece of bubblegum and slipped it into my pocket. Once home, I pulled it out and began to enjoy my ill-gotten gain when dad noticed it and asked, "Where'd you get the gum, son"? After we exchanged a few words I found myself standing directly in front of Gene – all 6 ½ feet of him – looking straight up. I stammered out the words, "I stole the bubblegum … I'm sorry" as I handed him the already-chewed gum in its wrapper. Now, one might think that he would have said, "Thank you for your honesty, young man," and then have returned the sticky mess so I could have enjoyed it a bit longer. But no! He kept the half-chewed gum and quipped, "You owe me a penny." Dad gave me the penny and I handed it to the giant man. In turn, I was given a list of chores, along with the words, "This will build character." I had no idea what the word *character* meant but by the day's end, I knew it was hard. Fifty-plus years have passed since that moment, and *character* is still hard.

Interesting word! A derivative of the Greek *charaktér,* the root word referred to a tool used for engraving that required the artisan to repeat the same stroke over and over again until the desired effect was achieved. Not too dissimilar to our vernacular, character-building is a lifelong pursuit requiring a person to do the "right" thing over and over again until it becomes a natural behavior. The challenge, of course, is *intentionally* behaving in certain ways in order to build a virtuous life – a life of character.

(a) Cardinal Virtues

Classical antiquity and Christian tradition have recognized at a minimum, four values that if practiced, would reflect a virtuous life – wisdom, justice, moderation, and courage.[41] And these "cardinal virtues" have served as a moral compass for the American people from the Founding era to the present day. It is no mystery, then, that certain core values – congruent with our Judeo-Christian teachings and stemming from these cardinal virtues – have been championed by those in the Profession of Arms as essential for military leadership.

(b) Core Values

The Department of Defense has not adopted a "single" set of core values; the Army, Navy, and Air Force are much too parochial for that. They each have their own. The Army lists seven: loyalty, duty, respect, selfless service, honor, integrity, and personal courage; the Navy and Marine Corps list three: commitment, honor, and courage; and the Air Force, also three: integrity, service, and excellence. A thorough study of all four expanded lists reveals a striking similarity.

For example, a partial definition of *Respect* by the Army is, "Treat people as they should be treated." The Navy defines *Commitment* as "Show[ing] respect toward all people..." The Marine Corps demands that all personnel show "respect for others" by living the core value of *Honor*. And the Air Force's *Service before Self* includes a subheading of "Respect for Others" with the explanation, "We must always act in the certain knowledge that all persons possess a fundamental worth as human beings."[42] Four core values: *Respect, Commitment, Honor,* and *Service before Self*; different in name only. And the similarities continue.

---

41 Referred to as the "cardinal virtues" these four values were first mentioned in Plato's *Protagoras 330b* and later by the Catholic theologian Thomas Acquinas in *Summa Theologica* II (I).61, 1133-1137.

42 The three official military websites listing the core values are: Army http://www.army.mil/values/; Navy http://www.navy.mil/navydata/nav_legacy.asp?id=193; Marine Corps http://www.marines.com/history-heritage/principles-values; and Air Force http://www.airforce.com/learn-about-our-values/ (accessed Aug. 25, 2012).

So what has this to do with the servant-leader? Everything! It is a vivid reminder that all successful military leaders have basically the same core values. In fact, these virtues have been so admired by all civilized cultures that there is no other list comparable; they are so broadly accepted they are universal, incommensurable, one of a kind! And all human cultures agree that only the most noble practice them; the operative word being *practice.*

Conclusion

Leadership *doctrine* is the teaching behind the blueprint– the body of principles that validate the strategic plan. As a way of reminding the reader of the leadership *doctrine* proposed in the preceding pages, note the three principles previously described:

1. The recommended leadership style is *Relational* – aspiring to nothing less than a transformation of organization by inspiring followers to fulfill their potential, enhancing their growth and increasing teamwork.

2. The recommended process is *Situational Leadership* – the understanding that the team's success is contingent upon the leader's ability to adapt his style to the follower's maturity.

3. And the recommended *modus operandi* of the leader – the reason he does what he does – is *Servant Leadership.* The servant-leader's natural inclination is to serve others and he believes the success of the mission is in direct proportion to the growth of the individual.

The successful leader exemplifies these three principles as he implements his plan by asking three basic questions: What is our destination? What is the road that will get us there? And how do we conduct ourselves on the journey?

Effective leaders do more than talk-the-talk; they walk-the-walk! They know what they need to do, they build the right plan, and they implement it with character. The challenge for the servant-leader is not choosing which list of core values to implement; the real challenge is just doing it! Character is developed no other way. One must repetitively do the right thing until it becomes a natural part of his daily walk.[43]

---

43 See Heb. 5:11-14. Ethical leaders are those who continue to practice godly values, as the author of

Living the core values is what separates the great leaders from all others. As Chaplain (COL) Paul Vicalvi (former Commandant of the Army Chaplain Center) reminded his audience in February 2006, "Some leaders just memorize them and some live them."[44]

---

the epistle to the Hebrews explained, "About this we have much to say but it is hard to explain, since you have become dull of hearing. For though by this time you ought to be teachers, you need someone to teach you again the basic principles of the oracles of God. You need milk, not solid food, for everyone who lives on milk is unskilled in the word of *righteousness*, since he is a child. But solid food is for the *mature*, for those who have their powers of discernment *trained by constant practice* to distinguish good from evil." In the biblical text, the Greek noun *dikaiosúnē* (righteousness) implies behavior such as "integrity, virtue, purity of life, rightness, correctness of thinking feeling, and acting"; in short, *character*. The adjective *téleios* (mature) described those who lived a complete life, exhibiting "consummate human integrity and virtue." The verb *gumnázo* (trained) meant "to exercise vigorously" and when coupled with the noun *héxis* (practice) the interpretation was unmistakable: If you want to be a person of strong character, you must do the right thing – for the right reason – over and over and over again. For the use of Greek, see James Strong, *The Exhaustive Concordance of the Bible: Showing Every Word of the Text of the Common English Version of the Canonical Books, and Every Occurrence of Each Word in Regular Order* (Ontario: Woodside Bible Fellowship., 1996), electronic edition, G.1343.

44 Paul L. Vicalvi was a former Commandant for the Army Chaplain Center and School at Fort Jackson, South Carolina. He delivered these remarks at a National Prayer Breakfast at Fort Lee, Virginia, on February 23, 2006. See electronic version of "Servant Leadership," *Army Logistician*, PB 700-06-03 Volume 38, Issue 3 (May-June 2006), http://www.almc.army.mil/alog/issues/May-June06/srvnt_leader.html (accessed May 9, 2012).

CHAPTER FIVE

A PRACTICAL THEOLOGY OF WORSHIP

We know God ... not through intellectual propositions, but through worship.[1]

John Chrysostom (AD 347-407)
Bishop of Constantinople

There are three broad areas of ministry for the military chaplain: ministry inside the walls of the chapel, ministry on the installation, and ministry on the battlefield. Arguing which one is more important is to miss the point. The chaplain is needed in all three places to facilitate the troops' religious freedom because that is precisely where we find the soldiers, sailors, marines, airmen, and coastguardsmen – on military bases in the United States and overseas, at sea, and on the battlefront.

In truth the warrior is either training for war or engaged in war, and the greater concentration of military personnel at any given time is in training. With over 1,414,000 military personnel on active duty in 2012, less than eleven percent found themselves in Iraq, Afghanistan, and the high seas.[2] The remaining 1.1 million were stationed on military bases throughout the United States and overseas. Arguably, there is no greater need for the military chaplain than on the battlefield, but the vast number of troops on military installations around the world, speaks volumes to the chaplain's responsibilities "inside" the walls of the chapel.

Pastoral counseling and prayer with soldiers occur everywhere – within the chapel, in work stations, on the flight line, at sea, and in the field –

---

1 John Chrysostom's response to Eunomius (fourth-century theologian) explaining the Christian's relationship to God. Cited in Robert Webber, "The Modes of God's Presence," *Liturgy* 6:4 (Spring 1987), 79.

2 Statistics gathered from several sources. See vetfriends.com at http://www.vetfriends.com/US-deployments-overseas/ (accessed Sep. 15, 2012).

but are considered in this study as ministry "outside" the walls (chapter nine). Moreover, these duties are not the exclusive domain of the chaplain. Professional counseling services are provided on every military installation, lay-led Bible studies and prayer meetings are commonplace, and chaplain assistants play a critical role on Unit Ministry Teams (UMT).[3]

There is only one ministry that remains the exclusive domain of the military chaplain – congregational worship. Though the chaplain and the civilian pastor have uniquely different callings, it is the worship ministry within the chapel walls that resonates with the military community, identifies the chapel as a "home church" and reminds the chaplain of the civilian pastorate. The venue for worship may differ but the chaplain's responsibility to facilitate a meaningful worship experience for the Christian soldier and his family is unchangeable.

America's warriors seek God's presence in worship. Perhaps no one appreciates the words of Jesus more than our military personnel – "For where two or three are gathered in my name, there am I in the midst of them."[4] In view of the soldiers' need for God's presence the Bible-believing chaplain would do well to examine the Scripture and implement practical theologies of sign and worship.

A Theology of Sign

If Jesus appeared in the flesh in full view of a chapel congregation during a Sunday service, worship would occur spontaneously with a symbol, not a word. Words could not express the Christian's love and adoration for the "King of kings" and "Lord of lords." Some people would bow while others kneel; still others would just fall prostrate upon the floor. In God's presence Moses, Isaiah, and Peter worshiped with words only after they covered their

---

3 Chaplain Assistants in the Army and Air Force, and Religious Program Specialists (RPs) in the Navy are enlisted personnel who do not require ordination, but are critical to the success of the chaplain's mission. They assist in ministry wherever the chaplains are stationed - in the field, on bases, in hospitals and in combat situations.

4 Mt. 18:20 (RSV)

faces and bowed before their Lord.[5] Perhaps the contemporary Christian song writer, Bart Milliard, said it best,

> Surrounded by your glory
> What will my heart feel?
> Will I dance for you Jesus,
> Or in awe of you be still?
> Will I stand in your presence,
> Or to my knees will I fall?
> Will I sing Hallelujah,
> Will I be able to speak at all?
> I can only imagine.[6]

(1) Symbols Convey Enormous Meaning!

There are moments in life when words just cannot express the depth of one's feelings but a symbolic gesture communicates clearly. Symbols convey enormous meaning! The rings a bride and groom exchange when taking their wedding vows are nothing more than small amounts of gold fashioned into two bands, but volumes have been written about that which they symbolize.

No single group of people appreciate the use of images more than those who serve in the Profession of Arms – service flags, unit guidons, personnel badges, rank, ribbons, and medals. Every symbol evokes personal, collegial, and professional pride. Similarly, Christian symbols serve as visual reminders of our relationship with God through Jesus Christ. In Christianity, the significance of a sign is that it has visible meaning through which the gospel of Jesus Christ is proclaimed. Both the Old and the New Testaments are rich in illustration of God communicating with His people through forms and signs. The Hebrew prophets literally acted out God's word[7] and since God's word was true, the actions were more than quaint symbols; they actually set in

---

5   *Cf.* Ex. 3, Isa. 6, Lk. 5

6   "I Can Only Imagine" was written by Bart Millard and first recorded by the Christian rock band, *MercyMe.*

7   *Cf.* Jer. 27-28; Ezek. 4

motion its fulfillment. The outcome, however, was always dependent on the faith and repentance of the people.

(2) God's Choice of Two Symbols!

The two most obvious forms in the New Testament – baptism and the Lord's Supper – are not meaningless externals but signs and symbols of a spiritual reality that draw value from the command of God and the presence of faith. One important fact to remember about water, bread, and wine is that these are God's signs, not ours. The Bible teaches that we are saved by grace through faith[8] but the symbols associated with baptism and the Lord's Supper, are God-given images to reenact our salvation in Christ.[9]

When Jesus instituted the Lord's Supper he took the bread, "and blessed, and broke it ... and said, 'Take, eat; this is my body.'" Then, "he took a cup, and when he had given thanks he gave it to them, saying, 'Drink of it, all of you, for this is my blood of the covenant, which is poured out for many for the forgiveness of sins.'" However, the words of Jesus did not end with death on a cross; they transitioned life from the cross – a promise that the next time He shared the "cup of blessing"[10] with His disciples they would be gathered "in [His] Father's kingdom."[11] For this reason, Paul reminded the Roman church that every time they celebrated the Lord's Supper, they proclaimed "the Lord's death *until* he comes."[12]

In many military locations, the evangelical chaplain faces austere conditions, and may choose to discourage baptism and the Lord's Supper even when asked by a soldier. Be creative! Bread, juice or wine, and water can be found

---

8   *Cf.* Eph. 2:8

9 For example, 1 Cor. 15:1-4 described the Gospel as the death, burial, and resurrection of Jesus Christ. The Apostle Paul in Rom. 6:1ff connected the Gospel with the image of baptism when he reminded the Roman church that they had died to sin, been buried with Christ in baptism, and arisen to walk a new life. The symbolic image of baptism as a watery grave is a perfect visual to demonstrate to the world that the "old has passed away, behold, the new has come" (2 Cor. 5:16).

10   1 Cor. 10:16 (RSV)

11   Mt. 26:26-29 (RSV)

12   1 Cor. 11:26 (RSV)

just about anywhere in the world. Breaking the Lord's bread with the chapel community is extremely meaningful to those who frequent the "valley of the shadow of death." Celebrating the Christian's salvation in Christ with "bread and wine" is as grounded in Scripture as prayer and preaching.

Baptizing in local rivers, lakes, streams, oceans, or creatively digging a shallow space in the desert floor, lining it with ponchos, and filling it with a few gallons of water from a military "water buffalo" will do more for the soldier than any other single act of worship. And for those who have taken an oath to "...support and defend the Constitution of the United States against all enemies" rising out of a watery grave to "walk in the newness of life"[13] is a defining moment for both soldier and church. Though water, bread, and wine are among God' chosen signs, there is no greater symbol that reminds the soldier "God is with us" than the Bible itself.

(3) In Scripture, God Speaks To Us!

Denominational traditions vary within Christendom, but the belief in Scripture as the primary source of God's revelation is common to all Christian churches. It seems only natural to remind the military congregation of the very heart of our common faith – the gospel of Christ as proclaimed and experienced in the New Testament.

In worship we speak praises to God both in prayer and song as we respond to Him seeking us through Jesus Christ. However, God also speaks to us in worship by the reading of His Word. It is strange that conservative Christians, who profess such a deep belief in the Bible as being the Word of God, seldom allot much time in the worship service to publicly read Scripture. And when time is allotted, the passages read are often poorly organized and haphazardly chosen.

The truth is "free worship" may not necessarily be free. Far too often congregations are bound to the biases of the preacher. The use of a lectionary (fixed reading) was adopted by the ancient church from synagogue worship

---

13 Rom. 6:4c (RSV)

rather early in its history as an effort to share the whole counsel of God without bias. The Scriptures were so precious to the early Christians that they were often read for hours at a time – as Justin Martyr, an early second-century apologist, explained, "The memoirs of the apostles [the Gospels] or the writings of the prophets [Old Testament] are read, as long as time permits."[14] From the second-century to the Reformation era, the sermon was primarily a means to explain the reading of the Word.

New Testament preaching is both "proclamation" (*kérygma*) and "teaching" (*didachē*). The proclamation of the gospel in the worship of the early church was intended to further dramatize the Christ-event through the application of the Scriptural text. The real meaning of preaching is set forth by the Apostle Paul in 1 Corinthians. He came to preach the gospel, which he identified as the message of the cross (1:8) – Christ crucified (1:23). In the context of worship, preaching reenacts the gospel which gives meaning to the worship experience. As Professor Webber explained,

> Primarily, preaching in the context of worship is not teaching (there are other occasions for that in the church). Rather, it is the time when the work of Christ (Creation, Incarnation, Death, Resurrection, and Consummation) is proclaimed and applied to the lives of God's people.[15]

When we remember that God is at work in the gospel message revealing His righteousness,[16] we should have a renewed appreciation for the sermon. Preaching is an act of worship that calls the Christian to reconcile with God, as Paul explained to the Corinthian church,

> All this is from God, who through Christ reconciled us to himself and gave us the ministry of reconciliation; that is, in Christ God was reconciling the world to himself, not counting their trespasses against them, and entrusting to us the message of reconciliation. So we are ambassadors for Christ, God making his appeal through us. We beseech

14   Justin, *Apology I*, 67.

15   Robert Webber, *Worship Old & New* (Grand Rapids, MI: Zondervan Publishing House, 1982), 125.

16   *Cf.* Rom. 1:16-17

you on behalf of Christ, be reconciled to God. For our sake he made him to be sin who knew no sin, so that in him we might become the righteousness of God. Working together with him, then, we entreat you not to accept the grace of God in vain.[17]

Appreciating the biblical use of symbols will build a solid foundation to ministry, and enable the chaplain to implement a practical theology of worship.

A Theology of Worship

This is the supreme paradox: God's very presence is necessary for our spiritual sustenance, yet, we cannot tolerate it. We were created in the image of God but frustrate ourselves with the impossible question, "Who is God"? We exercise dominion over nature by our God-given capacity to reason, but cannot understand God through intellectual propositions. Eunomius, a fourth century theologian, and his counterpart John Chrysostom, the distinguished bishop of Constantinople, argued about the human experience of God. Eunomius exclaimed, "I can know God even as God knows himself." Chrysostom countered with "We know God ... not through intellectual propositions, but through worship."[18] It appears we have no choice. Our human nature drives us to seek God, in whose image we were created.[19]

Abram, in God's presence, "fell on his face."[20] Moses, upon receiving the Ten Commandments, "bowed his head toward the earth and worshiped."[21] Isaiah, while receiving his prophetic call in the presence of the "Holy One" could only exclaim, "Woe is me."[22] Peter, forgetting all about the threatening storm, begged Jesus to leave, for the Lord's very presence sorely reminded him, "I am

---

17 2 Cor. 5:18-6:1 (RSV)

18 Webber, *Liturgy*, 79.

19 Ninian Smart, *The Religious Experience of Mankind* (New York: Charles Scribner's Sons, 1969), 499-537. Smart argued that the whole of human experience revolved around one's beliefs in a deity or the rejection of these beliefs; that human nature demanded it. What Smart referred to as "human nature," we submit is God's very image embedded in humanity at creation (Gen. 1:27). Our *Imago Dei* nature drives our innate longing to connect with that "something beyond ourselves."

20 Gen. 17:3 (RSV)

21 Ex. 34:8 (RSV)

22 Isa. 6:5 (RSV)

a sinful man."[23] What do these biblical heroes of the faith all have in common? They each witnessed the overwhelming power of God's presence! Apparently, when one occupies the same immediate space with the Creator, there is but one thing to do – worship!

It is important for the evangelical Christian to remember the intent of Christian worship. Working within such a religiously diverse community, one may be tempted to focus on a particular style of worship rather than "worship" itself. That would be a mistake. Whether one's church is located in a Nashville suburb, downtown Los Angeles, or Kunsan Air Base in the Republic of Korea, God's ministers need to "make worship, not the worship service, the goal of church life."[24] To this end, the Christian chaplain should lead the chapel community to:

- Experience Christ-Centered Worship

- Encourage Participation in Worship

- Express Unity of Spirit in Worship

- Enjoy the Celebration of Worship

(1) Experience Christ-Centered Worship

The music of heavenly worship – so beautifully set forth in Scripture – is directed toward God, not man. This is the key to worship whether through song or prayer, the reading of Scripture, or celebrating the Lord's Supper. The divine drama played out in Revelation 4-5 illustrates this perfectly. God is referred to as a precious stone. Around this invaluable gem are four living creatures (possibly the cherubim described in Genesis 3:24). Encircling these living creatures are twenty-four elders. Encompassing the twenty-four elders are millions of God's angels praising God and singing, "Holy, holy, holy, is the Lord God Almighty, who was and is and is to come!"[25]

---

23 Lk. 5:8 (RSV)

24 Cathy Townley, *Missional Worship* (St. Louis: Chalice Press, 2011), 9.

25 Rev. 4:8c (RSV)

God is holding a scroll sealed with seven seals. He majestically asks the heavens to answer the crucial question: "Who is worthy to open the scroll and break its seal"?[26] Absolutely no one moved; no one in heaven or earth came forward. Apparently, not a single angel felt worthy; the twenty-four elders (seated on thrones and wearing royal crowns) looked the other way; and the four living creatures with their flaming swords "which turned everyway" stood motionless!

As the Apostle John looked on, he began to weep. (One can appreciate the tears once understanding that the scroll contained God's plan of salvation for the world and unless someone was worthy to implement the plan, humanity was lost.) While John was overwhelmed with sadness, one of the twenty-four elders whispered, "Weep no more; behold, the Lion of the tribe of Judah, the Root of David, has conquered, so that he can open the scroll and its seven seals."[27] John turned, expecting to see a mighty lion but in its place was a lamb; not just any lamb, but a *paschal* lamb – a lamb fit for the slaughter.

The moment the Lamb took the scroll, the four living creatures, the twenty-four elders and all of the angelic hosts all bowed down and sang a new song,

> Worthy are you to take the scroll and to open its seals; for you were slain, and by your blood you ransomed people for God from every tribe and language and people and nation. And you have made them a kingdom and priests to our God, and they shall reign on the earth.[28]

All of a sudden, everyone around the throne and all of the angelic forces, "numbering myriads of myriads and thousands of thousands," continued this new song with a loud voice, "Worthy is the Lamb who was slain, to receive power and wealth and wisdom and might and honor and glory and blessing!"[29] And "every creature in heaven and on earth and under the earth and in the sea," shouted, "To him who sits on the throne and to the Lamb be blessing and

---

26 Rev. 5:2b (RSV)

27 Rev. 5:5 (RSV)

28 Rev. 5:9-10 (RSV)

29 Rev. 5:12 (RSV)

honor and glory and might forever and ever!" And the four living creatures said, "Amen!" and the twenty-four elders fell down and worshiped.[30]

Now, that is worship! If the chapel congregation misses this point, nothing else much matters: Worship must be centered on Jesus Christ, for He alone is worthy!

(2) Encourage Participation in Worship

Worship is an active experience! In many chapels the congregation is little more than an audience and the chaplain little more than a cheerleader. Far too often a chaplain will ask his supervisor, "Well, how did I do?" as if he was responsible for producing a program for people to come and watch, rather than participate. The Christian minister needs to be reminded weekly that if one does not "participate" with the risen Christ, worship has not occurred.

It was the Danish philosopher Søren Kierkegaard (1813-1855) who compared the divine drama of worship to the theater.[31] Though written in 1847, the analogy has resurfaced in recent decades, popularized by many Christian authors. In short, Kierkegaard defied the notion that the priest should play the role of the actor; the congregation, the audience; and God, some kind of heavenly director orchestrating the whole drama. Kierkegaard argued that it should be just the opposite; namely, the congregant stands before God as the actor, the priest (as director) prompts the actor, and God is the audience. Though the analogy breaks down biblically when God is relegated to "audience," the heart of Kierkegaard's challenge is on-target. Christian worship demands participation.

In Paul's polemic to the recently converted Corinthian pagans, the apostle argued that the Christian cannot "...drink the cup of the Lord *and* the cup of demons." Apparently some of the Corinthian Christians wanted it both ways – to enjoy the blessings of Christ yet continue to frequent a pagan altar. Paul considered that an anathema and appealed to the celebration of the Lord's Supper as his evidence.

---

30 Rev. 5:13-14 (RSV)

31 Søren Kierkegaard, *Purity of Heart* (SV XI 114-15), 180-81 reprinted in *Parables of Kierkegaard,* ed. Thomas C. Oden (Princeton NJ: Princeton University Press, 1978), 89-90.

Therefore, my beloved, flee from idolatry. I speak as to sensible people; judge for yourselves what I say. The cup of blessing that we bless, is it not a participation in the blood of Christ? The bread that we break, is it not a participation in the body of Christ? Because there is one bread, we who are many are one body, for we all partake of the one bread. Consider the people of Israel: are not those who eat the sacrifices participants in the altar? What do I imply then? That food offered to idols is anything, or that an idol is anything? No, I imply that what pagans sacrifice they offer to demons and not to God. I do not want you to be participants with demons. You cannot drink the cup of the Lord and the cup of demons. You cannot partake of the table of the Lord and the table of demons.[32]

His purpose was not to provide insight into the Lord's Supper, but rather to use its well-established meaning to illustrate his point. Everyone knew that the *Table of the Lord* demonstrated the unity of the Christian church; that every time the assembled church drank from the "cup of blessing" and broke the "one bread" they participated in the Lord's death and resurrection.[33] Paul's intentional use of the Greek *koinōnia* is significant. Translated into English as "fellowship," "participation," or "communion," its meaning is undeniable: it demands an active "sharing in something."[34]

Far too often (as in the civilian church), chapel worship is dominated by the chaplain. Military personnel and families long to participate if even by a simple "amen" or "praise the Lord." The chaplain who feels the burden to perform rather than lead the congregation in worship is doomed for failure before he begins for the simple reason that worship – by its very nature – must be experienced.

In his popular book, *Worship is a Verb*, Robert Webber devoted a whole chapter to the public reading of Scripture.[35] The God, who spoke, speaks! The God,

---

32 1 Cor. 10:14-21 (RS)

33 1 Cor. 11:26 (RSV)

34 Friedrich Hauck, *Koinōn in Theological Dictionary of the New Testament*, III, ed. Gerhard Kittel, trans. Geoffrey W. Bromiley (Grand Rapids: Wm. B. Eerdmans Publishing Company, 1965), 804.

35 Robert Webber, *Worship Is A Verb* (Peabody, Massachusetts: Hendrickson Publishers, Inc., 1985), 65-84.

who acted, acts! Scripture reading is no mere recital of past events but an opportunity to involve both the reader and listener in a continual reapplication of the Word, which is "living and active, sharper than any two-edged sword, piercing to the division of soul and of spirit, of joints and of marrow, and discerning the thoughts and intentions of the heart."[36] Worship that is imbued with this kind of power cannot be passively received. It deserves a hearty "Thanks be to God," "Amen," or any other appropriate affirmation of faith. If God is actually present in our worship, how can we sit passively? Worship begs for response.

(3) Express Unity of Spirit in Worship

Living in a military community, soldiers and their families often find themselves worshiping with strangers – mostly the result of frequent deployments, temporary duty, and permanent changes of station, but also due to the denominational diversity inherent in a chapel congregation. When chapel worshipers extend the hand of fellowship it is painfully clear that they are more-often-than-not shaking the hand of a stranger. Even in the civilian church getting to know the person sitting to one's side is difficult, but the transient and pluralistic nature of the military exacerbates this problem and challenges the military chaplain to be creative in worship, encouraging greater unity-of-spirit among the body of Christ.

Though many Christians feel the estrangement division has created, it is important to understand that the purpose of the worship assembly is not only reconciliation with God but with each other. Jesus told those who had a grievance against their neighbor to "...leave your gift at the altar and go. First be reconciled to your brother, and then come and offer your gift."[37] Paul reminded the church at Rome, that "Christ reconciled us to himself and gave us the ministry of reconciliation."[38] Unity of spirit is a challenge for both the

---

36 Heb. 4:12 (RSV)

37 Mt. 5:24 (RSV)

38 Rom. 5:10 (RSV)

civilian and military church, but denominational diversity found within the military congregation makes it an even greater challenge for the chaplain.

It is important for the evangelical chaplain to understand the difference between pluralism and ecumenism. Pluralism proposes that all religions (e.g. Christianity, Judaism, Islam, Buddhism, etc.) are equal; ecumenism aims for unity or cooperation among "Christian" denominations. Even when referring to the diversity of religious faiths within the military community, the chaplain needs to appreciate the distinction between the terms "pluralism" and "pluralistic" as both are tossed around as if they are synonymous.[39]

Accepting all soldiers' religious beliefs as equal to Christianity and working within a pluralistic setting are very different. However politically correct, it is biblically misleading for the evangelical chaplain to endorse pluralism and is counterproductive to the Christian chaplain's calling to "Go therefore and make disciples of all nations, baptizing them in the name of the Father, and of the Son, and of the Holy Spirit."[40] However, that is not to say that the Christian chaplain cannot fulfill his constitutional mandate to facilitate the soldier's religious freedom.

Though the evangelical chaplain knows that Jesus is "the way, the truth, and the life"[41] for all soldiers, he also understands that they have the constitutional (and God-given) right to believe as they choose. As military chaplains it is the chaplain's sworn duty to facilitate their right to believe and practice their faith. The proverbial bottom line is not complicated: The Christian chaplain can work within a pluralistic culture while not practicing pluralism.

Ecumenism is entirely different. Protestant chaplains have a unique opportunity to minister to Christians from many different denominations, but as in all opportunities, it is not without challenges. With over a hundred Christian denominations represented in the military, the evangelical chaplain

---

39 See chapter two.

40 Mt. 28:19 (RSV)

41 *Cf.* Jn. 14:6

may believe that "unity of purpose" is impossible. Yet in truth that depends upon the degree of unity pursued.

The Apostle Paul's appeal to the divided Corinthian church serves as a reminder to the chaplain that the Lord intended for His people to be united.[42] It is not within the scope of this study to debate whether or not denominationalism is good or bad, but it is a cultural fact that the Christian chaplain must deal with in order to be an effective minister within the military.

How can the evangelical chaplain conscientiously worship with denominationally-different Christian colleagues who may or may not be in complete doctrinal agreement? It is a question that every Protestant chaplain must address sooner or later. For me (Whittington), the challenge was immediate but rewarding.

Within the first week of active duty I was forced to deal with the issue as is every chaplain. I served on a medium-sized Air Force base with three other Protestant chaplains – Methodist, Presbyterian, and Christian Church. Along with two Catholic priests, we were one team ministering to one military community. Working within such ecumenism was relatively easy "outside" the chapel walls; no two chaplains were assigned the same squadron. All ministry of presence in hangars, on the flight line, and throughout the base community was free of doctrinal discussions. Simply put, our paths seldom crossed in the field; and when we did work together it was generally understood that theological differences of opinion would be discussed privately. However, worship "within" the walls of the chapel was a different story.

There I was, worshiping with chaplains from Christian traditions different from my own. Within weeks I noticed a recurring theme; though the worship style was different, the centrality of Jesus Christ was evident. Over time, I noticed that each of my colleagues was willing to forego many of their "traditions" in an effort to unify the team to reach the airmen for Christ. Granted, not every Air Force chaplain could boast of such a welcoming entrance into the military

---

42 *Cf.* 1 Cor. 1:10ff

chaplaincy, but these good experiences (with few exceptions) continued throughout my entire career.

There are those who contend that the strength of the military chaplaincy resides in its differences. While this may be true when considering the chaplain's skills as part of a team, there is no doubt that effective ministry demands a unified team.

The strength of the Christian chaplaincy does not reside in its differences, but rather in what binds it together – Jesus Christ. Over time, this singular credo: "I believe that Jesus Christ is the Son of God and my Lord and Savior" became my only test of fellowship. True to Scripture (e.g. John 3:16, 14:6; 1 Corinthians 12:3, Philippians 2:11) this confession of faith is at the heart of Christianity and is best expressed by Jesus' appeal to unite all believers.

> I do not pray for these only [apostles], but also for those who believe in me through their word, that they may all be one; even as thou, Father, art in me, and I in thee, that they also may be in us, so that the world may believe that thou hast sent me.[43]

Arguably, military Christians (who have set aside their denominational traditions to focus exclusively on the Lordship of Jesus Christ) have realized Jesus' prayer for unity "that they may all be one." And though the Protestant chaplain retains his own denominational identity (as do his parishioners), he recognizes the opportunity to serve all Christians a unique blessing!

(4) Enjoy the Celebration of Worship

People love to celebrate. As a nation we honor our national identity on several holidays – President's Day, Memorial Day, Independence Day, Labor Day, Veterans Day, and Thanksgiving. As families we celebrate life with birthdays, anniversaries, and graduations. Special occasions may call for our finest china or decorative paper plates, our finest silverware or colored plastic ware, champagne or fruit punch, gifts or balloons; but the one element that is

---

43 Jn. 17:20-21 (RSV)

common to every holiday and special occasion is a celebrative heart! In these special moments we reevaluate the meaning of our lives in the loving context of family and friends.

Celebrations provide an excuse to spend precious time with a child learning how to ride a bicycle, or laugh with friends while playing volleyball, or share a special gift with someone we love. As we slow our gait, we begin to smell the roses and are reminded of the world around us. It gives us perspective. Our mundane routines, however important, seem less significant when compared to those beautiful people with whom we celebrate life. The more momentous the occasion the deeper the appreciation for life's meaning. This is what elevates worship!

Biblical worship is rooted in God's interaction with His people and is highly festive and joyful. Even a quick perusal of the Old Testament reveals what God did for Israel and the celebration connected with each event, such as Passover, but the greatest celebration was yet to come. The prophets foretold the coming of the age when the Messiah would "bind up the broken hearted"[44] and establish a "new covenant."[45] A time of true fellowship realized through Jesus Christ!

According to the New Testament, reconciliation with God became possible with the realization of the good news, which the Apostle Paul affirmed as the death, burial, and resurrection of Jesus Christ.[46] The purpose of worship is not to prove the Christ it celebrates, but to enjoy our relationship with God through the risen Christ! As the gospel unfolds in worship the event becomes real to us. Any victory is worthy of celebration but a victory of that magnitude is incomparable as Paul exclaimed,

> But whatever gain I had [his enviable Jewish genealogy] I counted as loss for the sake of Christ. Indeed I count everything as loss because of the surpassing worth of knowing Christ Jesus my Lord … that I may

---

44 Isa. 61:1 (RSV)

45 Jer. 31:33 (RSV)

46 *Cf.* 1 Cor. 15:1-4

know him and the power of his resurrection. Thanks be to God who gives us the victory through our Lord Jesus Christ.[47]

Conclusion

In the autumn of 1993, Reverend Billy Graham wrote a letter to the Air Force Chief of Chaplains offering to "say a few words to our men and women in the armed forces"[48] stationed in the Japanese islands. On January 9, 1994, as a prelude to his four day crusade in the Tokyo dome, a worship service was planned at Yokota Air Base, Japan – headquarters of Fifth Air Force and United States Forces, Japan.

As project officer for the event, Colonel Whittington enjoyed the privilege of coordinating the worship service with the whole Protestant community, to include a sizeable contingent of U.S. soldiers, sailors, marines, and coastguardsmen, as well as thousands of airmen.

An added joy was planning the upcoming worship service with Dr. Graham, Henry Holley (Tokyo Mission 94 Director), George Beverly Shea, and a host of other incredibly gifted Christian servants working within the Billy Graham Evangelistic Association. Even more noteworthy than the obvious blessing of working with the greatest evangelist of the twentieth century, was the event itself – a vivid reminder that the military chaplaincy afforded a simple preacher the rare pleasure of experiencing Jesus' prayer for unity, "that they might all be one."[49]

On January 9, 1994, Christians from many different denominational traditions gathered to celebrate their common salvation through Jesus Christ. On this particular Sunday there were no other Protestant worship services – no general service, no gospel service, no liturgical service, no contemporary service, and no denominational worship of any kind on the entire installation. We were,

---

47 *Cf.* Phil. 3:7, 8a, 10a. 1 Cor. 15:57

48 Billy Graham letter (Sep. 23, 1993) to Ch, Maj. Gen., Donald Harlin; copy to Gen. Colin Powell and project officer, Ch, Lt. Col., Michael Whittington.

49 Jn. 17:21c (RSV)

in fact, the assembled church and our presence declared to the American and Japanese communities, "Jesus is Lord of all."

The worship itself was a glorious reenactment of the Christ-event. The congregation was called to worship by the Air Force Band of the Pacific – all volunteering their gifts of instrument and song. The call to worship was followed by a reading from the prophet Jeremiah quoting the Lord, when He promised,

> I will make a new covenant with the house of Israel and the house of Judah ... I will put my law within them, and I will write it upon their hearts; and I will be their God, and they shall be my people ... for I will forgive their iniquity, and I will remember their sin no more.[50]

The New Testament reading of John 1:1-18 reminded the congregation "how" God could forgive their iniquity and remember their sin no more – through Jesus Christ.

> In the beginning was the Word and the Word was with God, and the Word was God; all things were made through him, and without him was not anything made that was made. In him was life, and the life was the light of men ... And the Word became flesh and dwelt among us, full of grace and truth ... No one has ever seen God; the only Son, who is in the bosom of the Father, he has made him known.[51]

A community choir was formed – airmen, marines, sailors, soldiers, and coastguardsmen all asking to be a part of the celebration. The congregation's participation was evident throughout the worship with responsive readings, prayers, shouts of joy, and moments of deafening silence when one could have audibly heard a pin dropped in the middle of thousands. A prayer for the nation served as the preface for Reverend Graham's sermon; a powerful message taken from the 23rd Psalm, arguably the best known passage in the Bible and the one most often recited by the soldier in harm's way.

---

50 *Cf.* Jer. 31:31-34

51 Jn. 1:1, 14, 18 (RSV)

The Lord is my shepherd, I shall not want; he makes me lie down in green pastures. He leads me beside still waters; he restores my soul. He leads me in paths of righteousness for his name's sake. Even though I walk through the valley of the shadow of death, I fear no evil; for you are with me; your rod and your staff they comfort me. You prepare a table before me in the presence of my enemies; you anoint my head with oil, my cup overflows. Surely goodness and mercy shall follow me all the days of my life; and I shall dwell in the house of the Lord forever.

No one appreciates that particular psalm more than America's warriors. In times of peace, King David could calmly sing about his Lord in the third-person. *He* makes me lie down in green pastures. *He* restores my soul. *He* leads me in paths of righteousness. However, when the warrior King found himself in the valley of death it got personal and the psalmist shifted to speaking directly to God. I fear no evil for *you* are with me. *Your* rod and *your* staff they comfort me. *You* prepare a table before me. *You* anoint my head with oil. And so it is with the fighting men and women of America's armed forces. Both of your authors have shared the 23rd Psalm with literally thousands of troops, and more often than not, they would join us as we quietly whispered the words, "The Lord is my shepherd ...." As the noted evangelist closed his message, the whole congregation responded in tribute to Jesus Christ as we sang,

> Amazing grace! How sweet the sound
> That saved a wretch like me!
> I once was lost but now am found,
> Was blind but now I see.[52]

Irenaeus, a second-century Church Father, wrote, "The glory of God is a living man; and the life of man consists in beholding God."[53] Beholding God! What an interesting turn-of-phrase. It implies more than being a bystander watching God. It is a spiritual participation so intense that God and the one "beholding" become one in Spirit; true worship!

---

[52] The first verse to the Christian hymn, *Amazing Grace,* written by the English poet and clergyman John Newton (1725-1807).

[53] Irenaeus, *Against Heresies* 4. 34. 5-7.

Helping the soldier and his family experience God is the goal of the Christian chaplain. The best we can do is to ask the Lord for help, knowing that the Spirit "intercedes for us with sighs too deep for words"[54] as we plan a Christ-centered worship that encourages participation, expresses unity of spirit, and enjoys a heart-felt celebration of the greatest story ever told. May you be so blessed as to witness a soldier, sailor, marine, airman, or coastguardsman, behold God!

Rev. Billy Graham is transported by AF helicopter from his Tokyo hotel to Yokota AB, Japan early on Sunday morning, Jan. 9, 1994. The world-renowned evangelist preached to 2,500 military personnel and dependents assigned to the United States Forces, Japan.

---

54   Rom. 8:26b (RSV)

Lt. Gen. Richard Myers (right), Commander of the United States Forces, Japan and Brig. Gen. Michael McCarthy (374th Airlift Wing Commander) greet Rev. Graham before he enters the chapel for prayer and fellowship.

The worship service (Jan. 9, 1994) closes as Dr. Billy Graham and George Beverly Shea join the troops in the singing of "Amazing Grace."

CHAPTER SIX

BUILDING A PROTESTANT PROGRAM

*Being a chaplain in the military is not all about war, blood, and guts. Much
of the chaplain's work is the same as that of any parish priest.*[1]

Joseph F. O'Donnell, C.S.C.

———————————

Every military installation is unique. They may be grouped together under a
unified command such as United States Pacific Command (USPACOM), or a
major command within a single branch of service such as Pacific Air Forces
(PACAF), but no two installations have exactly the same mission parameters,
spiritual needs, or religious demographics.

When ensuring the free exercise of religion for all military personnel,
each branch of service has regulatory guidelines on how the chaplaincy
accommodates the soldier's constitutional rights. There is uniformity across
the Department of Defense when assessing "what" the chaplain should do;
namely, "perform or provide" pastoral care for all troops and spiritual advice
to commanders, but the "how" is as fluid as the "what" is firm.

A unified *field manual* on how to build a Protestant program simply does not
exist at a strategic level. The chaplains at every worldwide installation are
expected to build a program based upon the needs of their particular military
community, but every installation where military families live, work, and
worship have similar spiritual needs, no less than a civilian neighborhood
in a typical American town. Civilian churches do their best to meet these
demands by establishing viable worship services, Christian education classes,

———————————

1 Joseph F. O'Donnell, C.S.C. "Clergy in the Military – Vietnam and After: One Chaplain's Reflections,"
in *The Sword of the Lord: Military Chaplains from the First to the Twenty-First Century,* ed. Doris L. Bergen
(Notre Dame, Indiana: University of Notre Dame Press, 2004), 221.

and tailored programs to address the spiritual needs of the local community. Military chapels are no different.

Lack of a unified strategic plan should not preclude one from developing a general template for building a Protestant program, one that could be flexible enough to adapt itself to most peacetime military communities. The following fifteen-step model will equip a Protestant chaplain with such a template.

Airmen continually hear, "flexibility is the key to airpower." Truth be known, flexibility is the key to all success. Knowing that every installation has unique spiritual needs, the reader is encouraged to be flexible, adapting the various steps as needed.

Every Protestant denomination has its own interpretation of church ecclesiology – how the church should be organized. Based upon several New Testament texts, the first-century church had bishops, pastors, elders, deacons, and teachers,[2] yet regardless of how a certain church is organized, there must be a well-informed laity functioning as a working team – organizing, planning, and implementing worship services and programs. For most military chapel congregations this carefully-selected team is called the Protestant Parish Council (PPC). The council works directly with the Protestant chaplains in developing and implementing the Protestant program, and as such, is essential to its success.

The following fifteen-step plan was developed by Chaplain Davidson and implemented with MAJCOM-recognized success during his leadership at Eielson Air Force Base, Alaska. Though initially developed for Air Force chaplains, the template could easily be adapted to any military installation. It is based upon a single hierarchical premise: the parish council – consisting of all Protestant chaplains and selected lay leaders assigned to a particular chapel – is led by the senior protestant chaplain.

---

2 Many scholars believe that the terms bishop (Grk. *epískopos*), pastor (Grk. *poimēn*), and elder (*presbúteros*) are used interchangeably. Cf. Eph. 4:11-13; 1 Tim. 3:1-13; Tit. 1:5-9; Phil. 1:1

STEP ONE – Training the Council to See the Vision

The Bible teaches, "Where there is no vision the people perish."[3] The most important person at this stage of the process is the senior protestant chaplain. Jay A. Conger, a recognized expert on leadership, explained, "Leaders are individuals who establish direction for a working group of individuals, who gain commitment from these group members to this direction, and who then motivate these members to achieve the direction."[4] The senior protestant chaplain must have a clear biblical vision of the leadership direction of the Holy Spirit.

> The leadership design of any church [Brian Bauknight insisted] must not get too far from the Holy Spirit. Fully developed discipleship of in-reach and outreach demands a strong dependence upon the work of the Spirit. The gifts that God gives to believers are a manifestation of the work of the Spirit. Any church that desires a balanced ministry, therefore, is one where the people have some convictions regarding the work of the Holy Spirit.[5]

Every leader must begin by praying and seeking God's direction; then he (or she) will need to implement the chapel's vision based upon a solid biblical foundation. An ideal situation is for the council to develop a purpose statement that reflects the theology of all its members, but with a religiously diverse team, this is practically impossible. An experienced senior protestant chaplain will recognize this diversity and encourage the parish council to develop a vision statement, acceptable to all members of the council and theologically sound.

During every Summer Olympics the most popular race is the one-mile relay (4 x 400 meters); the highlight of the track and field events. Each nation assembles its fastest 400-meters' runners. The most critical part of the race, however, is

---

3 *Cf.* Prov. 29:18

4 Jay A. Conger, *Learning to Lead – The Art of Transforming Managers into Leaders* (San Francisco: Jossey-Bass Publishers, 1992), 18.

5 Brian Kelley Bauknight, *Body Building: Creating a Ministry Team Through Spiritual Gifts* (Nashville: Abingdon Press, 1996), 28.

not the speed of the runner but how well each person hands off the baton. If dropped, the team will lose the race. Successful leaders safely pass the vision to their team members.

Rick Warren, in his best-selling book, *The Purpose Driven Church* suggested five ways through which a leader could communicate a vision and a purpose: Scripture, symbols, slogans, stories, and specifics.[6]

> [Using Scripture] teach the biblical truth about the church. Teach the doctrine of the church passionately and frequently. Show how every part of your church's vision is biblically based by giving Bible verses that explain and illustrate your reasoning.[7]

In other words, preach sermons that are centered on the "vision." In relation to using symbols and slogans, Warren suggested "[these] can be powerful communication tools because they elicit strong passions and emotions."[8] Stories illustrate the purpose of the church, and specifics serve to accomplish that purpose.

STEP TWO – Developing the Parish Council Purpose Statement

After the senior protestant chaplain has helped the council understand and accept the chapel's vision, it is important to develop a plan for the next twelve months, outlining the Protestant chapel's purpose. This calls for a purpose statement, clearly defining the vision and purpose of the chapel's ministry. The Protestant Parish Council would do well to ensure the vision and purpose are biblical, clear and easy to follow, and quantifiable.

Rick Warren passionately argued, "An effective purpose statement expresses the New Testament doctrine of the church ... we don't decide the purposes of the church – we discover them."[9] The purpose statement must be centered on

---

6 Rick Warren, *The Purpose Driven Church* (Grand Rapids: Zondervan Publishing House, 1995), 112-114.

7 *Ibid.*, 112.

8 *Ibid.*

9 *Ibid.*, 100.

God's Word, clear, and easy to understand. Keep it short and include only those things that bring glory to the Lord and within the capability of the Protestant chapel. In his well-written book, *Master Planning*, author Bobb Biehl writes, "Determining a directional statement for your organization is one of the most critical and sometimes frightening ... moves in all of leadership. It is moving from 'just getting by' to 'winning big.'"[10]

Moreover, the purpose statement should be quantifiable, easily evaluated and measured with the help of surveys and performance measures. When used properly, it will provide the senior protestant chaplain and the parish council with an accurate means of evaluating ministry-success. Adapting quantifiable measures will alert both chaplain and council should there be a need to edit the purpose statement. Quantifiable measures should address certain questions:

1. Why does the Protestant ministry function? (Why are we here?)

2. What is our reason for having a Protestant ministry?

3. Who are we as chapel Protestants?

4. What are our goals for the Protestant ministry?

5. What are the ways to accomplish these goals?

If these questions are asked at a parish council meeting, the senior protestant could have a respected member take the lead and write the responses on a white board or poster paper. A thorough discussion should follow; afterwards, the senior protestant should take the lead in facilitating the council to write the purpose statement.

The following is an example of the purpose statement developed at Eielson Air Force Base (AFB), Alaska in the summer of 1999. Listed in the form of a creed, each statement identified the beliefs of the Protestant chaplains and the Protestant Parish Council. The statement read,

---

10   Bobb Biehl, *Master-Planning – The Complete Guide For Building A Strategic Plan For Your Business, Church, or Organization* (Nashville: Broadman & Holman, 1997), 72.

- We believe God is preparing us for very significant times as a congregation.

- We believe whatever direction we take as a body must be firmly grounded in His Word.

- We believe that the chapel's mission must be "The Great Commission" as stated in Matthew 28:19-20 to "Go and make disciples of all nations, baptizing them in the name of the Father and of the Son and of the Holy Spirit, and teaching them to obey everything I have commanded you and I will be with you until the end of the age."

- We believe "The body is a unit, though it is made up of many parts; and though all its parts are many, they form one body. So it is with Christ. For we were all baptized by one Spirit into one body."[11]

In the same council meeting at Eielson AFB, the senior protestant symbolically compared the chapel congregation to a tree. In order for any tree to flourish and bear fruit, it must be nourished and cultivated. We cannot be sincere in our worship of God without doing God's will. And we cannot do God's will without a vital, personal relationship with the Lord. In view of this truth, we were attentive to the spiritual development of our congregation; equipping them to bear fruit. To that end, we concluded that our purpose could be summarized as follows:

> To bring people into the membership of God's family through a relationship with Jesus Christ, develop them to spiritual maturity and equip them for ministry using their spiritual gift(s) in the chapel and life's mission in the world, in order to magnify God's name.

STEP THREE – *Organizing Monthly Meetings*

An often heard question is "How often should the parish council meet?" Too often and they suffer burn-out, too infrequent and the members lose interest. The following three suggestions are guidelines to consider when scheduling the Protestant Parish Council meeting.

---

11 1 Cor. 12:12-13 (NKJV)

(1) Is the meeting necessary?

Jerold W. Apps offered six tips to help the leader determine whether or not a meeting is necessary: study the situation, determine the specific purpose for the meeting, plan the agenda, prepare introductory remarks, make necessary arrangements, and decide on methods and equipment.[12] Is this a new group or have they been together for a while? What is the purpose of the meeting? What kind of authority does this group have and how does it relate to other chapel groups? What is the time limit? All of these questions can be easily answered once the senior protestant chaplain understands the dynamics of the council. Once answered, the chaplain and the parish president can determine how often the council needs to meet.

Once the meeting is established, the senior protestant would do well to follow his own checklist, ensuring that he has an agenda to include his introductory remarks describing the importance of the meeting, how the members will be involved, and administrative issues such as assigning a secretary and a time keeper. The venue is also important; making sure the room is the right size with appropriate lighting, seating arrangements, and necessary equipment.

Even more important than the agenda and administrative concerns is recognizing the possibility of conflict. Conflict must be acknowledged and dealt with as it occurs. To ignore it is not to eliminate it. This is where the senior protestant and the parish president can help. A wise chaplain will always allow the council president to assist in resolving conflict. Gaylord Noyce noted, "[the] chairperson facilitates the process of solving problems."[13]

(2) Schedule the Protestant Parish Council meeting at the same location

Try to schedule the PPC monthly meetings at the same location if possible. As creatures of habit, people generally prefer routine. At Eielson AFB the

---

12 Jerold W. Apps, *Ideas for Better Church Meetings* (Minneapolis: Augsburg Publishing House, 1963), 22.

13 Gaylord Noyce, *Church Meetings That Work* (Herndon, VA: The Alban Institute, 1994), 57.

Protestant Parish Council meeting was always conducted in the annex of the main chapel building.

(3) Schedule the date and time of the meeting

Working with each member to arrive at consensus, the date and the time should also be the same from meeting-to-meeting.

STEP FOUR – Accessing the Parish Council Members

All of our Armed Forces' organizations have a recall system for emergencies. Whenever there is an important event such as a military exercise, or a real-world emergency, the commanding general and all other subordinate commanders must be able to notify their troops, with priority given to mission essential personnel. The speed of the recall procedures may change with technology but the goal remains the same; contact personnel as quickly as possible!

The chapel also has recall procedures at every level, to include contacting the members of the respective parish councils. What if something were to occur that was urgent and the senior protestant or one of the parish council members needed to contact the membership? The chaplain and president of the council need to establish the same procedures that exist elsewhere on the installation. Depending on the available technology, this could be as simple as a telephone roster. In order for any type of recall to be initiated, there must be an up-to-date membership list with the appropriate information. Moreover, the senior protestant chaplain needs to ensure that every member of the council has been trained to receive and disseminate sensitive information with the appropriate protocol.

STEP FIVE – Developing an Organizational Chart

In order to manage a parish council in an orderly fashion it is necessary to develop an organizational chart. The authors of *Mastering Church Management* assert "Management is one way leadership manifest itself in the church. As most good leaders know, management is the process of getting things done through other people."[14]

An organizational chart provides members with a visual, informing them of whom to contact when developing and implementing specific programs or resolving conflicts. For example, during Davidson's leadership at Eielson AFB, the Worship division Leadership Team was responsible for recruiting, training, and budgeting. Listed under the Worship Ministry subheading were all of the Protestant ministries within this division. If a council member was asked by a local parishioner how one might be chosen to usher or read Scripture during worship services, the council member would consult the organizational chart and direct the worshiper to the right person. Bobb Biehl encouraged the leader to embrace organizational charts,

> An organizational chart makes clear to everyone who is responsible for what and who is responsible for whom. It is like a playing roster for a football team, a basketball team, or a baseball team. Everyone knows what his or her position is and what the relationship of the position is to all of the other positions on the team. It is this knowledge that lets people play together in precision, harmony, and unity.[15]

Organization is essential to a Protestant Parish Council. The council may recommend a great program but without the proper organization, it will be so confusing as to never be implemented. Continuing Biehl's sports analogy, imagine a head football coach taking eleven players, telling them to go on the field and win the game without assigning them specific positions. They would not only lose the game, the field of play would be utterly chaotic.

Dr. Jerry Falwell, renowned pastor of Thomas Road Baptist Church and founder of Liberty University in Lynchburg, Virginia told Chaplain Davidson on more than one occasion, "Charlie, if it is Christian it should be the best

---

14 Don Cousina, Keith Anderson, and Arthur MacDonald. *Mastering Church Management* (Kansas City: Watterich Publishers, 1956), 18-19.

15 Biehl, 88-89.

... don't ever settle for second-place in the Lord's work." Without the proper organizational structure, the Protestant ministry will always be second-best.

STEP SIX – *Writing the Guidelines*

Guidelines do precisely what the name proposes, they "guide" the processes of the organizational chart by providing the operational procedures to the council members as they develop and implement the chapel programs. All military branches have policy directives that guide their personnel. The nomenclature may change but regulations are prevalent in all armed services within the Department of Defense. In the United States Air Force these guidelines are called Air Force Instructions and they are written as procedural handbooks allowing airmen to perform everyday operations. The Protestant Parish Council Guidelines also serve as an operational tool to help the council members accomplish the chapel mission as defined in the purpose statement – to bring people into the membership of God's family through a relationship with Jesus Christ.

Barry McCarthy persuasively argued, "Successful meetings are possible only when there is an orderly consideration of business."[16] When preparing guidelines for the parish council, the senior protestant chaplain should consider McCarthy's recommendations.[17]

- Draft proposed bylaws

- Establish a guideline-committee

- Ascertain chapel needs

- Examine existing documents

- Write and review an initial draft

- Report findings to the council

- Adopt bylaws

---

16 Barry McCarthy, *A Parliamentary Guide for Church Leadership* (Nashville: Broadman Press, 1976), 19.

17 *Ibid.*, 16.

During this process, the senior protestant chaplain must ensure that the bylaws include the name, mission, members, officers, and the agreed-upon meeting arrangements of the parish council. Moreover, brevity and clarity are essential; the guidelines should be short and easy to understand. Nothing will stifle a ministry faster than too many rules.

I (Davidson) shared the following anecdote with my team in Eielson AFB to illustrate the need to write easy-to-follow rules.

> Summer finally arrives and dad decides to welcome the warm weather with a special family barbecue. There is nothing to it, right? The children get excited, mom purchases those great big steaks with all the trimmings and dad gets in the truck and heads to the nearest outdoor furniture store to buy the new barbeque grill. Sounds simple so far! Dad buys the grill and returns home. He pulls the huge box out of the truck and puts it on the patio to uncrate and assemble. Opening the box he smiles at his wife and children who are standing around the monstrous box laughing, having fun, and looking forward to a great meal that dad is going to cook on their new family grill. After ripping the layers of cardboard from around the grill, dad lays out all the different parts in a neat and orderly manner. He then begins reading the assembly instructions from a book the size of his wallet, in three languages. There are no fewer than a hundred steps to assemble, and after sweating bullets in the summer heat, he decides to toss the instructions and go it alone. By now, the wife and kids note the frustration and quietly slip away. You know how the story ends; of course you do, you've been there! The wife and kids gave up on good-ole-dad hours ago. As the sun is setting, the frustrated dad finally gets the grill together and then shouts to the heavens, "I will never buy another grill as long as I live!"

The moral of the story is clear: Instructions will only be used by the average "dad" if they are easy to follow. In the following example, the reader will note the Eielson AFB Protestant Parish Council Guidelines – a precise document that served the council well.

GUIDELINES OF THE PROTESTANT PARISH COUNCIL
EIELSON AIR FORCE BASE, ALASKA

GL-1.0 This governing body shall be known as the Eielson AFB Protestant Parish Council.

GL-1.1 This document shall be known as the "Guidelines of the PPC" and is created by the action and approval of the EAFB Wing Chaplain and applicable in all affairs of the council.

GL-2.0 MEETINGS AND ORGANIZATION

GL-2.1 The PPC shall meet monthly. The PPC President in consultation with the SPC may call other meetings.

GL-2.2 The Agenda for any meeting of the PPC shall be prepared by the SPC in consultation with the PPC President. The following is a suggested order of business:

1. Minutes from last meeting

2. Reports, oral and written, from each PPC Division

3. Expenditures form the previous quarter (month) and spending proposals for the next quarter (month)

4. After action reports, surveys, and quality performance measurements

5. Other business. Special meetings will follow a format that best meets its needs.

GL-2.3 PPC should faithfully attend all meetings unless excused because of duty/necessary requirement. PPC members should contact the PPC President or SPC before the scheduled meeting for an expected absence.

GL-3.0 PARISH COUNCIL STRUCTURE AND OFFICERS

GL-3.1 The purpose of the PPC is to coordinate, assist, evaluate, and promote all of the programs of the protestant parish. In order to accomplish this task, it is empowered to create Divisions, committees and Working Groups to accomplish its work.

GL-3.2 The PPC shall oversee the implementation of the vision, objectives and policies of the Chapel Program and assign responsibilities relating to the work of its Divisions. Within the guidelines established, Divisions shall be expected to and are authorized to function in the way they deem best to accomplish the assigned work. Their actions are always subject to review and approval by the PPC with final control placed with the SPC and WC. The Divisions shall refer matters that require administrative decisions to the PPC with recommendations for appropriate actions.

GL-3.3 The PPC shall be responsible for communication, strategy, long range planning, evaluation, budget planning/review and stewardship. It shall develop and propose to the SPC an annual budget to be presented at the August meeting.

GL-3.4 The Officers of the PPC shall be:

1. President-Selected by the SPC in consultation with other active duty chapel attendees. (All PPC Presidents thereafter will be elected by the PPC.)

2. Vice-President-Elected by the PPC from the PPC membership.

3. Secretary- (Optional)-Elected by the PPC from the PPC membership.

4. All Officers elected or selected are required to attend a leadership-training course and complete the Spiritual Gift Inventory. Service in each office will ordinarily be one year.

GL-3.5 Selection and election of the PPC President, Division Chairman's, Members at Large and the Alternates will be accomplished in the month of May. The PPC meeting in June will serve as a time for transition and the meeting in July will be designated the first official business meeting of the new PPC.

GL-3.6 The voting membership of the PPC shall be as follows:

1. The President

2. The Vice-President

3. The Four Division Chairmen

4. The Members at Large

5. The Alternates will vote when filling in for another member

6. The total voting membership of the PPC is eight if using this format. However, the number of PPC members will be determined by the SPC. An assessment of the Protestant Chapel Ministry will mandate the size of the PPC.

GL-3.7 The non-voting advisory members of the PPC shall be all PC's with the SPC acting as the primary advisor to the PPC.

GL-3.8 A quorum shall consist of a majority of the voting membership.

GL-4.0 THE DIVISIONS OF THE COUNCIL

GL-4.1 The Four Divisions of the PPC shall be:

1. The Worship Division

2. The Religious Education Division

3. The Nurture and Outreach Division

4. The Lay Division

GL-4.2 The number of persons serving on each Division will be determined by the PPC in consultation with the Division Chairman and the Chaplain Advisor to that Division. Membership in each Division shall be drawn from a list of Chapel attendees from the different worship services. Each member will attend an annual leadership-training course or will be trained by the Division Chairman and the Chaplain Advisor for that Division. Each Division is responsible to the PPC and shall report directly to the PPC.

GL-4.30 Each Division will be organized to accomplish its work and shall have committees and or working groups as necessary.

GL-4.31 WORSHIP DIVISION

GL-4.312 The Worship Division Chairman will work with the Worship Division Chaplain on all matters pertaining to the Worship Ministry.

GL-4.313 Each Worship Service will have its own Worship Committee, responsible for the same areas as the Division and organized for the purpose of coordination and teamwork within each worship service and the total Protestant Worship Community. This is to include the Protestant Purpose Statement, goals and objects.

GL-4.40 RELIGIOUS EDUCATION DIVISION

GL-4.41 The Religious Education Division shall be responsible for all of those areas that pertain to recruiting, training, evaluating, budgeting and planning in religious education. This is to include as a minimum Sunday School, Vacation Bible School, and all other Children/Adult educational ministries.

GL-4.42 The Religious Education Division Chairperson will work with the Religious Education Chaplain and the Religious Education Coordinator (if one is hired) on all matters pertaining to the Religious Education Ministries.

GL-4.50 NURTURE AND OUTREACH DIVISION

GL-4.51 The Nurture and Outreach Division shall be responsible for all of those areas that pertain to recruiting, training, evaluating, budgeting and planning in the nurture and outreach arena. This is to include as a minimum spiritual development opportunities, fellowships special events and designated offerings.

GL-4.52 The Nurture and Outreach Division Chairman will work with the Nurture and Outreach Chaplain on all matters pertaining to the Nurture and Outreach Ministries.

GL-4.60 LAY ORGANIZATION DIVISION

GL-4.61 The Lay Organization Division shall be responsible for all of those areas that pertain to recruiting, training, evaluating, budgeting and planning in all lay organizations. This is to include as a minimum Protestant Men of the Chapel (PMOC), Protestant Women of the Chapel (PWOC), Protestant Singles of the Chapel (PSOC), and the Protestant Youth of the Chapel (PYOC).

GL-4.62 The Lay Organization Chairman will work with the Lay Organization Chaplain on all matters pertaining to the Lay Organization Ministries.

GL-4.70 MEMBERS AT LARGE

GL-4.71 The Members at Large will be responsible for the following areas of ministry.

1. To be the eyes and hears of the Protestant Worship Service they attend. In other words each Member at Large will give a report on the atmosphere of that service.

2. To check with the parish members who are leading the various areas in that service and make sure they have the materials needed in order to do the work.

3. To make sure that the Worship Service Surveys are given quarterly in the service.

4. To get with the chaplain of that service and tally the surveys and be ready to give a report at the next PPC meeting.

5. The Member at Large is not a position for complaining. The Member at Large is to help make things run smoother.

GL-4.80 THE ALTERNATES FOR THE PPC

GL-4.81 If and when an Alternate is needed he/she will resume the responsibilities of the position they fill within the PPC until the regular PPC member returns.

GL-4.82 If for some reason a regular PPC member cannot or does not return then the Alternate who is currently filling the position may become a regular PPC member upon voting approval with a quorum by the PPC membership.

STEP SEVEN – *Writing Job Descriptions*

In order to run a race one must know which way to run. Moreover, there is a need to know how to run, how far to run, and when to stop running. In the Protestant Parish Council, every member must have a job description – a statement of what is required of the individual as a designated member of the council. Harold Westing offered several benefits of job descriptions in his informative book, *Church Staff Handbook – How to Build an Effective Ministry Team.* He explained,

> Job descriptions spell out duties, responsibilities, and limits of authority in a particular position. Even though every possible situation cannot be written out showing where authority needs to be displayed, some guidelines must be provided for doing so. Here is where role clarification exercises can be helpful. More staff conflict arises here perhaps than any other place. To whom and under what circumstance is a person to be accountable is one of the major ingredients to be clarified.[18]

Frankly, asking someone to perform a task without the proper guidance is a misuse of people resources. A clearly defined job description helps communicate expectations and demonstrates confidence in the ability of others to perform the job. Additionally, it provides the leader with an additional means of communicating the team's vision and describing how that particular member can help the team realize the vision. In *The Every Church Guide to Growth,* the authors asserted, "The pastor-leader must effectively communicate his plan

---

18 Harold J. Westing, *Church Staff Handbook – How to Build an Effective Ministry Team* (Grand Rapids: Kregel Publications, 1997), 95.

so that the followers see [understand] the plan, buy into the plan, desire to implement the plan, and will pay the price to make it happen."[19] This is an essential step for the senior protestant chaplain. The job description must not only be written well but communicated well.

Another important reason for having a job description is that it holds the member accountable. Once a particular person's job description is written by the senior protestant chaplain, the member should understand its gravity – the Christian member is accountable to God, the parish council, and to the whole of the Protestant community. Towns, Wagner, and Rainer prioritized "accountability" as the fifth law of leadership.

> People [the authors insisted] must be involved in the journey. If the pastor tries to take [control of] the journey, he'll never arrive at the destination. The pastor and the people must do it together. The law of accountability says in slogan, "Followers don't do what the leader expects (by vision or dream): they do what the leader inspects."[20]

STEP EIGHT – *Preparing the Agenda*

An agenda – a plan of things to be considered – provides a team with a clear direction. Without it, the members' time and energy are wasted and the meeting serves little purpose. The agenda should include a list of items and programs the senior protestant needs to discuss; and if warranted, to develop and implement. Gary McIntosh's book, *Staff Your Church for Growth-Building Team Ministry In The 21st Century,* argued a well-written agenda "provides for sharing of reports and feedback on each team member's ministry."[21] It is important, however, for the leader to have taken the time to have prioritized the agenda items. What he lists first will be read by the council as most important; conversely, the last item will be considered least important whether the senior protestant chaplain intended it or not.

---

19 Elmer Towns, C. Peter Wagner & Thom S. Rainer, *The Every Church Guide to Growth* (Nashville: Broadman & Holman Publishers, 1998), 172.

20 *Ibid.*

21 Gary L. McIntosh, *Staff Your Church for Growth-Building Team Ministry In The 21st Century* (Grand Rapids: Baker Book House Co, 2000), 126.

STEP NINE – Reporting Procedures

In the parish council meeting it is helpful, when giving a report on a particular ministry, to ensure the information directly relates to the topic of interest. No less important is in the "hearing" of the report by the other members. To facilitate every member's retention of the facts, the chaplain or the council's president should request the report be written and distributed to everyone present. The benefits are many – fewer questions need be asked, the committee member giving the report is more focused and less likely to ramble, and in the need of follow-up every member has a written reminder of the issue; even the secretary benefits by being able to participate without having to continually take down the information in the form of minutes.

Though there is a place for last-minute issues to surface, it is rarely the case that "declared immediacy" is justified. It is simply not a good practice for the senior protestant chaplain to regularly allow for members to give impromptu reports on major issues. No matter how experienced the spokesman, important information will be omitted and the proverbial rabbits will be chased, taking valuable time from the more important issues.

Every parish council division chairperson should be held accountable for providing written reports to every member of the council. A recommended series of questions could serve as a general template for all written reports:

- What is the program, event, or endeavor being reported?

- Who is leading the event?

- How many are expected to attend?

- When is the event to take place (date, time, schedule)?

- Where is the event to take place (location)?

- How is the event being sponsored?

- Are they budgetary concerns (transportation, youth permission slips)?

This brief litany of questions will provide direction and continuity for all members. Keeping these simple tips in mind will help the PPC member cover the main objectives.

STEP TEN – *Developing a Lay Ministry List (Recruiting Volunteers)*

One of the major complaints from many senior protestant chaplains, responsible for building a Protestant program, is a lack of resources – time, money, and people – but the most important of the three is people. Volunteers may be an additional benefit allowing some civilian church programs to excel, but they are absolutely essential for the military chapel to exist.

Post and base chaplains have enormous responsibilities "outside the chapel walls." Their presence is demanded in the work places throughout the installation. As explained in *Part Three,* the chaplain's responsibilities outside the walls of the chapel are exponentially more energy-consuming than his time within the chapel walls. In view of this fact, the chapel's ministries – worship, education, adult/youth programs – depend exclusively on the lay volunteer. With military regulations and fiduciary restraints preventing paid-professional ministry teams, it is extremely important for the Protestant Parish Council to appreciate the need for volunteers.

Without the laity volunteering for chapel ministries, the chapel's purpose to "bring people into the membership of God's family through a relationship with Jesus Christ" is thwarted. Unfortunately, volunteers are few and the chaplain needs to be aware of the danger of burnout. The general rule of "twenty percent of the people doing eighty percent of the work" is proven every day in churches all over America. Volunteer-burnout should be a real concern for the Protestant chaplain trying to build a viable ministry program.

The senior protestant chaplain, in concert with his fellow clergy and the Protestant Parish Council, must address this concern. Better to cancel a program than endanger the spiritual (and physical) health of a volunteer who doesn't seem to know the word "no." Could the chaplain persuade the volunteer to "keep on keeping on"? Of course, but ungodly guilt should never be used by God's pastors. A good shepherd takes care of his flock.

To help prevent the temptation to use the same volunteers over and over again, the senior protestant chaplain with the help of the parish council should develop a Lay Ministry List Form and strongly encourage the congregation to complete the form. One need not reinvent the wheel to come up with an appropriate form. A quick search on the Internet would produce a dozen examples within minutes.

The form should allow the worshipper to identify his or her ministry interests within the large headings of Worship, Religious Education, Nurture/Outreach, Lay Organization, and Recreational Interests. Under each major heading, the form could list the sub-headings (such as greeter, usher, lay-reader, etc.). The congregation could then be asked to complete the form at regular intervals – during worship services, Bible classes, special events, and so forth. These names would then be added to a Lay Ministry List and updated as needed. However elementary this process may sound, one would be amazed at the number of military chapels that have not implemented this simple procedure.

An additional process to identify volunteers is the parish council itself. There is a synergistic creativity in all groups. And it is up to the chaplain to foster a dynamic within the parish council that unleashes this synergy. One model to build a Lay Ministry List calls for the senior protestant chaplain to "brainstorm" with the parish council encouraging them to suggest innovative ways to not only build a particular program, but provide a way to recruit volunteers to implement it.

For example, if the Protestant chapel community is going to start a youth group and the goal is to have at least fifty youth from grades 7-12 attend on a weekly basis, the parish council's responsibility is to figure out how many people are needed to handle this size of ministry. Once planned, the council begins actively recruiting the volunteers. The council engages the chapel congregation with the simple fact, "without the volunteers, the Protestant chapel will have no youth program."

Working with the parish council in an intentional "brainstorming" process will help resolve other program issues as well. How many teachers and sponsors are needed? How many people are needed to help with refreshments? The proverbial bottom line is easy to understand – every aspect of the chapel ministry is dependent on lay volunteers.

The need for the body of Christ working together is as ancient as the New Testament church. We need each other to be what God called us to be – one body of believers using all of God's spiritual gifts. In Romans 12 and 1 Corinthians 12, the Apostle Paul speaks of certain gifts that the Lord gives to His children for the purpose of building His kingdom. It is necessary for all Christians to use the gift (or gifts) God has given them because simply put, the church cannot function when Christians choose to be spectators and not participants. Scripture is replete with the biblical admonition to work together, but the Apostle Paul's solution to the Roman church centered on the members of the congregation pulling together and using their spiritual gifts. In Paul's words, "Having gifts that differ according to the grace given to us, let us use them."[22]

STEP ELEVEN – Developing a Survey

All successful chapel ministries are predicated on the findings of a meaningful survey. Acquiring and assessing "spiritual-needs" information from the local military community is as essential in building a successful chapel program as a surveyor analyzing the rock, soil, and water availability to determine the feasibility of a geothermal heating system. Lucrative business owners spend exorbitant monies discovering the needs of their target-audience. Though marketing agencies across the world use state-of-the-art technology to uncover the needs of the marketplace, it still comes down to one question: "How can we provide what the people need?"

---

22 Rom. 12:6 (RSV)

Some chapel leaders tend to ignore the question all together and just hope that everything will go well. If *status quo* is the chaplain's goal, then the spiritual needs of the soldier or the military family really do not matter, but if the chaplain's ministry is to introduce the soldier to God and God to the soldier, knowing the needs of the military community is prerequisite. Chaplains who pursue excellence ask the tough questions: What does our community need? How do we get the information? Once ascertained, how can we as a congregation, meet those needs? If asked, "How are things going?" a great leader knows the answer. Even though the means of discovering the information continues to evolve with every technological update, the real substance never changes; you have to ask the people. The best information-gathering tool available to the chaplain and the parish council is the old-fashioned "survey."

Surveys validate what the chapel ministry is doing well, challenge what is done poorly, and shed light on what ministries are needed but not provided. Successful senior protestant chaplains and parish councils take surveys seriously and use the feedback judiciously. The survey itself need not be that complicated to achieve outstanding results. Biehl noted "If you ask the right ten people to take ten minutes and fill out this form you will get 50 to 80 percent of the information you need to improve [your ministry]."[23] This would work exceptionally well if the chapel is small; if however, the congregation is several hundred worshipers, it would be prudent to have a larger sample of about twenty percent.

Distributing the survey is not rocket-science; for example, many successful military chaplains still use the ushers to distribute the surveys to the worshiping congregation with a return-goal of twenty percent. This percentage of returns is practical and provides ample information to validate or challenge present programs and recommend future ministries. Further information could be gleaned from the surveys, such as knowing where the congregation stands on the large headings of mission and purpose statement, worship services, religious education, nurture and outreach, and lay ministry.

---

23   Biehl, 146.

Senior protestant chaplains and protestant parish councils who are secure in their faith receive constructive evaluation as if from the Lord Himself. Ministries that have a God-honoring purpose statement with biblical goals and objectives trust the congregation to provide honest and constructive feedback. It is important that the survey is prepared well – concise and prioritized. There is no shortage of materials in the religious marketplace that would help the chaplain and parish council develop a quality survey.

STEP TWELVE – *Developing a Quality Improvement Form*

A completed survey begs the question, "What do we do with the feedback?" It is a great question and one that all successful chaplains and parish councils answer routinely. To that end, the senior protestant chaplain would do well to consider these ten recommendations:

1. If the survey has a scoring system (for example 1-5 with 5 being the best), set an overall goal of averaging 4.5. This would equate to a 90% satisfaction rate, comparable to most military standards for quality-of-life programs.

2. Score the numbered surveys by individual worship services and then score the surveys as a collective group. This will provide the Protestant Parish Council with the satisfaction level (or lack of) for each worship service and the overall combined satisfaction rate.

3. Write down every comment made by the parish for the individual worship services and prioritize these comments from most-mentioned to least-mentioned.

4. Give the information to the Protestant chaplain in charge of each particular worship service.

5. Require the chaplain to inform his/her congregation of these survey recommendations and ask them for additional help by prioritizing the top five recommendations from the most needed to the list needed.

6. Use this prioritized listing of the top five congregational recommendations and share this information with the parish council at the next meeting (ensure it ranks high on the agenda) and seek the council's consensus to validate the congregational priority of the recommendations.

7. The Protestant chaplain in charge of the recommended changes should lead the parish council in a time-controlled brainstorming session suggesting ways to implement the recommendations. If the area for improvement falls under a major ministry division, the chairperson and advisor-chaplain should monitor the progress to ensure the council is on-track.

8. Facilitated by the same Protestant chaplain, the council needs to form an opinion on the improvement to be made, and if needed, develop a plan of action.

9. Inform the congregation of the action plan and continue to keep the church family abreast of its progress.

10. Continue to report on the progress of the action plan to the Protestant Parish Council until the plan is fully implemented.

Every successful organization has a quality control team that continually monitors its business practices in an effort to validate the purpose of the company's existence. Everything the chapel does must relate to the purpose of the Lord's church. Why expend the energy to have a Quality Improvement Form second-to-none? Because the chapel's purpose – leading the military troop and his family to Jesus Christ and equipping them for ministry – is the most noble and important mission in the world!

STEP THIRTEEN – *Quality Performance Measures (QPM)*

If you were to enter the New York Stock Exchange at 11 Wall Street in Lower Manhattan, the first thing you would notice is what the traders call the "Big Board." Its purpose is clear, to reflect in real-time the rise and fall of nearly 4,000 stocks. Metrics serve an important function of providing information necessary for decision-making. Imagine an F-16 pilot charged with intercepting an enemy aircraft without being given the appropriate coordinates, or a marathon runner not knowing the race route. By having charts and statistics on certain topics of interest, an organization can plan future moves. So it is with the military chapel.

The information may be a boring read but utilizing the results to further God's

Kingdom should excite every Christian. A well-prepared performance metric can assist the Protestant Parish Council in understanding both attendance and offerings – two quality measures that provide guidance to all successful chapel leaders.

Quality performance measures are simple to create by using a computer spreadsheet application such as Microsoft Excel. The chapel's administrative staff is trained to design the charts and input the appropriate statistics. A good quality performance measure is essential for the chapel team to build a Protestant program.

It is important to use the QPM on ministries that can be measured. A parish council must avoid the trap of using performance measures in every service program, but the QPM is ideally suited for worship service attendance, offerings, and analyzing statistical surveys.

Using the attendance and offerings quality performance measures at Eielson AFB, the senior protestant chaplain was able to analyze the drop in worship attendance and offerings, investigate the timing of the decrease, and make the appropriate changes. In one particular case, the chaplains and parish council presumed the worship attendances were falling due to poor preaching or an unknown problem among divisive members. Once investigated, it was discovered that one of the fighter squadrons had deployed. The quality performance measure provides only statistics; what one does with the information determines the real value of the QPM.

STEP FOURTEEN – *Protestant Parish Council Flowchart*

Every military person understands and respects the "chain of command." In fact, every civilian organization employs some form of organizational structure; without it, the company cannot be productive. When problem-solving is required, the first tool the senior protestant chaplain should consult is the Protestant Parish Council Flowchart. Who holds the first-level of responsibility for the ministry in question? As in all military organizations, problem-solving begins at the lowest level and elevates up the chain-of-command only if needed.

Though the highest ranking chaplain on the installation is responsible to the military commander for all chapel programs, the senior protestant chaplain is responsible for all Protestant programs. Having determined the chain-of-command's highest chaplain level, the flowchart reflects the senior protestant chaplain as the second-highest ranking chaplain within the Protestant chapel. With the other Protestant chaplains appropriately listed within their particular areas, the flowchart should reflect the members of the Protestant Parish Council. This would be divided into the large division headings with the appropriate chaplains and council members assigned to each. Each chapel base of operations will have a different flowchart. What is important for the reader to understand is its importance, especially when problem-solving.

STEP FIFTEEN – Writing the Fund Operating Instruction

The final step in building a Protestant Program involves establishing policy and procedures regarding the operation and the use of chaplain non-appropriated funds. It should be noted here that there are two kinds of funds that are used in military chapels.

Appropriated funds are annual or periodic appropriations by Congress given to the Department of Defense who, in turn, allocate them between the military services. Each branch of service will then apportion the monies to its respective agencies, to include the chapel. Though there are strict regulations governing both funds, appropriated monies generally are authorized for the operational side of the house – education and training for chaplains, and upgrades to the chapel facility.

Non-appropriated funds augment monies appropriated by Congress and are primarily given to the chapel through the weekly worship offerings. In general, the chaplains use this income for charitable giving and the funding of all chapel programs.

Both funds are regulated with service policy directives[24] and these regulations provide strict guidance when using appropriated funds but only a general framework when providing direction for non-appropriated monies. This is intentional because every base or post is unique; moreover, the government has no desire to entangle itself in the freewill religious offering of its military troops. A wise chapel leadership, however, will provide very clear instructions for the use of non-appropriated funds. The worshiping Christian wants to know that his tithes and offerings are used as intended – to glorify God and help those in need.

The fund Operating Instructions (OI) should be clearly written and easy to follow. On most military installations where families live, work, and worship, the fund OI provides specific guidance in nine general areas. Though a list of specific instructions would be irrelevant to the reader (since every installation is unique), the nine general areas of responsibility are listed below:

1. Wing Chaplain (title varies within branches of service but this refers to the senior chaplain of the installation) Responsibilities: The Wing Chaplain is responsible for all monies disbursed. (Generally the Wing Chaplain delegates authority to the senior protestant chaplain for all Protestant expenditures.)

2. Parish Advisor Council Responsibilities: Includes meeting annually for the purpose of creating an annual budget and to meet periodically, if necessary, to review the budget.

3. Non-Commissioned Officer In Charge (NCOIC) Responsibilities: The NCOIC's main responsibility is to ensure the chaplain assistants are properly trained. The NCOIC may also have an additional responsibility to inspect the Chaplain Funds at monthly intervals.

4. Fund Custodian Responsibilities: Track all non-appropriated income and expenditures, establish contractual guidelines for non-appropriated paid personnel, and ensure the security of fund assets.

5. Bookkeeper Responsibilities: Assist the Fund Custodian by writing and tracking purchase orders for the buying of materials and other related items for the respective parish to conduct ministry.

---

24   AR 165-1, AFI 52-101, SECNAVINSTR 1730

6. Chaplain Fund Requests: Non-appropriated forms that must be used before any purchase can be made.

7. Chaplain Fund Credit Cards: Sometimes referred to as IMPAC cards (Air Force) the credit card is authorized to be used in lieu of a Purchase Order.

8. Accounting for Receipts: This is a set of instructions on how to receive, handle, and deposit worship service or other types of offerings that are collected at the chapel.

9. Accounting for Disbursements: This is a set of instructions on how to pay the bill.

As children of God, all Christians should contribute their tithes and offerings, "not reluctantly or under compulsion, for God loves a cheerful giver."[25] The Christian minister, however, has an even greater responsibility. The chaplain's fiscal charge from the military exclusively pertains to the proper handling of the non-appropriated monies, but the chaplain's calling from the Lord to fulfill one's pastoral ministry[26] demands even greater attention. He has a spiritual duty to ensure that the soldier's offering is suitably used to share the love of Christ with the military community.

Conclusion

With the uniqueness that every military installation brings to the table, one may argue that there is simply no procedural template available to build a Protestant program. Obviously, your authors beg to differ and propose that these aforementioned fifteen steps will provide a valid framework for the Protestant ministry at any military installation. The operative word is "framework," a scaffold for the senior protestant chaplain to stand upon while laying the bricks for the Lord's house.

The most important part of any structure is the foundation. And when it comes to the worship and ministry of the military chapel, that foundation is Jesus Christ. If we fail to be attentive to the foundation, the house will not stand.

25 2 Cor. 9:7 (RSV)

26 *Cf.* 2 Tim. 4:5

The foundation is Christ, and the walls are an inspirational worship service and a viable spiritual program. Together they form a congregational home for the soldier and his family. And from the strength of this home church, the military pastor fulfills his ministry in the workplace and on the battlefield.

- PART THREE -
MINISTRY "OUTSIDE" THE WALLS

Chaplain's Role, Faith Issues, Foxhole Ministry

MATTERS OF CONSCIENCE

CHAPTER SEVEN

THE ENIGMATIC ROLE OF THE CHAPLAIN – OFFICER OR CLERGY?

"The man of God and the man of war:
what have they to do with one another?"[1]

Professor Harvey Cox
Harvard University

Chaplains wear rank but have no command authority.[2] They don the uniform of the warrior but are noncombatants.[3] They attend the same professional military schools[4] and undergo the same rigorous training as their fellow soldiers, airmen, sailors, and marines,[5] but do not carry a weapon.[6] They go to war but do not kill the enemy. They are in a word, an *enigma* to many civilian critics as well as proponents. However, if you ask the ones that matter – the troops – they understand the role of the chaplain.

Ask the soldier in battle who just lost his buddy in a firefight. Ask the Air Force pilot steadying himself the night before his first combat mission. Ask the

---

1 Cox, v.

2 10 U.S.C. Sec. 3581 (2012). It should be noted that the words "and shall be on the same footing with other officers of the Army, as to tenure of office, retirement, and pensions" were "omitted as obsolete, since there is no distinction between the status of a chaplain as an officer and the status of other officers of the Army."

3 Geneva Conventions: Protocol 1, June 8, 1977, Article 43.2.

4 In all branches of service, chaplains attend the same professional military education (PME) schools as other commissioned officers to include Command and Staff College and War College. Though the nomenclature and foci are commensurate to the specific military branch (land, air, or sea), both schools are 10-month residencies focusing on leadership and ethics, international security studies, national and military strategy, and joint/coalition operations.

5 Such as readiness, chemical warfare, survival, airborne, and combat, etc. Generally speaking, the chaplain's training is contingent to the needs of the military. For example, if the chaplain is in an airborne unit he will need to attend the basic parachute course.

6 Though Protocol 1 of the Geneva Conventions is clear on the noncombatant status of the chaplain, it is silent on whether or not chaplains may bear arms. However, the present policy directives of all three armed services clearly indicate that "Chaplains will not bear arms in combat or in unit combat skills training." See AR 165-1, Chapter 3-1.f (2009).

young marine returning home from a lengthy deployment discovering his wife is gone, or the commander searching for just the right words before delivering a death notification. Ask the young sailor working launch-and-recovery on the flight deck of an aircraft carrier, or the maintenance crew working on an F-15 fighter jet at midnight in a hangar on a remote stretch of runway, or a Special Operations field commander trying to understand the religious culture of a local Afghan village. Ask them if they understand the role of a chaplain and listen carefully. They may have never read a single word in a distant regulation filed on some remote shelf in a Pentagon office, but they know what their chaplain brings to the table – a "visible reminder of the Holy."[7]

Who Am I?

In truth, when there is tension within the chaplain's role, it is generally not the soldier's problem; it belongs to the chaplain. When the Lord spoke from the burning bush telling Moses, "Come, I will send you to Pharaoh that you may bring forth my people, the sons of Israel, out of Egypt," Moses retorted, "Who am I that I should go to Pharaoh, and bring the sons of Israel out of Egypt?" The Lord answered, "But I will be with you." Moses countered, "If I come to the people of Israel and say to them, 'The God of your fathers has sent me to you,' and they ask me, 'What is his name?' What shall I say to them?"[8]

For centuries the Church has criticized Moses for reluctantly obeying God but good *exegesis* demands that we give credence to Moses' reluctance. He did, after all, ask two very important questions. It is as if the Lord's servant was challenging *Yahweh*, "Lord, before I confront the most powerful king on the face of the earth – from whom (I might add) I barely escaped with my life, will you please answer this question, 'Who am I?' And while you're at it, 'Who are you?'" Two reasonable questions; in fact, *critical* questions for all servants of God!

One can only presume that Christian chaplains entering the military know

---

7   A description the U.S.A.F. Chaplain Corps has used for decades. See AFI 52-101 (2005) 2.1.

8   *Cf.* Exodus 3:10ff.

the God who called them, yet expecting them to know their role within the military is naïve at best; a prescription for failure. The chaplaincy is unlike any ministry calling within Christendom. Regardless of seminary education and experience within the civilian pastorate, there is a significant learning-curve for the newly appointed chaplain. The Chiefs of Chaplains of the Army, Navy, and Air Force are fully aware of this shortfall and have designed basic courses for all incoming chaplains, an "introduction to the 'nuts and bolts' of being an entry level chaplain."[9]

The civilian minister entering the military chaplaincy would do well to read carefully the chaplain policy directives of his respective service. These regulations, coupled with the Constitution's First Amendment and the Geneva Conventions' First Protocol, provide a necessary framework to appreciate the role of the chaplain. Once read, there are three distinctions that need to be remembered; each contributing to the unique role of the military chaplain – rank without command, non-combatant status, and the dual role of staff officer and clergy.

(1) Rank Without Command (Chaplain Whittington)

I was preparing for a remote assignment to Saudi Arabia when my Wing Chaplain showed up at my front door in the spring of 1981. "I have good news and bad news for you," he quipped. "Which one do you want to hear first?" "The good news, boss," I replied. He said, "You're not headed to Saudi!" My immediate thought was, "Whew, dodged a bullet there." I had already done a little "assignment-recon" so I knew the desert heat was unbearable with summer highs averaging from 113 to 122 degrees Fahrenheit. I then asked, "And the bad news?" I can still hear his laugh when he said, "You are on your

---

9 The names may change – Chaplain Basic Officer Leadership Course (Army), Naval Chaplains Basic Course (Navy), Basic Chaplain Course (AF) – but the curriculum is similar. Described by the AF Chaplain Corps, "BCC is an introduction to the 'nuts and bolts' of being an entry level chaplain. You will study counseling techniques, history of chaplaincy, deployed ministry, chapel management, budgets, religious accommodation, AF Core Values, legal responsibilities, and readiness. You will be certified in several programs that range from marriage counseling to suicide intervention." See http://usafchaplain.blogspot.com/2007/01/basic-chaplain-course.html.

way to Gila Bend Air Force Auxiliary Field," which (of course) begged the question, "Where is Gila Bend?"

Aerial view showing an F-15 above Gila Bend Air Force Auxiliary Field, AZ and the Luke Air Force Range in the Sonoran Desert (1982).

Located in the Sonoran Desert, this remote auxiliary airfield supported the largest gunnery range in the free world[10] and was considered by the Air Force in 1981 as one of the few isolated bases in the Continental United States (CONUS). It didn't take more than a day on station to know the descriptive term *isolated* was no exaggeration – 70 miles from Phoenix, 120 miles from Tucson, and 125 miles from Yuma. One of the most inhospitable and largest deserts in North

---

10   Formerly Luke Air Force Range, the Barry M. Goldwater Air Force Range consists of 1,900,000 acres of undisturbed Sonoran Desert and 57,000 cubic miles of airspace where pilots practice air-to-air maneuvers and engage simulated battlefield targets on the ground. The primary users of the range included aircraft from Luke Air Force Base, Davis-Monthan Air Force Base, and Marine Corps Air Station Yuma. Secondary users, however, included Air Forces from all over the free world. Various types of jet fighters trained on the range over the years. The supersonic F-100 replaced the subsonic F-84; the F-4 and A-7 later replaced the F-100, while the F-5 and F-104 were introduced for foreign pilot training. The F-15 was used from 1974 to 1993, and the F-16 replaced the F-4 in 1983. The primary aircraft operating at the airfield are F-16 and A-10 aircraft, as well as AH-64, AH-1F, OH-58, CH-47, and UH-60 helicopters associated with Air Force and Marine training exercises. See http://www.globalsecurity.org/military/facility/goldwater.htm (accessed 15 Dec 2011).

America, the vast Sonoran Desert covers an area of 120,000 square miles, and reaches temperatures of – you guessed it – 122 degrees.

With less than five hundred airmen, our mission was to provide all range operations and maintenance support for the fighter pilots to practice air-to-air maneuvers and engage simulated battlefield targets on the ground. A small community in the midst of a vast desert, the *Bend* was the perfect setting for relational ministry and a vivid reminder that the chaplain's role is unlike all other commissioned officers. Of the five hundred airmen, only five were commissioned officers – the commander and his deputy, the civil engineer, the logistician, and the chaplain.

I had been on base less than a month when a Master Sergeant (E-7) driving an M-880[11] dashed in front of me. Not knowing who I was, and noticing only the bars on my subdued fatigues, he hollered: "Captain, sir, we need an officer." I jumped in the bed of the truck with a dozen other airmen as the non-commissioned officer in charge (NCOIC) yelled to a subordinate, "Tell the captain what's up." Trying to listen to an airman over the grinding gears and jarring ride of a military transport is about as easy as holding a quiet conversation in the middle of a frenzied rock concert. Nonetheless, the gist of what the airman was telling me was that a German-piloted F-104 had gone down over the range[12] and a team had been quickly assembled to provide the proper protocol – cordon off the area and provide command and control until the response team from Luke Air Force Base (AFB) took over.

My only question was, "Where's the pilot?" Once I was told he had safely ejected and was being transported back to Luke AFB, in my mind I was there solely to provide spiritual support to the first responders. The moment we arrived at the crash site, the NCOIC said, "Sir, what do we do?" No sooner had he asked the question, he noticed – for the first time – the subdued cross

---

11 The M-880 was a Commercial Utility Cargo Vehicle (CUCV) used by the military in the 1970-80s as a light utility vehicle.

12 The F-104G crashed on August 4, 1981 due to engine failure caused by Foreign Object Damage (FOD). The pilot safely ejected. See http://www.ejection-history.org.uk/aircraft_by_Type/GermanF104.htm (accessed Dec. 20, 2011).

on the uniform. His fallen countenance was telling. "Oh, my God," he roared, "you're a chaplain!"

Having served four years as an enlisted airman prior to the chaplaincy, I was fully aware that an NCO with his experience knew exactly what to do; he just needed a firm reminder that he was in command and should conduct himself accordingly. And he excelled! As for me, I did what I was trained to do as well. I provided spiritual care to the team and to the NCO in command.

Ch. Whittington engaged in ministry of presence. The German-piloted F-104 crashed nearby on Aug 4, 1981 and a small team of Gila Bend AFAF airmen secured the crash site.

Whether I knew what to do or not is not the point. Granted, there are chaplains with expertise in more than one discipline but it is essential for the chaplain to understand that his only *legal* role is as a cleric. Several of my colleagues also had prior military service and civilian professions. Prior careers in law, psychology, social work, education, and aviation were not uncommon, yet regardless of the chaplain's knowledge base, the Department of Defense had commissioned him *solely* on his religious qualifications. A quick perusal of the entry-requirements for the Army, Navy, and Air Force reveal nothing about advanced degrees in law, psychology, or any of the sciences. The professional prerequisites for the chaplaincy are (understandably) religious: ecclesiastical endorsement, seminary degree, and two years of religious leadership experience.[13]

Some of my colleagues, prior to their appointments as a chaplain, flew combat missions, served as medics on the battlefield, and prosecuted criminal cases in the courtroom. To the discerning eye, one cannot help but notice prior badges worn with pride on the uniform of many chaplains. As an Air Force chaplain I noticed a few of my colleagues wearing their *wings* in addition to the *cross;* however, what the clergyman did prior to his commissioning as a chaplain is irrelevant, even if his prior commissioning carried rank *with* command.[14]

By law, chaplains are commissioned officers *without* command authority.[15] This is often misunderstood by many outside of the military community. As a commissioned officer the chaplain does not abdicate the protocol commensurate to his rank, general military authority extended to all personnel, or the authority to supervise his own staff, but he cannot "order a subordinate unit to execute directives or orders."[16]

The chaplaincy is considered one of three professional appointments in the military; the other two, medicine and law. Unlike all other commissioned officers who can cross-train into other specialty codes, the chaplain, judge advocate, and physician are appointed to provide a specific professional

---

13 The general qualifications for all chaplains in the armed services: ecclesiastical endorsement, two years religious leadership, U.S. citizenship (no dual citizenship), a Bachelor's degree, a seminary degree (or equivalent), maximum age of 42 (active duty) and 44 (reserve), commissioning physical, security background investigation, and the ability to work in the Department of Defense directed religious accommodation environment.

14 As an interesting aside, AFI 36-2903, Chapter 10.2.1 (2011) clearly states that the "Chaplain badge is worn in the highest position ... Aeronautical, space and cyberspace badges are worn above occupational and miscellaneous badges, but not above the chaplain badge." Not even the Air Force *wings* can be worn above the *cross.* Frankly, the symbolism speaks volumes to America's heritage and the level of respect our nation has for religious freedom.

15 See 10 U.S.C. Sec. 3581 (2012).

16 Army FM 1-05, *Religious Support,* Section 3-106, cited in Sekulow and Ash (July 10, 2011).

service. If the physician loses his license to practice medicine, or the lawyer is disbarred, or the chaplain, defrocked; *ipso facto*,[17] they are discharged from the military.

Though I clearly outranked the MSGT at the crash site of the F-104, he was in command. My congressional mandate was clear, "ensure that the 'free-exercise' rights of religion are not abridged."[18] I was the only commissioned officer at Gila Bend AFAF without command authority; then again, I had something far more unique – moral authority given by *Deo et Patria*[19] and earned through ministry. To be fair, on that particular day it meant that I helped pick up debris at the crash site, carried water to the airmen, and occasionally provided advice to the NCOIC; still, it was his command. When the mission was completed late that night, the MSGT dropped me off at the chapel. As I jumped out of the M-880, he was determined to walk with me to my car where he said "thank you" and out of respect, rendered a salute. Upon later reflection, I thought, "Rank without command; what a perfect setting to reflect the teachings of Christ."

> And they [disciples] came to Capernaum; and when he [Jesus] was in the house he asked them, "What were you discussing on the way?" But they were silent; for on the way they had discussed with one another who was the greatest. And he sat down and called the twelve; and he said to them, "If anyone would be first, he must be last of all and servant of all."[20]

(2) Non-Combatant Status

Though the Geneva Conventions and the Law of Armed Conflict (LOAC) are clear on the non-combatant status of the chaplain,[21] they are silent on whether or not the chaplain may bear arms. Given to interpretation, one might presume

---

17 Latin: "by the fact itself."

18 AR 165-1, Section 1-6.d.

19 Latin: God and Country

20 Mk. 9:33-35 (RSV)

21 "Members of the armed forces of a Party to a conflict (other than medical personnel and chaplains covered by Article 33 of the Third Convention) are combatants, that is to say, they have the right to participate directly in hostilities." Geneva Conventions, Protocol 1, Article 43.2 (June 8, 1977).

that the chaplain could carry a weapon for defense as long as he did not "participate directly in hostilities,"[22] but as Carl von Clausewitz emphasized in his celebrated classic *On War*, "war is the realm of uncertainty."[23] The chaplains bearing arms for defensive measures could easily be caught up in the fog-of-war and in a moment's notice, become combatants; though it is possible that "Much of the motivation for [bearing arms] may be to identify with their soldiers as well as self-preservation."[24] Regardless of the reasons a chaplain may have, brandishing a weapon could easily compromise the chaplain's non-combatant status and jeopardize his mission to "nurture the living, care for the wounded, and honor the dead." For this reason, all three Chiefs of Chaplains have made it clear, "Chaplains will not bear arms in combat or in unit combat skills training."[25]

For centuries, warfighters have "generally agreed that it is in everyone's best interest to 'treat certain people, property and places exempt from armed conflict.'"[26] From the Council of Ratisbon in A.D. 742 to our present day Law of Armed Conflict, the chaplain's non-combatant status has slowly evolved, as Chaplain Steven Schaick succinctly explained in an Air War College essay (2009).

> At the Council of Ratisbon chaplains were first authorized to serve in times of war but were clearly instructed to do so as noncombatants as they were prohibited from carrying weapons. Chaplain William Emerson, for many the "father" of the chaplaincy, distinguished himself during the American Revolutionary War as having made the personal choice of ministering without a sidearm even as many of his peers elected to arm themselves. The Continental Congress officially

---

22 *Ibid.*

23 Carl von Clausewitz, *On War*, eds. Michael E. Howard and Peter Paret (Princeton, NJ: Princeton University Press, 1976), 120. This text continues to be required reading in the United States' military war colleges.

24 Donald W. Kammer, "The Unique Prophetic Voice of the Army Chaplain" (paper presented at the International Society for Military Ethics, January 25-26, 2007) at http://isme.tamu.edu/ISME07/Kammer07.html (accessed Mar. 5, 2012).

25 AR 165-1. Chapter 3-1.f. See also AFPD 52-101, Para. 2.1; SEC NAVINST 1730, Para. 4-b.

26 Steven A. Schaick, "Examining The Role of Chaplains As Noncombatants While Involved In Religious Leader Engagement/Liaison," (Air War College essay: February 17, 2009) at http://www.dtic.mil/cgi-bin/GetTRDoc?AD=ADA539854 (accessed 4 Mar 2012). Quotation within Schaick is taken from Law of Armed Conflict Lecture, MS-1C, given at the Judge Advocate General School, Maxwell AFB, AL.

recognized chaplains with military status and pay on July 29, 1775. But it was not until 1863 that Francis Lieber first penned a code of conduct for armed conflict ... [these rules were] instrumental in developing the Hague Conventions on land warfare in 1899 and 1907 ... [And] at nearly the same time of Lieber's work was a man named Henry Dunant, writing and submitting similar laws of warfare ... He was also a key author of the first Geneva Convention in 1864 ... Though the Geneva Conventions underwent revisions in 1906 and 1929, World War II demonstrated that the Conventions were not yet as strong as they needed to be as nations were still doing whatever they deemed necessary to achieve victory. Thus, the Geneva Conventions were greatly strengthened in 1949 and this revision remains today the basis of our laws for armed conflict.[27]

The Chaplain is a non-combatant; easy enough to understand. What became far more challenging in the War on Terror was trying to understand the role of religion at the heart of the conflict, as Douglas Johnston identified in "Religion and the Global War on Terrorism."

As made clear by the experience of September 11 and its aftermath, the United States is operating at a distinct disadvantage when it comes to dealing with conflict that involves a significant religious component. Indeed, the principal reason religious terrorism poses such a difficult challenge is because we as a nation-state have virtually no capability to understand this phenomenon, let alone deal with it. For most of our country's existence, religion has effectively been off the policymaker's screen—a victim of enlightenment prejudice and its accompanying assumption that religion would have a declining influence in the affairs of state ... As a result and as made abundantly clear by our experience in Iraq, the United States has little, if any, ability to deal with religious differences in a hostile setting.[28]

For the last two decades American troops have been engaged in a war on two fronts – Iraq and Afghanistan – and Islam is the indigenous religion to both

27 *Ibid.*, 9.

28 Douglas M. Johnston, "Religion and the Global War on Terrorism," *The Journal of Religion, Conflict, and Peace*, Volume 1, Issue 1 (Fall 2007), http://religionconflictpeace.org/node/6 (accessed May 10, 2012).

regions. The very fact that Islam, one of the major religions of the world, is at the cultural heart of the conflict, has involved the chaplains in ways never before considered.

In Schaick's essay, he shared a story not at all atypical to many deployed chaplains. In the summer of 1995 he was assigned as the Combined Joint Task Force Chaplain with a mandate to provide a ministry of presence to the American Special Forces located in Northern Iraq. The commander of the unit asked the chaplain to accompany a small team to a Kurdish village in northern Iraq. After boarding a Blackhawk helicopter "flying low and fast above the barren Iraqi landscape"[29] the Blackhawk landed at a remote Kurdish village in northern Iraq with the intent to better appreciate the religious culture and improve relations with the local leaders. In the course of their meeting, the chaplain was pointedly introduced as the soldiers' "holy man," which garnered a few laughs from the local villagers because they too had their mullah seated at the meeting. To the Special Forces commander's pleasant surprise, the chaplain's presence had "set the conditions for a noticeably more successful visit."[30] Chaplain Schaick later reflected, "My being 'at the table' crushed preconceived notions that Americans were little more than arrogant and Godless crusaders."[31]

This expanding role for the chaplain as liaison to the indigenous religious leaders will continue to increase in direct proportion to the military's presence in theocratic cultures. However, there is a danger of crossing the line into Information Operations (IO) and arguably, engaging in an element of combat power, no less a violation of military doctrine than for the chaplain to strap an M9 to his belt. As Chaplain Kenneth Lawson explained,

---

29 Schaick, 2009.

30 *Ibid.* Joint Publication 1-05 "Religious Affairs in Joint Operations" (2009) asserts, "In many situations, clergy-to-clergy communication is preferred by the indigenous religious leader. Military chaplains with the requisite knowledge, experience, and training/education have religious legitimacy that may directly contribute positively to the JFC's [Joint Force Commander] mission, www.dtic.mil/doctrine/new_pubs/jp1_05.pdf (accessed May 10, 2012).

31 Schaick, 2009.

Army chaplains are not in the intelligence gathering business. Chaplains, as religious advisors, must not allow themselves to drift too far into the realm of IO. It is one thing to interact with local religious leaders to facilitate dialogue and understanding to better advise the commander on the impact of local religions on the military mission. It is another thing altogether for a chaplain to gather information in a religious liaison capacity that unethically could be used for targeting or other offensive operations. Afghan religious leaders place a high value on clergy. The U.S. Army chaplain can engage in a respectful dialogue and exchange of ideas and cultural sensitivities in discussions with indigenous clergy. But the sacredness of such dialogue must not be compromised by IO personnel eager to glean any information from the chaplain that may help their mission. A military chaplain who compromises the sacred bond between clergy will be instantly discredited by Afghan clerics, promoting distrust and disdain of all U.S. personnel.[32]

As long as American interests are threatened by enemies steeped in religious fanaticism, regulations governing the chaplain as a *Religious Leader Liaison* must continue to be revised to protect the non-combatant status of the chaplain while continuing one of the chaplain's core competencies – advising leadership. When the opportunity arises for the chaplain to serve as a religious liaison, Lawson recommended the following guidelines:

1. A religious liaison mission must be endorsed by the commander.

2. The chaplain must state his intentions with the G2, G3, G5 and G9 sections.[33]

3. Only chaplains of field grade (Major) or higher should participate.

4. Emphasis should be on common humanitarian and religious concerns and not on political/military matters.

5. After the mission, chaplains are not to provide information related to targeting or offensive operations to the command. Some non-lethal

---

32 Kenneth Lawson, "Doctrinal Tension: The Chaplain and Information Operations," *Military Intelligence Professional Bulletin* 35, no. 2 (April-June 2009), 27.

33 G2 (Military Intelligence), G3 (Operations), G5 (Plans and Strategy), G9 (Civil Affairs).

targeting information may be appropriately shared with the command, such as the location of schools, religious sites, and orphanages.[34]

Wars change from generation to generation. Technology drives weaponry, weaponry drives doctrine, and doctrine drives strategy and battlefield tactics. The only constants are the principles of war and the warrior's spiritual needs: hope for tomorrow, faith in one's country, and a *Band of Brothers'* bonding with the one fighting at your side. The presence of the chaplain is a visible reminder of all three.

In his Pulitzer award-winning novel, *Truman*, author David McCullough weaves a delightful story of Captain Harry S. Truman engaging in a light-hearted conversation with his chaplain (Father Tiernan) during a forced march of nearly 100 miles in the great Meuse-Argonne offensive during World War I.

> The march went on for a week. "The weather was bad, rainy, and we would sleep in the daytime in thickets or in woods and then take off at dusk and march all night," said Private Rickens. They passed places called Ourches, Loisy, and Rembercourt, which were nothing but ruins. Sometimes Harry and Father Tiernan walked together at the head of the battery, talking about "the history of the world and I don't know what all," Harry remembered. If all priests were like him, he told Tiernan, there wouldn't be any Protestants.[35]

Truman was not alone in his admiration for the chaplain. The priest endeared himself to the whole battery. McCullough – a masterful storyteller – shared another riveting (and humorous) example of the high esteem the soldiers had for their chaplain.

> Colonel Klemm, in a state such as the men had never seen, kept riding up and down the line shouting orders "like a crazy man" and at one point senselessly ordered an advance at double-time up a long hill. Had he not been wearing a yellow rain slicker, some of the men later speculated, he might have been shot in the back. But because Father

---

34   *Ibid.,* 26.

35   David McCullough, *Truman* (New York: Simon & Schuster Paperbacks, 1992), 127.

Tiernan had on the same color coat no one would have risked making a mistake in the dark.[36]

One need not explain the relevance of those two excerpts to an experienced chaplain. Even without the context, the meaning is clear. Father Tiernan was doing exactly what he was called to do; a noncombatant armed only with love for his soldiers, faith in God, and duty to his country, he marched side-by-side easing fears and bolstering courage by talking about "I don't know what all." No one knows if the priest's presence protected Battery D of the 129th Field Artillery but McCullough does share an interesting statistic. On the eleventh hour of the eleventh day of the eleventh month, 1918, the Germans signed an armistice agreement and the Great War was ended. "For the 129th Field Artillery the war had been the Meuse-Argonne offensive and it had cost the regiment 129 battlefield casualties." Captain Truman's battery suffered only three wounded.[37]

(3) Dual Role – Officer or Clergy? (Chaplain Whittington)

My first week as an Air Force chaplain was nearly my last week on active duty! Having just moved into my office at the Tactical Fighter Wing (TFW) Headquarters, I was summoned to meet with the Wing Commander – a crusty, foul-mouthed, ill-tempered, arrogant fighter-pilot – the likes of which (to the credit of the Air Force) would never again cross my path.

Thinking the visit was nothing more than a courtesy call to meet his new *Flight Chaplain,* I entered with a smile. I was wrong. This was not a courtesy visit. As I stood in front of the boss' desk, he told me that one of his senior staff officers was soon to be married and that I would be officiating at the ceremony. It was not a request. It was an order. I simply nodded and asked if the officer could give me a call to set up a pre-marital appointment. The Commander's response was telling, "He's a full colonel, chaplain. You call *his* office." With an automatic, "Yes, sir," I walked out of his office, down the corridor, and entered

---

36 *Ibid.,* 126.

37 *Ibid.,* 135.

the office of the groom-to-be. He was kind enough to invite me in where he provided a succinct *pre-brief* of the situation.

> I've been married and divorced four times and my fiancé has been married multiple times as well. We are not Christians. In fact, we don't believe in God at all. But I want to be married in the chapel by a chaplain. After all, I've earned that perk, wouldn't you agree, chaplain?

I remember thinking, "Good Lord, when I said 'Here am I, send me,' this is not what I had in mind." I explained to the colonel that neither my conscience nor my interpretation of Scripture would allow me to perform the wedding. I then offered to set up an appointment with another chaplain or provide the phone number for the local Justice of the Peace. I had no sooner returned to my office (in the same HQ building) when the commander's secretary was on the line, "The boss wants to see you," she said, "immediately."

As I stood in front of his desk – for the second time within the hour – he used even fewer words than our first visit. "Chaplain, what in the blazes do you think you're doing"? The next words out of my mouth were not nearly as eloquent as Martin Luther's defense in the famous trial before the Holy Roman Emperor in A.D. 1521, but the sentiment was similar.[38] I explained to the boss that it was neither "right nor safe" for me to violate my conscience or the Word of God – neither of which held any sway with the Wing Commander. It wasn't until I added, "And it also violates Air Force regulation," that he began to take notice. As I remained standing (at attention) he telephoned the Installation Senior Chaplain and Major General Dick Carr, the Air Force Chief of Chaplains – both of whom defended my right to say "no." Upon hearing this, the Commander of one of the Air Force's premier Fighter Wings dismissed me and the incident was never mentioned again.

---

38 Luther's response to the Archbishop of Trier (prosecuting counsel) should be memorized by all Christian chaplains. Archbishop Eck asked the accused Luther, "Martin – answer candidly and without horns – do you or do you not repudiate your books and the errors which they contain?" Luther replied, "Since your Majesty and your lordships desire a simple reply, I will answer without horns and without teeth. Unless I am convicted by Scripture and plain reason ... my conscience is captive to the Word of God. I cannot and I will not recant anything, for to go against conscience is neither right nor safe. Here I stand. God help me. Amen." Cited in Roland H. Bainton, *Here I Stand: A Life of Martin Luther* (New York: Abingdon-Cokesbury Press, 1950), 185.

Though it is important for military commanders to understand the dual role of the chaplain, it is the chaplain's responsibility to be well-versed in the regulations that govern his ministry in the armed forces. He serves as both staff officer and chaplain – commissioned by the military and ordained by his denomination – and his influence as a minister of the Gospel of Christ is contingent upon how well he wears both hats. Donald W. Hadley and Gerald T. Richards were on-target when writing, "Newly commissioned military chaplains must learn to comfortably wear a uniform that sets them apart as both military officer and endorsed representatives of a particular faith group.[39]

Some churchmen have considered the two mutually exclusive. As the Vietnam War was drawing down in 1971, Professor Harvey G. Cox of Harvard rhetorically asked, "The man of God, and the man of war: what have they to do with one another?"[40] On the heels of this unpopular war, Cox argued that the system was too corrupt for a chaplain to survive with integrity. How can a minister of Christ answer to the government? How can the chaplain don the uniform of a warrior and the cross of a priest? Or in the words of Cox, "proclaim a prophetic gospel when he is wearing the uniform of the military, is paid by the state, and furthermore is dependent on his superior officers for advancement"?[41] On the surface, these appear to be good questions, but at the risk of showing disrespect to those who live in ivory towers, the questions are simply bogus. The chaplain answers to *both* the Church and the State to alleviate this very tension.

Two decades before America declared its independence, a young George Washington commanded a Virginian regiment. As commander, he was particularly concerned with the immoral behavior of his men, who, "in despite of the utmost care and vigilance, are, so long as their pay holds good, incessantly drunk, and unfit for service."[42] Not only did he believe that a

---

39 Donald W. Hadley and Gerald T. Richards, *Ministry with the Military* (Grand Rapids, MI: Baker Book House, 1992), 24. Italics in original. Cited in Michael T. Jones, Lt. Col, USAF, "The Air Force Chaplain: Clergy or Officer?" (unpublished essay, Air War College, April 1996), 11.

40 Cox, v.

41 *Ibid.,* x.

42 Washington to Virginian Governor Robert Dinwiddie (September 23, 1756).

chaplain's presence would help resolve the moral dilemma, he understood the import of the chaplain being "one of the men" and highly recommended that he be appointed as an officer of the corps. In a letter written to Governor Robert Dinwiddie on September 23, 1756, Washington complained,

> The want of a chaplain does, I humbly conceive, reflect dishonor upon the regiment, as all other officers are allowed. The gentlemen of the corps are sensible of this, and did propose to support one at their private expense. But I think it would have a more graceful appearance were he appointed as others are.[43]

In the twenty years that followed, the chaplains' presence became a familiar site in the colonial militias. Understanding the need for the chaplain to serve as a "soldier " in order to minister to soldiers, the Continental Congress on July 29, 1775 officially established the Army chaplaincy, creating the second oldest military unit next to the infantry.[44] The move was validated – with constitutional authority – when the First Amendment was ratified in December 1791, prohibiting the government from forming its own clergy while guaranteeing the soldier's religious freedom.

Without the institution of the military chaplaincy, the government is in a quandary. To avoid contravening the *Establishment Clause* of the First Amendment, Sekulow and Ash argued that the national government has no choice other than commissioning the civilian clergy.

> It is constitutionally inappropriate for the government to delve into the details of religious belief and clergy qualification within a specific faith group ... Hence, *denominational affiliation is the irreducible essence of membership in the chaplaincy of the US armed forces, and as such, military chaplains are intentionally hired, and hence expected, to represent a specific denominational view within the military.* Military chaplains are, in the final analysis, members of the clergy of their specific faith groups who conduct their ministries in uniform.[45]

---

43 *Ibid.*

44 Drazin and Currey, 9-10.

45 Sekulow and Ash (July 10, 2011). Italics in original.

In a *Memorandum Opinion*, issued on April 30, 2007 (*Larsen v. U.S. Navy*), U.S. District Judge Ricardo M. Urbina concluded,

> The realities of maintaining a military in a religiously pluralistic nation places the government in a delicate constitutional position given the Establishment Clause and the Free Exercise Clause. On the one hand, "[s]pending federal funds to employ chaplains for the armed forces might be said to violate the Establishment Clause" … "Yet a lonely soldier stationed at some faraway outpost could surely complain that a government which did not provide him the opportunity for pastoral guidance was affirmatively prohibiting the free exercise of his religion." It is in the space between the constitutional command against practices respecting an establishment of religion and the command against practices which prohibit the free exercise thereof that the military chaplaincy rests.[46]

Though the Department of Defense is constitutionally bound to provide its personnel with the free exercise of their religious rights, could it not accomplish this by allowing the civilian religious organizations access to the troops? In a word, no!

Without being held accountable to military regulations, the civilian cleric could actually undermine the religious freedoms of the soldiers in a number of ways.

- Refusing to provide religious support to those who differ from one's own faith.

- Being unwilling to assist the commander in developing programs to provide for the spiritual care of the unit.

- Choosing to avoid being placed in harms' way thereby denying the soldiers the presence of a chaplain, abrogating their constitutional freedom of religion.

To be candid, it is one thing for a civilian minister to enjoy working with the soldiers on post, or the airmen, sailors, and marines on their respective peace-

---

46 *Larsen v. U.S. Navy* (2007). For online transcript of Memorandum Opinion by Judge Urbina, see https://ecf.dcd.uscourts.gov/cgi-bin/show_public_doc?2002cv2005-59 (accessed May 5, 2012).

time bases. It is entirely different to expect that same civilian pastor, priest, imam, or rabbi to undergo rigorous military training, be willing to move to a foreign country, suffer through an unaccompanied remote tour, brave sea duty, or deploy to the battlefield. The chaplain doesn't just minister *to* the soldier; he is a soldier! He *is* a sailor! He *is* a marine! He *is* an airman!

The Founders ensured that the government would "make no law respecting an establishment of religion, or prohibiting the free exercise thereof..." Both clauses work in tandem; one, dependent on the other. The state cannot prohibit the soldier's access to his religious freedoms but it has no clergy of its own. The government, therefore, must turn to its citizenry to facilitate the soldier's constitutional freedom of religion and the civilian minister voluntarily takes the same oath of office as all commissioned officers in order to provide pastoral care to the soldier; a promise, by the way, to both country and God.

One of the most memorable moments of my life occurred when I raised my right hand and promised to "support and defend the Constitution of the United States against all enemies ... So Help Me God." The oath is personal. *I* promised to support and defend the Constitution. So help *me*, God! Administered by a close friend (a decorated war hero and retired Army colonel), he reminded me "this isn't a promise to be taken lightly."

Here I Raise Mine Ebenezer[47] *(Chaplain Whittington)*

As a daily reminder of this not-to-be-taken-lightly promise, I started an early morning tradition that visually reminded me of my dual-role as a minister and an officer. When serving at CONUS and overseas bases where the Air Force Class B uniform was generally worn, I would offer short prayers as I pinned on the various parts of my shirt at 0530 hours. The Class B uniform was a simple blue shirt requiring only the officer's badge, name tag, and rank

---

47 When Yahweh secured a victory for the Jews by confusing the Philistines, the prophet Samuel took a large stone and placed it between Mizpah and Jeshanah to symbolize God's help. He called the stone, *Ebenezer*, which means "stone of help." In 1758, the lyricist Robert Robinson penned these now-familiar words: "Here I raise mine Ebenezer; hither by thy help I'm come; and I hope, by thy good pleasure, safely to arrive at home." As I prepared myself for daily ministry, the uniform became my *Ebenezer*.

(ribbons were optional). This little procedure became my *Ebenezer* – a visual reminder that I was not alone in my ministry to God, family, and nation. I pinned each in order of my personal priorities.[48]

The first accessory was the chaplain's cross worn just above the left pocket – over the heart. As I pinned the cross to the uniform I whispered something like, "Lord, good morning. As I pin this cross over my heart I am reminded of my ultimate allegiance to Jesus Christ. God forbid that I should have to choose between being a good officer or a Christian, but if the choice has to be made, give me the courage to choose the latter. Help me fulfill my calling, through Christ my Lord. Amen."

The name tag came next. A simple blue plate with the airman's last name engraved in plastic. The name, however, etched in the cheap plastic was priceless. Though the name I carried represented many generations, I generally thought only of those closest to me – my father who entered World War II six weeks after his wedding, my mother who waited faithfully for his return four years later, my wife who chose to wear my name proudly, and my three sons. I understood that my behavior that day would reflect upon all of them. And so – as I pinned on the name tag – I prayed, "Lord, you know the love and respect I have for my dad, mom, wife, and sons. Yet you also know that far too often I say what I should not say, or leave unsaid what I should have had the courage to say. At times I've behaved well; at other times, I've struggled and sinned. Please help me this day live a life worthy of my father's name. May my life, this day, bring glory to You and honor to my family's name."[49]

Signifying the last priority of the three, I would pin the rank on the uniform. Though the cross and name remained constant, the rank changed. And with every promotion, the prayer I whispered evolved. If you stay around long

---

48 The practice of preparing the uniform shirt in a certain order – cross, name tag, rank – was presented during a course at the Chaplain's School early in my career. I am indebted to Ch. Col. Al Hockaday, former Commandant of the Air Force Chaplain School for sharing such a visual reminder of the chaplain's priorities.

49 The two (glory to God and honor to one's name), go hand-in-glove. Once a chaplain's reputation is tarnished (even if undeserved), his ministry to the troops is significantly damaged. The Christian chaplain would do well to put the Apostle Paul's admonition to memory, "Abstain from all *appearance* of evil" (2 Thess. 5:22, KJV).

enough, eventually you will be responsible for others. Toward the end of my career, my prayer was simple, "Lord, you have promoted me into leadership. You must think that I can handle it. You called me as a minister of Jesus Christ *and* as an Air Force senior officer. Help me lead as I want to be led – empowering those around me to excel! Amen."

The ritual helped ground me in my calling as both minister and officer. It was important for me to be reminded that God was my help in troubled times. Most of the time I fulfilled my calling honorably but there were moments, I failed miserably. Still, every morning as I hung the uniform shirt on the bathroom door and began placing the cross, name, and rank, I felt the Lord's presence and was afforded one more day to "get it right."

All three of these elements were visually present at my last promotion ceremony; the day I pinned on the iconic rank of colonel – the American *eagle* – worn on both shoulders with the left epaulette located directly above the cross. Collegial prayers were said, and then my family pinned on the eagles (my wife on one side and my dad on the other) – the cross, the name, the rank. Present at the ceremony was one of my former bosses who had distinguished himself as a senior military officer and a faithful Christian servant. As the ceremony ended and the festivities began, he congratulated me and then quietly whispered, "Don't let the eagle 'defecate' on the cross" – or some word to that affect. Perhaps crude to the evangelical ear, but a much-needed visual for a newly-promoted servant of God!

Conclusion

Chaplains wear rank but have no command authority, don the uniform of the warrior but are noncombatants, and deploy to the battlefront but do not kill the enemy. An enigma for sure! Unlike all other commissioned officers the chaplain has a dual allegiance – God and country. The challenge is significant, but once the two roles are in sync, the servant of Christ is well-equipped to attend to the soldier's spiritual needs, to handle matters of faith, and be that visible reminder of the Holy in foxholes, at home, and overseas.

CHAPTER EIGHT

CONTROVERSIAL MATTERS OF FAITH

*Every part of Scripture is God-breathed and useful one way or another –
showing us truth, exposing our rebellion, correcting our mistakes, training
us to live God's way. Through the Word we are put together and shaped up
for the tasks God has for us.*

2 Timothy 3:15-16 (The Message)

———————

Truth! Interesting word, is it not? In His defense before Pontius Pilate, Jesus declared, "Everyone who is of the truth hears my voice." Dismissively, Pilate snapped, "What is truth?"[1] In the New Testament, truth implied "that on which one can rely" (referring to Holy Scripture).[2] The reference to the Bible as the authoritative source for moral truth has seldom been challenged by the American public; that is, until recent generations.

The official seal of Harvard University prominently displays the Latin word *veritas*,[3] but its meaning on many of our campuses and throughout American society has become blurred. If this blurring were relegated to an academic discussion among ivory-tower scholars and a few students – as it was among the philosophers of Classical Greece – then there would be no problem. Truth flourishes in the soil of controversy and learning is maximized when the student is encouraged to articulate his or her thoughts. It is altogether different, however, when the goal shifts from seeking moral truth (i.e. facts upon which one can rely) to seeking recognition for certain lifestyles, one's personal conduct, or society's collective immoral behavior.

———————

1   Jn. 18:37-38 (RSV)

2   R. Bultmann, "*Alētheia*," ed. Geoffrey W. Bromiley, Theological Dictionary of the New Testament: Abridged in One Volume (Grand Rapids, Michigan: William B. Eerdmans Publishing Company, 1985), 38-39. *Cf.* Jn. 17:17

3   Latin: truth

Search for a New Standard of Truth

If the present understanding of truth challenges immorality (and the culture is unwilling to consider guilt as an option) then that society has two choices: condemn the immoral behavior or change the standard of measure that denounced it. And in America, that standard has always been our Judeo-Christian heritage based upon the values grounded in the Bible. With many Americans wanting to legitimize behavior considered sinful in Holy Scripture, a new search for truth has attracted recent generations to consider any alternative to the Bible regardless of fact. Dr. Gene Veith, Director of the Cranach Institute at Concordia Theological Seminary, offered a helpful example,

> In their search for a more palatable Jesus, novelists such as Dan Brown of *The Da Vinci Code,* feminist theologians such as Elaine Pagels, and their acolytes in the media and pop culture are turning to the apocryphal gospels of the early heretics. These are alleged to contain a valid, alternative version of early Christianity, one that can support today's feminism and moral permissiveness ... But comparing the New Testament Gospels to those written centuries later only confirms that these writings are works of history. Do you remember the furor over the recent discovery of an ancient manuscript entitled *The Gospel of Judas?* The media reported that the document presented Judas as a good guy who turned Jesus over only because Jesus told him to. The reports implied that the church had gotten it wrong over all these centuries; that Judas was no sinister betrayer but a leading disciple to whom Jesus imparted special knowledge ... The media coverage indicated that we would now have to re-evaluate our knowledge of Jesus. The translation became a best-seller and National Geographic, which was behind the publication of the text, made a TV documentary on the subject ... But have you heard the rest of the story? [Scholars have accused] the National Geographic of "scholarly malpractice" ... The National Geographic translators rendered the text so that it read the opposite of what it actually said ... The false Gospels, and the novels and scholarship that supports them, are pure fiction.[4]

---

4 Gene Edward Veith, "The Gospel of Reality," *Table Talk Magazine* (February 1, 2009), http://www.ligonier.org/learn/teachers/gene-veith/ (accessed March 23, 2013).

Beyond the search for a new scripture, many in society continue to look for an alternate religious philosophy that sanctions their behavior; such as materialism, universalism, skepticism, and most recently, moralistic therapeutic deism – a belief that argues "being nice" is the only requisite for going to heaven. However appealing when first heard, it is a total misunderstanding of the nature of sin and the need for a savior.

Why is this discussion important for the evangelical chaplain? Because all worldviews – the lens through which we observe life and act accordingly – are built on a foundation; and a foundation built on fiction will fell a house. It is virtually impossible for any two people, including Christians, to view the world through the same lens; but if we believe the Bible to be the Word of God, we have our foundation built on the rock that neither "rain nor wind" can collapse.[5] To stand firm the evangelical chaplain must ensure his actions are congruent to his worldview, regardless of the consequences.

Christian Worldview

The Christian's worldview is foundational to all of life and critical for success in today's military chaplaincy. Whether you choose to pursue the military as a career or simply experience this ministry for a few years, our best advice is to know *who* and *whose* you are. And never forget it! Only this will sustain you in crisis and provide a "lamp to your feet and a light to your path."[6] This is true not only for the chaplain, but for all Christians. God forbid the reader should ever have to choose between being a good officer or a good person, but if it is forced upon you, choose the latter.

In remembering who you are in Christ, it is a good practice to remind yourself of certain milestones along your journey of faith. For example, I (Whittington) vividly recall a conversation I had with Dr. W. Paul Jones, the Director of Doctoral Studies at Saint Paul School of Theology. As I was attempting to impress this prominent theologian I remember admitting that I had repeatedly

---

5   *Cf.* Mt. 7:24-27

6   *Cf.* Ps. 119:105

begged the Lord to quiet the storms of my life, allowing me to pursue my post-graduate studies in peace. No sooner had I said those words than Paul motioned for my silence and said, "You're asking for the wrong thing. We never experience God's grace in the calm, only in the storm. Peace is not the absence of conflict; it is the discovery of God's presence within the struggle. Pray that God will reveal Himself in the storm."

A few years later he authored *Theological Worlds – Understanding the Alternate Rhythms of Christian Belief*, wherein he suggested that a person's Christology is directly connected to his worldview. This insightful book arms the reader with a keen self-awareness of his particular theological world and helps him understand his perception of life. In his text, Dr. Jones described five theological worlds.[7]

The first theological world is *Separation and Reunion* – the feeling of isolation and the longing to be connected with something greater than humanity. These people seek God to lead them home. The second is *Conflict and Vindication* – the feeling of anger and the need to fight against evil as a soldier fights terrorism. In this theological world Jesus appears as a King – one anointed to liberate the warrior's rage and provide a "new" earth upon which to live and be happy. *Emptiness and Fulfillment* are the third theological world. Before coming to Christ, this person felt like an outcast, needing to be made whole and yearning for a sense of belonging.

Interestingly, both of your authors identified with the fourth theological world, *Condemnation and Forgiveness*. Guilt runs rampant with most of us, and we feel powerless to overcome our sin. In fact, we are powerless. We seek forgiveness and warmly receive Jesus as Savior, who redeems us from our mistakes. We claim the biblical promise that "Though your sins are like scarlet, they shall be as white as snow."[8]

---

7 W. Paul Jones, *Theological Worlds – Understanding the Alternate Rhythms of Christian Belief* (Nashville: Abingdon Press, 1989), 42-43.

8 Isa. 1:18 (RSV)

The last theological world Professor Jones described was *Suffering and Endurance*. Understanding this Christian perspective will help the chaplain deal with those soldiers who feel overwhelmed with life. They are victims and refugees in search of a *suffering servant* who understands their pain and ensures them that with God's help, they will endure.

Though every Christian's theological needs contribute to his unique salvific journey, the conservative Christian – believing the Bible to be the inspired Word of God – grounds his worldview on Scripture. Such a biblically-grounded theology provides the wherewithal for the chaplain to address the soldier's questions, the same questions that have been discussed by philosophers from the beginning of human history.

- Where did I come from?

- Why am I here?

- Where am I going?

In today's world where Christianity is largely relegated to myth and its ministers considered unenlightened, it takes courage for the military chaplain to appeal to Scripture and boldly proclaim truth.

- **Where did I come from?** In the beginning, God created the heavens and the earth ... then the Lord God formed man of dust from the ground, and breathed into his nostrils the breath of life; and man became a living being (Gen. 1:1; 2:7. RSV)

- **Why am I here?** But you [have been called] out of darkness into his marvelous light (1 Pt. 2:9. RSV). For by grace you have been saved through faith; and this is not our own doing, it is the gift of God (Eph. 2:8. RSV). For this is the message which you have heard from the beginning, that we should love one another (1 Jn. 3:11. RSV). We love because He first loved us (1 Jn. 4:19. RSV).

- **Where am I going?** The dust returns to the earth as it was, and the spirit returns to God who gave it (Eccl. 12:7. RSV). [Upon death] God will dwell with them, and they shall be his people, and God himself will be with them; he will wipe away every tear from their eyes, and death shall be no more, for the former things have passed away (Rev. 21:3-4. RSV).

We have shared these passages at countless gravesides of fellow warriors. Death is always tragic, but there is a decided note of joy with those present when the body of a Christian is put to rest. When the bugler sounds taps and the casket is lowered into the grave; family, friends, and war-buddies take solace in knowing that their paths will cross again, in the sure and certain hope of the resurrection.[9]

One's worldview and the socio-political issues that chaplains deal with on a daily basis are inseparable, but the biblical principle of seeking God's help in prayer and appealing to Scripture is sufficient for the challenge. Still, there are three controversial issues that continue to trouble our conservative military chaplains – the repeal of Don't Ask, Don't Tell, command-sponsored prayer in the name of Jesus, and evangelism.

The First Controversy – Repeal of Don't Ask, Don't Tell

A Brief History

On May 5, 1950 the Uniform Code of Military Justice (UCMJ) – a major revision of the military criminal code – was signed into law by President Harry S. Truman.[10] The code, which included discharge rules for homosexual military members, was validated by President Ronald Reagan in 1982 in a defense directive stating "homosexuality is incompatible with military service." Under conservative political pressure, President Bill Clinton was unable to keep his campaign promise to lift the ban but in 1993 issued a compromise in a defense directive forbidding applicants from being asked about their sexual orientation.[11] Codified in 10 U.S.C. § 654, the policy was known as Don't Ask, Don't Tell (DADT), and remained in effect for eighteen years.

---

9 *Cf.* 1 Cor. 15:20-22

10 Uniform Code of Military Justice Legislative History in Military Legal Resources," at http://www.loc.gov/rr/frd/Military_Law/UCMJ_LHP.html (accessed Mar. 24, 2013).

11 Mary Kate Cannistra, Kat Downs, and Cristina Rivero, "A history of don't ask, don't tell," *The Washington Post* (Nov. 30, 2010) at http://www.washingtonpost.com/wp-srv/special/politics/dont-ask-dont-tell-timeline/ (accessed Mar. 24, 2013).

A congressional bill to repeal the directive was enacted in December 2010 but required the president, secretary of defense, and the chairman of the Joint Chiefs of Staff to certify that the repeal would not harm military readiness. President Obama, Secretary Panetta, and Admiral Mullen sent the certification to Congress on July 22, 2011 and DADT was subsequently repealed the following September.

In typical military fashion, all of America's armed forces successively instituted education and training programs for military chaplains with the goal of helping them deal with the new directive. Some conservatives argued that the scripts used in conjunction with the training slides (e.g. Army DADT tier III education slides) inferred that the chaplain should agree with the policy or resign his commission. Yet what appeared to be coercive language by the Army, Navy, and Air Force chaplaincies was in fact a valid reminder that a chaplain is also an officer, commissioned by the President of the United States; and if he can no longer conscientiously serve as a military chaplain, he should resign his commission and return to civilian ministry.

The challenge for the biblically conservative chaplain may stem more from his personal belief that homosexuality is sinful behavior than it does from believing that the repeal of DADT inhibits his ministry to the troops. This is not to dismiss the seriousness of one's biblical faith. Your authors have already argued that a conservative Christian worldview must be grounded in Scripture, and all of life viewed through that particular lens. It is important, however, for the chaplain to distinguish between the government's validation of immorality and his ability to perform or provide ministry to all military personnel. Whether one is successful or not depends heavily on the chaplain taking the words of Jesus to heart, "Behold, I send you out as sheep in the midst of wolves; so be wise as serpents and innocent as doves."[12] In view of these two dynamics – one's personal belief and the ability to work within military boundaries – two questions need to be asked. (1) What does the Bible teach

---

12   Mt. 10:16 (RSV)

about homosexuality? (2) How does the repeal of DADT affect the chaplain's military ministry?

(1) What Does The Bible Teach about Homosexuality?

The Bible is strangely silent about the homosexual condition but its condemnation of the conduct is explicit in Leviticus 18:20 and Romans 1:26-27. A thorough *exegesis* of these passages would no less corroborate what the casual Bible student interprets in a single reading; homosexuality in the Judeo-Christian scripture is considered a sin. Liberal and conservative scholars generally agree that the Bible condemns the behavior, but they ardently differ on its relevance to twenty-first century society.

In an effort to dismiss Scripture as archaic, there are those who argue that certain lifestyles are not a matter of choice but chosen for them at birth. In the risk of over-simplifying a complicated issue, if a loving and just God condemned a behavior then the person must be able to make a choice, or be forced to indict God.

The Apostle Paul addressed this principle – God's love and justice will not let us be tempted beyond our strength to endure, "But with every temptation will also provide the way of escape."[13] True, one may insist that they were born with a predisposition toward homosexuality and therefore, have no choice; but they have no less of an argument than a promiscuous heterosexual who claimed he was born with an over-active libido, or a driver engaged in road-rage arguing he was not responsible for his action because he was born with an uncontrollable temper. However strong the impulse to engage in immoral behavior, according to the Bible, we have a choice.

The operative question becomes, "Who cares what the Bible says?" And frankly, it is a valid question for those who do not believe the Scripture to be the inspired Word of God. In a 2011 Gallup poll, only "three in ten Americans

---

13 1 Cor. 10:13 (RSV)

interpret the Bible literally, saying it is the actual word of God."[14] At a casual glance, this may discourage the evangelical Christian but once the ambiguous term "literal" was removed from the question, the poll revealed that one out of two Americans believed the Bible to be "inspired by God" and an overwhelming eighty-three percent revered it as coming from God, not man.[15] The operative question of "Who cares what the Bible says?" is answered with, "Most soldiers believe it is the Word of God and if shared in a non-judgmental manner, will listen!"

When the chaplain encourages a soldier to live a Christian life, does this imply that the chaplain is sinless? Of course not! No one understands the wages of sin more than the conscientious Christian, as the Apostle Paul confessed, "I am the least of the apostles, unfit to be called an apostle, because I persecuted the church of God."[16] All Christian ministers (especially your authors) should freely confess, "We are all in the same leaky boat." The words of Scripture, written two thousand years ago, still resonate true today; "Everyone has sinned and is far away from God's saving presence."[17] Apart from God's grace through Jesus Christ, no one would be saved; but prerequisite to repentance is accepting a certain behavior as sinful, then "changing one's mind" and seeking God's forgiveness.[18]

From a biblical perspective the greater issue for the conservative Christian chaplain (and soldier) is not the repeal of DADT, but working within a system that condones a behavior decried by Scripture as immoral. The practical question for the evangelical chaplain, therefore, is "How does the change of military policy affect my ministry?"

---

14 "In U.S., 3 in 10 Say They Take the Bible Literally," *Gallup* (July 8, 2011) at http://www.gallup.com/poll/148427/say-bible-literally.aspx (accessed Mar. 24, 2013).

15 *Ibid.*

16 1 Cor. 15:9 (RSV)

17 Rom. 3:23 (TEV)

18 J. Behm, "*metanoéō*," ed. Geoffrey W. Bromiley, *Theological Dictionary of the New Testament: Abridged in One Volume* (Grand Rapids, Michigan: William B. Eerdmans Publishing Company, 1985), 641.

(2) How Does the Repeal of DADT Affect the Chaplain's Military Ministry?

In addition to the conservative Christian, Jewish and Muslim personnel have expressed concerns over the repeal of DADT. One of the frequently asked questions identified by the U.S. Navy in the *Military Support Plan for the Implementation of the Repeal of Don't Ask, Don't Tell* was, "Does repeal of Don't Ask, Don't Tell affect the speech, morals or religious rights of Sailors?" The admiralty's answer was unmistakably clear, "No."

> There will not be any modifications or revisions to policy regarding Sailor protections and obligations with respect to free speech and free exercise of religion. The Department of Defense recognizes the right of all members of the Military Services to hold individual beliefs consistent with their moral foundations and conscience and does not seek to change them.[19]

One can hope that the same protections extend to the chaplain. Under the present regulatory guidelines, "Chaplains will not be required to take part in religious services, rites, sacraments, ordinances, and other religious ministrations when such participation would be at variance with the tenets of their faith."[20] But the playing field has changed since these regulations were written.

Before the repeal of DADT the Uniform Code of Military Justice provided legal support to many of the moral concerns voiced by conservative Christians; not the least of which, were sexual improprieties. With the ban against homosexual behavior lifted, the evangelical chaplain has a legitimate fear. If the chaplain preached against the sin of same-sex marriage from a military pulpit, or provided biblical counsel to gay or lesbian soldiers encouraging them to repent and change their behavior, will he suffer reprisal? All three service branches believe they have addressed the chaplain's unease and reassured them,

---

19 *Military Support Plan for the Implementation of the Repeal of Don't Ask, Don't Tell,* Appendix D, Q7. See *The Washington Post* (PDF), http://www.washingtonpost.com/wp-srv/politics/documents/Training_FAQs.pdf (accessed Mar. 23, 2013).

20 AR 165-1, Ch. 3.3-5.b

Chaplains will continue to have freedom to practice their religion according to the tenets of their faith. In the context of their religious ministry, chaplains are not required to take actions that are inconsistent with their religious beliefs (e.g., altering the content of sermons or religious counseling, sharing a pulpit with other chaplains or modifying forms of prayer or worship). Chaplains of all faiths care for all Service members and facilitate the free exercise of religion for all personnel, regardless of religious affiliation of either the chaplain or the individual. Chaplains minister to Service members and provide advice to Commanding Officers on matters of religion, morals, ethics and morale in accordance with, and without compromising, the tenets or requirements of their faith. If, in chaplains' discharge of their broader duties within the unit, they are faced with an issue contrary to their individual faith, they may refer [the troop] to other appropriate counsel.[21]

Of course, every military member has access to the Inspector General (IG) and can lodge a complaint against anyone if they choose. If a chaplain preached on the Leviticus 18:22 text declaring the homosexual lifestyle to be sinful behavior, one could easily imagine an angry parishioner filing an IG complaint claiming hate speech or accusing the chaplain of promoting dissension within the ranks (affecting unit good order and discipline). Though the chaplain may need to remember the words of Jesus to be "wise as a serpent" and address such volatile issues on a person-by-person basis, the content of his sermons is protected by military regulation and the IG would be challenged to substantiate the complaint.

A much greater concern for the evangelical chaplain is "unofficial reprisal" by those in his chain of command. With some Christian denominations ordaining homosexuals, and the repeal of DADT allowing them to openly serve, gay and lesbian chaplains will continue to be recognized within the military chaplaincy. And irrespective of one's own personal lifestyle, a heterosexual supervisor may disagree with the evangelical's biblical position and strongly believe that they have no right serving as a military chaplain.

---

21 *Ibid.*, Appendix D, Q6.

Chaplains – as all commissioned officers – are promoted or passed over to promotion based primarily on their annual officer performance reports. Every military member understands the subjective nature of these evaluations. However difficult it is for a supervisor to avoid subjectivity when evaluating a fellow chaplain, both supervisor and subordinate need to be fully cognizant that the temptation for unofficial reprisal is always present. The best an evangelical chaplain can do is to be aware of the possibility and establish an open and honest relationship with his rater or those whom he rates. However, in the end, if one believes that his performance report has been unduly downgraded because of his biblical belief, the chaplain has the same right to appeal to the IG as all other service members. More importantly, he should embrace the Word of God, "If you do suffer for righteousness' sake, you will be blessed. Have no fear of them nor be troubled."[22]

In today's chaplain corps, where conservatives outnumber all other Christian traditions, perhaps the greater onus falls on the evangelical supervisor. They too must be equally guided by the Word of God. When rating a subordinate who ardently disagrees with your conservative beliefs, it is important to remember the scriptural injunction, "Do not return evil for evil or reviling for reviling; but on the contrary bless, for to this you have been called."[23] Though it will take several years to determine how the repeal of DADT affected military readiness, the chaplain works in the present; and as of today, it is the official policy of the Department of Defense. If the chaplain's conscience allows him to continue his ministry within the present policy guidelines – and he has reached supervisory level – he must rate all subordinate chaplains based solely upon their duty performance, not sexual orientation.

Your authors can only presume what they would do if still on active duty, but one thing is obvious; if a Christian chaplain cannot conscientiously serve within the present policy, there remains no recourse other than to resign one's commission and return to civilian ministry. If on the other hand, the evangelical

---

22 1 Pt. 3:14 (RSV)

23 1 Pt. 3:9 (RSV)

chaplain chooses to remain in uniform; there will be ample opportunity to humbly share the love and teachings of Christ when asked by one's colleagues.

The Second Controversy – Prayer in the Name of Jesus

"In the blessed name of Jesus, the Savior of the world, I pray. Amen." These words closed a prayer for Air Force Academy cadets attending a Protestant worship service during field training at Jack's Valley in the summer of 2004. Fervent prayers, passionate testimonies of faith, and Christ-centered sermons were considered stridently evangelical and the Senior Staff Chaplain was strongly encouraged to censor the chaplain's speech (chapter three). After considering the criticism, the senior chaplain dismissed the recommendation without taking any action.

On a separate occasion at an overseas location, another Air Force chaplain was asked to offer an invocation at a command-sponsored event. To the disquiet of the Wing Chaplain, the content of the prayer was much too long, overly sectarian, and zealously closed in the name of Jesus.

In fair assessment of the two occasions, the chaplain supervisor – the same person in both incidents – had strikingly different responses. The strongly-worded memorandum at the Academy was naïve and reflected an ignorance of the official policies governing the role of the military chaplain. According to regulations, the chaplain has every right to persuasively share the tenants of his faith during a voluntarily-attended worship service. The same regulations, however, are intentionally silent regarding prayer at command-sponsored events. The rationale provided in 2005 by Navy Chief of Chaplains Louis Iasiello remains applicable today. In an interview at the Pentagon's Navy Annex, the admiral explained,

> We train our people to be sensitive to the needs of all of God's people. We don't direct how a person's going to pray. Because everyone's own denomination or faith group has certain directives or certain ways of doing things, and we would never – it's that whole separation-of-

church-and-state thing – we would never want to direct institutionally that a person could or couldn't do something.[24]

Extremes beget extremes. A few secular, atheist, and politico-religious organizations believe that prayer has no place in military formations though "such prayers have been permitted since the founding of our nation."[25] Yet they argue that even if permitted, the prayer should never close in Jesus' name as the mere mention of Jesus on a government platform, promotes one religion over another and violates the establishment clause. In a word, Jay Sekulow, Chief Council of the American Center of Law and Justice, called such thinking "absurd."[26]

On the opposite extreme are a few fundamental Christians arguing that unless the evangelical chaplain verbally promotes the Christian belief and closes his prayer by audibly using the name of Jesus, he compromises his faith. Equally unreasonable, the military chaplain finds himself in a quandary as the battles persist in our nation's capital.

Those opposed to any appearance of religion on our military installations continue their efforts to remove prayer altogether from command-sponsored events, while a few congressmen persevere in their fight for the constitutional right of the chaplain to pray according to the tenants of his faith.

Section 590 of House Resolution (H.R.) 5122 initially included a phrase allowing chaplains to pray according to the dictates of their own conscience but was omitted from the final bill signed by President Bush on October 17, 2006.[27] Similarly, on January 7, 2009, Representative Walter B. Jones of North Carolina introduced H.R. 268 as an amendment to Title 10, United States Code,

---

24 Cited in Alan Cooperman, "Military Wrestles With Disharmony Among Chaplains," *Washington Post* (August 30, 2005), at http://www.washingtonpost.com/wp-dyn/content/article/2005/08/29/AR2005082902036_2.html (accessed Mar. 28, 2013).

25 Sekulow and Ash (July 10, 2011).

26 *Ibid.*

27 Initial wording can be found at http://www.gpo.gov/fdsys/pkg/BILLS-109hr5122eas/pdf/BILLS-109hr5122eas.pdf. See H.R. 5122 (109th): John Warner National Defense Authorization Act for Fiscal Year 2007 at http://www.govtrack.us/congress/bills/109/hr5122/text (accessed Mar. 20, 2013).

"to ensure that every military chaplain has the prerogative to close a prayer outside of a religious service according to the dictates of the chaplain's own conscience."[28] Though introduced, the bill was never referred to committee. Re-introduced as H.R. 343 on January 22, 2013, it was assigned to a congressional committee which will consider it before possibly sending it on to the House or Senate as a whole. The bill is given a six percent chance of getting past committee and a one percent chance of being enacted.[29]

As is always the case, the political battles are fought within congressional corridors while the military salutes smartly and presses on with the business at hand. The conservative chaplain needs to apply a practical theology; one that encourages the minister to remain faithful to his Christian calling while not insisting on a sectarian prayer or closing in the name of Jesus. In the words of evangelical Chaplain (LTC) John Laing,

> The chaplain who chooses to take a stand on this issue should realize that he may be missing opportunities to offer public prayers that could have an impact on soldiers within the unit he serves ... Thus it seems to me that it is better to offer a prayer to the Lord in front of the soldiers of the unit, than to not offer a prayer at all ... [adding the all-important] this is subject to one's conscience.[30]

In over fifty years of combined active duty, your authors can count on one hand the number of times evangelical chaplains took undue advantage of a prayer platform at a military formation. Granted, one's interpretation of what constitutes proselytism is subjective, but there is no doubt that the vast majority of liturgical chaplains would corroborate that statistic. Unfortunately, prayer in Jesus' name is no longer the central issue; the dispute is quickly approaching prayer itself. With the undue attention surrounding prayer at military formations, the Christian chaplain would do well to carefully weigh one's personal freedom in Christ (as reflected in Scripture) and the missed opportunity to pray.

28 H.R. 268 at http://www.govtrack.us/congress/bills/111/hr268 (accessed Mar. 20, 2013).

29 H.R. 343 at http://www.govtrack.us/congress/bills/113/hr343 (accessed Mar. 20, 2013).

30 Laing, 67.

Does Scripture Shed Any Light on the Issue?

When reading conservative Christian authors on the issue of "military chaplains and prayer," the two most referenced biblical passages are John 14:13-14 and 1 Corinthians 9:22-23.

> Whatever you ask in my name, I will do it, that the Father may be glorified in the Son; if you ask anything in my name, I will do it. *Jesus – John 14:13-14 (RSV)*

> I have become all things to all men that I might by all means save some. I do it all for the sake of the gospel, that I may share in its blessings. *Apostle Paul – 1 Corinthians 9:22b-23 (RSV)*

John 14:13-14

Scripture must be understood in context. At this point in John's narrative of Christ, the reader finds Jesus on Thursday of Holy Week with less than one day to live on earth. Our Lord had already washed the disciples' feet and given them the *mandatum* to do "as I have done to you." He then celebrated the Passover meal – popularly depicted in Leonardo da Vinci's *Last Supper* – and said to Judas, "What you are going to do, do quickly." The rest of the conversation revolved around Jesus returning to the Father to "prepare a [heavenly] place" for His followers. It was in this context, that Jesus assured them "Whatever you ask in my name, I will do it."[31] What a comfort this must have been for the disciples, knowing that even though Jesus would be absent in body, He would be powerfully present in Spirit.

The operative phrase in John 14:13, is "in my name." Even the most casual reader would not presume this was some magical formula providing *carte blanche* to the one who prayed – as biblical scholars William MacDonald and Arthur Farstad explained, "To ask in Jesus' Name is not simply to insert His Name at the end of the prayer. It is to ask in accordance with His mind and will."[32]

---

31 *Cf.* Jn. 13-14

32 William William, Arthur Farstad, *Believer's Bible Commentary : Old and New Testaments* (Nashville : Thomas Nelson, 1997, c1995), S. Jn. 14:13.

Jesus' whole point in prayer is to remind the disciples of the real source of the Christian's power – God! In ancient thought, the source of one's power was affiliated with his family's wealth and possessions; and as such, the two thoughts were often connected. When the apostles Peter and John healed the lame beggar at a temple gate, the rulers used the two words interchangeably and asked "By what *power* or by what *name* did you do this?"[33]

Associating the believer's prayer with the power of God, Dr. John MacArthur provided a framework that could be applied by the evangelical chaplain offering a public prayer for the soldier. MacArthur certainly encouraged all Christians to audibly pray in the name of Jesus but he also cautioned the Christian against using it as a mere formula.

- The believer's prayer should be for His purposes and kingdom and not selfish reasons.

- The believer's prayer should be on the basis of His merits and not any personal merit or worthiness.

- The believer's prayer should be in pursuit of His glory alone.[34]

Consider the following chaplain's prayer at a preflight briefing where attendance was mandatory.

Almighty God, we ask your blessings upon these pilots who go forth this morning, not because it is their wish but because it is their duty. We ask you to be with them every step of the way and to grant their safe return. Help them to be at their very best – cautious, alert and capable in their mission. More importantly, remind them of your presence, as the Bible says, "The horse is made ready for the day of battle but the victory belongs to the Lord." Hear our prayer gracious Lord, for it is in your most holy name, we pray. Amen.[35]

---

33 Acts 4:7 (RSV); emphasis (italics) is ours.

34 John MacArthur, *The MacArthur Study Bible* (Nashville: Word Pub., 1997), S. Jn. 14:13.

35 Modified from "Preflight Briefing," *Book of Prayers* (Maxwell Air Force Base, Alabama: USAF Chaplain Service Resource Board, n.d.), VII-13.

If you had been one of the pilots that brisk morning before takeoff, would you have climbed into your jet without knowing the chaplain unselfishly asked for God's presence to be with you in the dangers ahead and that his prayer was based on his Christian faith, even though he closed without mentioning the name "Jesus"?

The chaplain's heart was centered on the aviator's need for Christ. Knowing he would not be asked to pray again if he audibly closed in the name of Jesus, the chaplain willingly put the pilot's need for prayer over his own freedom of speech. With that in mind, one might argue that he would find an advocate in the Apostle Paul who chose to restrain his freedom in order to reach unbelievers with the gospel.

1 Corinthians 9:22

The context of 1 Corinthians 9 reveals Paul's adamant belief that he had every right to receive material support for his ministry. He rhetorically asked, "Who serves as a soldier at his own expense? Who plants a vineyard without eating any of its fruit? Who tends a flock without getting some of the milk?"[36] Still, Paul and his companions did not ask for remuneration; on the contrary, they balanced authority with discipline. The great apostle deliberately forfeited his "right" for the sake of others. Warren Wiersbe, a prolific Christian writer, expressed it more eloquently when he said "[Paul] did not have the right to give up his liberty in Christ, but he did have the liberty to give up his rights."[37]

Granted the contexts are different – the right to receive pay for services rendered and the right to pray according to the dictates of one's faith – but the biblical principle is hard to ignore. In the words of John MacArthur,

> [The apostle] stooped to make the gospel clear at the lower level of comprehension, which Paul no doubt had done often while dealing with the Corinthians themselves. Within the bounds of God's Word, he

---

36 1 Cor. 9:7 (RSV)

37 Warren W. Wiersbe, *The Bible Exposition Commentary* (Wheaton, Ill.: Victor Books, 1996, c1989), S. 1 Cor. 9:22.

would not offend the Jew, Gentile, or those weak in understanding. Not changing Scripture or compromising the truth, he would condescend in ways that could lead to salvation. Liberty cannot be limited without self-control.[38]

Is it any different with the evangelical chaplain? Must one always demand his religious right even if it means he loses the opportunity to pray with the very people that God called him to serve?

Some extreme conservatives have argued that the chaplain who has chosen to pray at command-sponsored events without closing his prayer "in Jesus' name" has, in effect, denied Christ. That is not only irrational, mean-spirited, and a flagrant misuse of scripture; such absurdity aligns them with their opponents on the far left who assert the extreme opposite – mentioning the name "Jesus" in public prayer is tantamount to the government's endorsement of a state church. Both are ludicrous and serve neither God nor country.

There is absolutely no doubt that a chaplain's uniformed presence – with the cross prominently pinned over the heart – identifies his faith to every person within sight of the podium. It is not only the uniform that speaks volumes to America's warriors; they know their chaplains through a ministry of presence. They see them daily in garrison and deployed, on flight lines and in maintenance hangars, in the workplace and aboard ship. Whether one prays in the name of Jesus or chooses to close with an abrupt "Amen" has no bearing on the chaplain's identity with Christ. Without a word being spoken, the soldiers know if their chaplain is Christian.

The Third Controversy – Evangelizing the Troops

Though the repeal of Don't Ask, Don't Tell and praying in the name of Jesus, have received greater public scrutiny in recent years, they are no more controversial than the ill-defined debate on Christian evangelism within the military.

In media coverage and related articles from both sides, two words are tossed

---

38 MacArthur, *Study Bible,* S. I Cor. 9:22.

about as if synonymous – proselytism and evangelism – but among experienced chaplains there is a definite distinction between the two. The former carries a negative connotation implying an implicit misuse of one's rank and power while the latter (evangelism) is more a reflection of one's actions than words.

Even in the New Testament there is a subtle difference. The Greek verb *euangelizomai* (evangelize) does indeed mean to "proclaim" the good news but the proclamation is a comprehensive picture of the whole activity of one's life, not only the spoken word.[39] As for the meaning of proselytism – "to make or try to make converts"[40] – the New Testament uses its adjectival form (proselyte), and then, only four times. In all four instances it signified converts to Judaism; and in its first occurrence (Matthew 23:15), Jesus denounced the legalistic missionary work of the Pharisees as hypocritical.[41]

Regardless of the chaplain's regulatory right to adhere to the tenants of his faith, even the most ardent evangelical would not argue that a chaplain (or any Christian) should force his religious views on the powerless. Western history is replete with the ungodly action of Christian leaders supported by a nefarious church, such as the notorious Charlemagne (A.D. 742-814) who offered the Saxons death or Christian baptism.[42] Imposing the gospel on another is not only a contradiction in terms, but has absolutely no place in a Christian's ministry. Accepting the working definition of proselytism as unbecoming to a Christian, how does one evangelize?

For the evangelical chaplain, the issue is not "should" the good news of Jesus Christ be proclaimed to military personnel, but "how" can the chaplain preach the gospel within the regulatory boundaries. Implementing the "how" calls for

---

39 Gerhard Friedrich, "εὐαγγελίζομαι," *Theological Dictionary of the New Testament*, II, ed. Gerhard Kittel, trans. Geoffrey W. Bromiley (Grand Rapids: Wm. B. Eerdmans Publishing Company, 1964), 718.

40 *The New Lexicon Webster's Encyclopedic Dictionary of the English Language*, Deluxe ed. 1991, s.v. "proselytize."

41 Karl Georg Kuhn, "Προσήλυτος," *Theological Dictionary of the New Testament*, VI, ed. Gerhard Friedrich, trans. Geoffrey W. Bromiley (Grand Rapids: Wm. B. Eerdmans Publishing Company, 1968), 742.

42 Philip Schaff, *History of the Christian Church*, Vol. 4 (Peabody, MA: Hendrickson Publishers, Inc., c.1885, 2006), 242.

the chaplain to (1) consider the biblical principle that actions speak louder than words; and (2) appreciate a commonsense approach to military ministry.

Chaplains are often called upon to pray at special events and greet visiting dignitaries – to be that "visible reminder of the Holy" to both soldier and guest. Ch. Whittington and his wife Debbie enjoy a moment with the Honorable Walter Mondale (U.S. Ambassador to Japan) at the Special Olympics, Yokota Air Base, Japan (1994).

(1) Actions Speak Louder Than Words

Apart from John 3:16 and the Lord's Prayer of Matthew 6, the Great Commission is one of the most recognized passages in all of the New Testament. Prior to His ascension, Jesus charged the disciples,

> Go therefore and make disciples of all nations, baptizing them in the name of the Father and of the Son and of the Holy Spirit, teaching them to observe all that I have commanded you; and lo, I am with you always, to the close of the age.[43]

---

43 Mt. 28:19-20 (RSV)

Generally, the passage is read with the emphasis on the verb "to go" as if the command from Jesus is for His followers to drop whatever they are doing and "Go to all nations" preaching the good news of salvation. However, in the original biblical text, the words "go, baptizing, and teaching" are participles, modifying the imperative command to "make disciples"[44] as Greek language scholar, Barclay Newman, explained,

> *Go ... baptizing ... teaching* (verse 20) are each participles dependent upon the main verb *make disciples of.* But in such a construction it is not uncommon for the participles themselves to assume the force of an imperative. However, the command to *make disciples* is the primary command.[45]

The imperative command from Jesus was to "make disciples," assuming the listener would automatically be going. Scholars Robert Hughes and Carl Laney reasoned that Matthew 28:19 could be translated, "As you are going, make disciples ...."[46]

Implied in this popular text, is the understanding that "proclaiming the good news" is reflected in one's behavior *and* the spoken word. Its application to the military chaplain – working within evangelistic constraints – is significant. To the military Christian the "Great Commission" is saying, "As you go about your daily work in garrison, deployed, flight line, work units, or aboard ship, imitate Christ in word and action." To the chaplain, the charge from Jesus Christ is fulfilled during worship services *and* in a ministry of presence outside the walls of the chapel.

Many Bible passages corroborate this interpretation. For example, the Apostle John told his Christian community in 1 John 3:18 that real love is expressed not

---

44 James Swanson, *et al. The Swanson New Testament Greek Morphology: United Bible Societies' Fourth Edition.* (Bellingham, WA : Logos Research Systems, Inc., 2003), S. Mt. 28:19-20 19 (πορευθέντες, μαθητεύσατε, βαπτίζοντες, and διδάσκοντες).

45 Barclay Moon Newman; Stine, Philip C.: *A Handbook on the Gospel of Matthew* (New York : United Bible Societies,1992) in UBS Helps for Translators; UBS Handbook Series, S. 886

46 Robert B. Hughes; Carl J. Laney, *Tyndale Concise Bible Commentary* (Wheaton, Ill. : Tyndale House Publishers, 2001), S. 422

by "word or speech" but by one's behavior. The apostle chose to use the active verb *agapáō* (love) reminding his Greek reader that love is demonstrated by what you "do" not what you "say."[47]

In Peter's first epistle, the apostle informed the Christian wife that her unbelieving husband "though [he does not] obey the word, may be won without a word ... when [he sees] your reverent and chaste behavior."[48] Biblical scholars agree that by using the noun *anastrophē* (behavior), Peter is telling the Christian church that unbelievers can be won to Christ not only with the spoken word; but by imitating the manner of life of those they love and respect.[49]

When Jesus was tested by a religious leader asking which commandment was the greatest, our Lord overlooked more than six hundred statutes meticulously explained in Jewish writings and quoted the simple *Shema* of Deuteronomy 6:4-9, "Love God with all of your heart..." and then added, "And love your neighbor as yourself."[50] When the chaplain's behavior "outside the walls" reflects the love of Jesus Christ, his demeanor proclaims the gospel with no less power than his words in the pulpit on any given Sunday. With "actions speaking louder than words" military evangelism becomes a commonsense approach.

(2) Commonsense Approach to Military Ministry

One would be hard-pressed to find a specific regulation prohibiting the chaplain from talking about his Christian faith with a soldier. For that matter, there are legal experts who argue that even "Commanders and other leaders may speak of religious matters with subordinates" providing they do not impose their religious views on them.[51] It is not "evangelism" that is under scrutiny;

---

47   In today's Christian culture, one need not know an *alpha* from an *omega* to have heard the word *agápē* and to know that it is the kind of love that God has for us, and expects us to have for each other – an unselfish love, one that gives to others asking nothing in return.

48   1 Pt. 3:1-2 (RSV)

49   ἀναστροφή (translated as "behavior" in RSV) conveyed "manner of life or conduct." See James Strong, *The Exhaustive Concordance of the Bible: Showing Every Word of the Text of the Common English Version of the Canonical Books, and Every Occurrence of Each Word in Regular Order.* electronic edition (Ontario : Woodside Bible Fellowship, 1996), S. G391

50   *Cf.* Mt. 22:34-40

51   Sekulow and Ash (July 10, 2011).

it is the misuse of power. The problem is exacerbated when the conversation occurs within a hierarchical structure such as the military. Practically every word from a senior officer could be considered a directive to a subordinate. For that reason, every military leader must always be cognizant of his rank and position.

This principle cuts straight to the crux of the evangelism issue. Every soldier, sailor, marine, airman, and coastguardsman knows that the chaplain – as a commissioned officer – is due the protocol commensurate to his rank. If the chaplain began sharing his Christian faith with an airman working on a C-130, the young mechanic may think he has no choice but to listen to the officer until dismissed. If the airman, on the other hand, started the conversation about faith, the situation would be entirely different.

For this reason, your authors advise against *initiating* a testimony of faith when engaged in a ministry of presence. This is not to say that the chaplain could not exchange a Christian greeting, such as, "Have a blessed day!" or "God bless you!" or "If you'd like to pray, just let me know!" For even the most liberal of critics would not argue that this friendly exchange breached professional conduct.

Imposing one's faith on an unsuspecting subordinate is not only wrong but, frankly, unnecessary. There will be thousands of opportunities for the chaplain to boldly proclaim the Christian message. Every time you hear the words, "Chaplain, do you have a minute?" the Lord provides you with one more opening to share the good news. Your authors have experienced the privilege of witnessing thousands of military personnel receive Christ as their Lord and Savior. They have offered countless prayers and baptized hundreds in rivers, lakes, oceans, seas, and makeshift pools all over the world.

And practically every conversation seemed to begin with those six words, "Chaplain, do you have a minute?" Marriage problems, emotional distress, drug-addiction, fears, and failures – all are opportunities to provide Christ-centered counsel. Granted, there may be an occasion when a lonely sentry notices the cross on the uniform and asks for help from a stranger, but as Major General Bob Dees explained, most soldiers talk to the chaplain whose "voice they recognize in the dark."[52] Though the chaplain has a great opportunity every Sunday to evangelize the soldier in the pew, the one who engages the troop-in-the-trench is the chaplain whose voice is recognized in the dark.

This is ministry in a foxhole, a metaphor describing the place where the chaplain introduces the soldier to God and God to the soldier. Foxholes are everywhere – on the battlefield and foreign runways, in military motor pools and bomb dumps, at home and abroad, aboard ship and on remote Pacific islands whose names would be forgotten, if not for the marines engaged in a battle study. God's presence is experienced in foxholes all over the world – every time the chaplain and the soldier share a word. To this end, your authors invite the reader to step into the trenches and witness the glory of Christ.

---

52   See MG Dees' remarks in the Foreword of *Matters of Conscience.*

The U.S. Coastguard Loran Station on Iwo Jima was transferred to the Japanese on Sep. 29, 1993. AF chaplains from Yokota AB, Japan traveled to the iconic island to offer prayers in memory of the American and Japanese who died during the battle.

Standing on Mount Suribachi, Iwo Jima on Feb. 9, 1994, the USFJ Marines begin their annual combat study of the heroic battle of 1945. Lt. Col. Whittington and his fellow AF chaplains from Yokota AB provided spiritual guidance through prayer and ministry of presence (1994-1996).

CHAPTER NINE

MINISTRY IN THE FOXHOLE

Jesus ... primarily conducted his ministry out among the people, preaching on the hillsides and plains; from a boat on the Sea and in the Judean wilderness ... He went into the "trenches" with his ministry.[1]

John D. Laing, Chaplain (LTC), TXARNG
Seminary Professor and Author

———————

Noticing the chaplain's cross on the Air Force service dress of Colonel Whittington, the Slovakian general turned and faced a small group of American pilots visiting from the United States Air War College (AWC) and politely asked, "Why is the priest here?" Looking surprised, one of the American pilots – an F-16 driver – bellowed, "A priest? We thought he was a pilot!" And then with a smile, added, "General, where we go, the chaplain goes." With these words the foreign general shrugged his shoulders and continued his welcoming remarks while proudly standing in front of an Su-22M4 Fitter K – a thirty-year old Soviet attack aircraft exported to the Slovakian Air Force.

The general's surprise at the sight of a clergyman on official orders was echoed by many other foreign dignitaries in February of 2000. As a member of AWC Seminar 10, Chaplain Whittington not only accompanied his classmates through Slovakia, the Czech Republic, and Poland; but as the senior officer, was their spokesman. The chaplain's presence – a shock to every foreign host during the central European visit – was a familiar sight to the line officers he accompanied from AWC.

———————

1 Laing, 3.

AWC Seminar 10 standing in front of a Su-22M4 Fitter K in Bratislava, Slovakia (2000).

As the senior-ranking officer of Air War College Seminar 10, Col. Whittington receives a memento from the commanding general of the Czech Republic military (2000). The fact that chaplains attend U.S. war colleges is unique among the world's armed forces and demonstrates the importance America places on our freedom of religion.

Though the history of warfare abounds with field commanders demanding the blessings of the gods before marching off to war, the colonial soldiers of early America expected their Christian chaplain to accompany them into battle. And that expectation – unique in world military history – continues to present day.

However heightened the soldier's need for God in a battlefield trench, a minister of Christ understands the need for God's presence in war *and* peace, and the experienced chaplain sees "foxholes" everywhere! In the context of John 4 (the "Woman at the Well" narrative) Jesus was disappointed in his disciples because they were so preoccupied with the ordinary that they missed the extraordinary! As they were arguing with each other over food, Jesus saw the Samaritans running toward Him – their white robes glistening against the hot Palestinian sun – appearing as a field of grain in full bloom. Silencing the disciples, He exclaimed, "Do you not say, 'there are yet four months, then comes the harvest'? I tell you, lift up your eyes, and see the fields white unto the harvest." Without any further word, the disciples looked out upon the horizon and saw the crowd approaching the well. Before the sun set that day, the Bible recorded, "Many Samaritans ... believed."[2]

Foxholes are everywhere; but the chaplain must lift his eyes to see these extraordinary opportunities. Reflecting the light of Christ in the trenches, at home, and overseas demands that the chaplain attends to the warrior in settings where few want to go, and at those ungodly hours when most others want to sleep.

If You Ain't Ammo, You Ain't Special!

With few exceptions, Army, Navy, and Air Force chaplains are responsible for visiting all assigned military personnel – on base, aboard ship, and deployed. The size and location of the work unit may differ and each of our armed services may call similar work units by different names, but the chaplain's

---

2 *Cf.* Jn. 4:35, 39, 42

responsibility is the same – providing pastoral care to the soldiers, sailors, marines, and airmen assigned to the unit.[3]

If every chaplain visited his assigned units without fail, the constitutional mandate to facilitate "free exercise" would be fulfilled; and all troops, accounted for, but that must be an intentional goal. Visiting the large operational hubs on any given day is not much of a challenge; these are the most visible centers where the majority of the troops work. On a typical Air Force base, these work areas would include Headquarters, support offices, maintenance hangars, hospitals, and flight operations.

One could easily dedicate his entire ministry of presence to these facilities and be confident that he is providing pastoral care to all, but in fact there are troops scattered all over the installation who seldom see a chaplain; such as the troops who work in the Bomb Dump.

> One of my favorite places to go visit was the Bomb Dump [writes Chaplain, Major General Charles Baldwin]. It is really the "Ammunition Storage Area" – the place where we store all the bombs and bullets. It is always "at the far end of the base … far, far away from any populated area." Not many people go there; perhaps because it is far away or it is a dangerous place. Then again, maybe most chaplains think "no one important" works out there. The "Ammo troops" are a little different. They even have a special "cheer" that is often yelled at Official functions – Awards Ceremony, Dining Out, and Promotion Events. The acronym is "IYAAYAS." I had visited several bomb dumps at remote sites all over the world during my career, so, when I became the Chief of Chaplains, I determined I would visit every Bomb Dump of every base I visited, if it were at all possible. For example, when I was asked to speak at the National Prayer Breakfast on a given base, I would ask the host chaplain to take me to the Bomb Dump. It was one of the most rewarding parts of my ministry. These young airmen were doing dangerous work every day, and were oftentimes neglected by the others on the base. I thought, "…this is exactly where Jesus would have wanted to go – the faraway

---

3 With the consolidation of several Army and Air Force bases the chaplain would do well to learn the organizational structure of his joint base. The differences are many and reflect how the two services are best deployed in combat.

place where people risked their lives to prepare for the daunting task of combat." Ammo troops had many great signs around the squadron. One of my favorites was "If you see an Ammo guy running, follow him." After we exchanged "coins," I would take note of their motto, and yell out "If You Ain't Ammo, You Ain't SPECIAL!" which would always follow with laughter from the troops because they knew that was the "chaplain's version" of their revered motto.[4]

As the Command Chaplain for the Pacific Air Forces, Colonel Whittington was aware first-hand of the pastoral visits General Baldwin made to the "ammo troops" in the Pacific theater. A former rescue helicopter pilot (HH-53) in Vietnam, Chaplain Baldwin understood the need to be that "visible reminder of the holy" to America's warriors serving in remote places. The reports of his pastoral visits were appreciated by both chaplains and airmen, and serve as a reminder to the reader to "Go out to the highways and hedges"[5] and reflect the light of Christ.

In the Trench at Home

Not every visit is as pleasant as the ammo troop laughing with his chaplain. By regulation, the chaplain is called upon to accompany his commander in death notifications. Generally, the heart-wrenching duty calls for the commander to notify the surviving spouse and children with a chaplain and a medical caregiver present. Once notified, the chaplain offers spiritual comfort and the medical expert stands ready if needed. It is stressful enough when there is one notification, but when the unspeakable happens – a major accident – the strain can be overbearing for all present.

During *Operation Desert Shield* on August 29, 1990, a C-5 Galaxy crashed seconds after takeoff from Ramstein Air Base, Germany. Of the seventeen souls aboard, only four survived. Nine of the casualties were from the 433rd Military Airlift Wing at Kelly Air Force Base, Texas. When word of the crash reached the base during the night hours, the information was incomplete; still,

---

4 Written narrative from Charles Baldwin to Michael Whittington (March 20, 2013).

5 *Cf.* Lk. 14:23

the commander decided to form two special teams to notify the families of the unknown status of their loved ones. As the senior protestant chaplain for the Kelly community, Chaplain Whittington accompanied the lead team as they notified five of the ten families. No sooner had the families been notified of the accident, the word reached base headquarters that nine of the ten Kelly airmen onboard, had died in the crash.

One can only imagine the horror on the faces of each family member when they heard the doorbell ring for the second time; not just the sight of tears but cries of anguish from the wife and fear in the faces of the little children cowering behind their mother. Words always fail in moments like this. The best one can do is to be that visible reminder of the Holy and beg the Lord to embrace the suffering. Within a few days, a special memorial service was conducted in a C-5 hangar, the large opening facing the familiar flight line. Taps echoed within the metal walls and thousands of fellow airmen offered their final salute to the fallen heroes. Not every foxhole is found in some distant desert. Some of the most unpopular trenches are at home, where families live, and children play.

Around the Crud Table

Few chaplains would be found on Friday night at the bar, the flight line rec-room, or the softball field; that is, unless they were there for reasons other than a drink, or to engage in a fast-paced game of Crud,[6] or be applauded for their softball skills.

Most chaplains in a peacetime setting, reserve Friday night for family or chapel activities. Preparation for Sunday services, choir practices, Bible studies, or one's own family night generally took precedence over spending additional time with the airmen. After all, the chaplain had already dedicated a full week visiting and counseling with the troops; still, the chaplain's presence at the

---

6   Crud is a popular game in many of the world's air forces – to include USAF, Navy, and Marine aviators. Played without pool cues on a snooker or pool table, the rowdy game involves a player running around the table trying to strike the shooter ball before it stops moving (snooker table) or sinks in a corner pocket (pool table).

fun-times – relaxing in the club lounge, laughing with the pilots while racing around the pool table, competing on the softball field – validates the chaplain/airman relationship. And when a serious need presents itself, this is the pastor the airmen call.

Ministry in times of joy (as well as sorrow) solidifies the bond between chaplain and troop. And as an additional blessing, provides unique opportunities unavailable to the civilian pastor. At every operational CONUS and overseas assignment, Chaplain Whittington accompanied the aviators on flying missions – frequently on helicopters and heavy transports, and occasionally on jetfighters. Twice, he was invited to take the back seat of a T-38 and an F-15 during air-to-ground, escort, and air-to-air training sorties. Yet as exhilarating as the missions were for a chaplain, they served a much higher purpose.

For example, his inaugural flight in the F-15D model was the direct result of a camaraderie he enjoyed with the airmen of the 32nd Tactical Fighter Squadron (TFS), Camp New Amsterdam, The Netherlands (1983-1986). Soon after the mission, the chaplain deployed with a small team of support personnel and F-15 pilots to a remote location in Greece. Within days, the Greek government became embroiled in a political dispute with the North Atlantic Treaty Organization (NATO). As a result, the deployment was curtailed and the small American unit was detained. Working within a community as transient and unpredictable as the military, one quickly appreciates the adage, "If you want to hear God laugh, tell Him what you'll be doing tomorrow." Not a single 32nd TFS airman could have possibly envisioned a scenario where American jets would be grounded by a friendly nation, and its aviators, detained.

Though never in apparent danger, some of the men were angered at the thought of a third-world power confining the world's greatest air force, others laughed about it while playing sports, and a few others enjoyed a rare nap in the middle of the day. Still, whether angry or napping, all work ceased, and within a day or two, boredom set in. The military mission may have ended, but Christian ministry was exponentially heightened. In the days to follow, a bored (but voluntary) audience afforded the chaplain ample opportunity to reflect the light of Christ not only in worship, Bible study, and prayer; but on fields of play. After all, it all started around the crud table.

434th TFTS aviators congratulate Capt. Whittington following an air-to-ground training mission in an AT38B (1981). It was the last sortie for the pilot, Maj. Dan Cecil (wearing a squadron T-shirt) and Whittington's first supersonic flight. Moments like this provide a tight pastoral bond between airmen and their chaplain.

Ch. Whittington exits the F-15D at Camp New Amsterdam Air Base, The Netherlands (1985) following a two-hour air-to-air training sortie. After building a pastoral relationship with the squadron, the chaplain was given the opportunity to deploy with a small support team and pilots to Greece.

Delay The Sortie Until The Chaplain Arrives!

Attending America's warriors at zero-dark thirty on a foreign runway, not only separates the conscientious chaplain from his colleagues, but distinguishes the military minister from his civilian counterpart.

Many church leaders believe the chaplaincy is a contradiction. How can the minister, as a person of peace, serve a war machine? "Good question," wrote Reverend Gary Smith, retired Air Force chaplain and author of *Letters from Boerdonk.*[7] Smith, whom Whittington lauded as, "A master storyteller and the most creative chaplain I worked with in 30 years" answered the question, with – as the reader would expect from a storyteller – a riveting anecdote.

In his book, Lieutenant Colonel Smith shared the story of one of his Air Force chaplain colleagues – a Lutheran minister. Before serving on active duty, he was an anti-military activist scouring the Midwestern landscape looking for America's Intercontinental Ballistic Missile (ICBM) silos in order to protest the use of nuclear weapons. With dogged intent the Lutheran pastor finally had the chance to confront a young Air Force missile officer surfacing from an underground silo. The activist asked the young lieutenant, "How can you come to work each day wanting to go to war and knowing you could push that button and destroy millions?" The young officer gently replied, "Sir, I come to work each day PRAYING ... I don't have to."[8]

The missileer's heartfelt words so disarmed the activist that upon further prayer and reflection, he decided to enter the Air Force as a chaplain. According to Reverend Smith, he later distinguished himself in *Operation Desert Storm.* In the author's own words,

> The chaplain always stood in the same spot at [0200 hours] each morning as flight crews went out to their planes for early morning missions ... One morning the flight crews had to scramble early and

---

7   Gary Layne Smith, *Letters from Boerdonk* (Dripping Springs, Texas: HighPoint Publishing, Inc., 2007), 217-218.

8   *Ibid.*, 218. Emphasis is in original.

the chaplain had not yet been notified. When he heard the sirens go off, he grabbed a truck at 0130 hours and raced to the flight line. The pilots were purposely delaying their take-off … they felt better with the nightly send-off ritual of the chaplain. They had run by "the chaplain's spot on the flight line, and he was not there." [When he arrived] the chaplain climbed the ladder of every fighter jet in the dark and shook the hands of each pilot and prayed with each one.[9]

Conscientious chaplains make a difference, but it demands intentional ministry! Getting out of bed at zero-dark thirty to pray with the pilot on the runway, or the soldier standing watch, or the sailor aboard a ship are defining moments for one's ministry. And to reiterate, these trenches are to be found everywhere – in the desert heat and the arctic cold – anyplace where the chaplain is least expected, but most appreciated.

All Work Stops at 40-Below

"Everyone loves to visit us in July when the salmon are running," said the Wing Commander at Eielson AFB, Alaska, "But when the temp dips to 40-below, suddenly the distinguished visitors disappear." He was right. Few senior officers wanted to visit Fairbanks, Alaska in the middle of winter, and the Pacific Air Forces (PACAF) Command Chaplain was no exception. This was one of those many occasions when Davidson and Whittington's paths crossed. As the Wing Chaplain for Eielson, Lieutenant Colonel Davidson asked the Command Chaplain to visit his airmen – not in July, but in February – in temperatures so cold that water thrown from a glass would freeze before it hit the ground.

One frigid winter night, the Eielson Wing Commander and the Command Chaplain were walking through a row of aircraft hangars visiting the maintenance troops working on the A-10 *Thunderbolt*, affectionately nicknamed, *Warthog* because "it is slow, ugly, and can't be stopped" according to the jet mechanic holding the wrench. Knowing how young airmen took pride in their jobs, the chaplain (shivering from the bitter cold) encouraged

9   *Ibid.*, 218-219.

him to talk as long as he wanted. After walking about the jet and visiting for an hour or so, he thanked the airman for his service to America and shared a brief prayer.

Inside the hangar the temperature was hovering around zero. As they were walking out of the metal building, slowly moving toward the tarmac the commander said, "It looks like I'll have to call a down-day later this morning; the temperature is predicted to drop another five degrees." "Do the planes not function well when it's this cold?" asked the chaplain. The commander smiled and assured his PACAF guest that the jets loved subzero temperatures. "It's a human factor," he said, "the body can only take so much. All work stops at 40-below." The general was surprised the mechanic had the energy to talk at the end of a long shift, but added, "He was probably in shock to see you at this hour and 35-below zero. He won't forget this visit."

No Greater Love

"It doesn't take a hero to order men into battle. It takes a hero to be one of those men who goes into battle" exclaimed General H. Norman Schwarzkopf, two weeks after American and coalition forces liberated Kuwait in *Operation Desert Storm*.[10] Throughout the history of this great nation, millions of such heroes have been sent into battle and though the number is impossible to calculate, as many as 1.3 million have paid the ultimate price.[11]

Reminders of the fallen are everywhere – from our nation's capital to the battlefields of Europe to remote islands in the Pacific. Prayers at national memorials, funeral services for veterans of yesteryear and yesterday, and prayers for the sick and dying scattered in military hospitals, at home, and overseas are commonplace for today's chaplain. But unlike other Americans reading about a casualty in a local newspaper or hearing about a soldier's death on cable news, it is "up close and personal" for the one whose duty calls him

---

10 Taken from a television interview with Barbara Walters, March 15, 1991; cited in H. Norman Schwarzkopf, *It Doesn't Take A Hero* (New York: Bantam Books, 1992), xiii.

11 "America's Wars: U.S. Casualties and Veterans," *Infoplease* at http://www.infoplease.com/ipa/A0004615.html (accessed Apr. 9, 2013).

to console family and friends. To be candid, it is one of those unique settings where the chaplain's dual role as priest and warrior is understood by all.

At the graveside the only visual distinction between the one reading the 23rd Psalm and the troops standing around the casket mourning the loss of their buddy is the clerical stole draping the chaplain's uniform or the cross prominently placed over his heart. One need not have personally known the fallen hero to mourn the loss, but there are many occasions when both "face and name" are known and the memory of a friend is forever embedded in the chaplain's memory.

The Lord's Prayer, the 23rd Psalm, and the oft-used Johannine text where Jesus reassured Martha that her dead brother Lazarus would rise again[12] are all comforting words to those who mourn. Yet when death occurs on the battlefield, the chaplain will more often-than-not open his remarks with a different passage from John's Gospel; the words of Jesus already in the hearts of those standing by their buddy's graveside – "Greater love has no man than this, that a man lay down his life for his friends."[13]

This was the verse that resonated with Major General Baldwin one week after visiting the Explosive Ordnance Disposal (EOD) squadron at Kirkuk Air Base, Iraq. Experienced chaplains, familiar with every Specialty Code,[14] understand the danger of being a member of an EOD team. In the Air Force, these are the airmen who handle improvised explosive devices (IED) and unexploded pieces of ordnance; a dangerous job "that requires a great deal of knowledge and exacting attention to detail" according to Air Force leadership.[15] They would often travel with military caravans disarming any IED along the roadside. Knowing the dangers the airmen faced daily, Chaplain Baldwin decided to

---

12 *Cf.* Jn. 11:25

13 Jn. 15:13 (RSV)

14 The Air Force Specialty Code (AFSC) is a four or five-digit code used to identify a specific military occupation. The nomenclature differs within each major branch of service but all services employ specialty codes – e.g. Army Military Occupational Specialty Code (MOSC) and a system of naval ratings in the U.S. Navy along with the Navy Enlisted Classification (NEC).

15 See "Explosive Ordnance Disposal (EOD)," *Careers* (official Air Force website) http://www.airforce.com/careers/detail/explosive-ordnance-disposal-eod/ (accessed Apr. 9, 2013).

visit the EOD squadron at every opportunity. During one of his many trips to the Middle East, the Air Force Chief of Chaplains found himself in the desert of Kirkuk engaging in a ministry of presence with these dedicated heroes.

> On this particular day, I met an EOD team of three Air Force airmen – one Technical Sergeant, one Staff Sergeant, and one Senior Airman. The team leader said to the female airman, "Tell the chaplain what you did yesterday." She very humbly told me how it was her turn to do the final disarming of the IED. She had to wear the heavy bomb "suit" to walk up to the bomb and do the final step to make the bomb safe. I was extremely impressed with her courage and her devotion to her team and to the mission. When I gave her my Chief of Chaplains coin, she said, "Oh, Chaplain, I do not deserve this; I was only doing my job." I got very emotional when I tried to thank her and her team for what they were doing. She told me they had only two more weeks to go on this deployment. When I got home from that visit to the AOR, I learned that all three airmen on that EOD team were killed by an IED the week after I met with them. They had one week to go.[16]

Upon hearing the news, this former rescue-helicopter-pilot-turned-Baptist-chaplain welled up and thought of the words of Jesus from John 15:13. Then he added, "What a privilege for a chaplain to be able to visit people who live such amazing lives."[17]

The military is a dangerous business. Our troops put themselves in harms' way on a daily basis, in training and war, but it isn't just the tip-of-the-spear that lands in a combat zone. Support personnel – including chaplains and their armed assistants – deploy with their soldiers. There is no arguing that the greater number of chaplains engaged in America's war against terrorists (Iraq/ Afghanistan) belong to the Army; due in no small part, to the uniqueness of land, sea, and air operations. And as retired Air Force chaplains, your authors have tremendous respect for their Army colleagues. When it comes to battlefield ministry, they are the world's best.

---

16 Baldwin (March 20, 2013).

17 *Ibid.*

But their greater numbers do not diminish from our brave Navy chaplains at risk on sea or in a bombed-out house in Afghanistan conducting a worship service for combat marines, or America's courageous Air Force chaplains who find themselves in harms' way at remote air bases scattered throughout the world. The following three stories share a single deployment in multiple foxholes. Your co-author, Charlie Davidson, found himself at God's place in God's time reflecting God's presence.

Shock and Awe – The First Leg

Major Davidson was sitting at his desk at Lackland AFB, Texas when he was summoned to the Wing Chaplain's office. He was aware of the build-up of American and coalition forces in the Middle East in preparation for a military offensive toward Baghdad, so there was little surprise when the boss said to prepare for deployment to the AOR in December 2002.

At the close of the duty day, Chaplain Davidson returned home, hugged his wife and together they lifted the deployment before the Lord. It was at that time, he and Roydene "accepted the call for him to go." "Accepting" the call may sound peculiar to the reader; after all, it isn't as if he had the choice to say "no." True, but even though all military personnel must obey orders, every soldier has the choice to accept mediocrity or pursue excellence "as they go." During his prayer, God reminded Charlie, "The horse is made ready for the day of battle, but the victory belongs to the Lord."[18] And with that word from the Lord, Chaplain Davidson shared the news with each of his three children living in Lynchburg, Virginia, and assured them of a father's eternal love.

With mobility bag in hand, Davidson began his twenty-hour flight to Al Udeid, Air Base in Qatar, arriving on January 16, 2003. Located west of Doha, Qatar, the air base hosted a large U.S. military presence. As part of his personal memoirs, Davidson recorded,

The ministry here consisted of conducting several weekly worship

---

18 Prov. 21:31 (RSV)

services complete with prayers, music, scripture, brief sermon, and altar call. We always concluded by praying for one another and all of the soldiers, airmen, marines, and coalition forces in the Middle East and around the world. As the number two chaplain at Al Udeid, I was assigned to provide a ministry of presence to all flight line personnel. Many times I would just walk around encouraging the airmen working on the aircraft and praying with the troops. It wasn't long before I established a great rapport with the maintenance crews, pilots, and commanders. They appreciated the prayers so much that I made a few business-type cards with a brief written prayer for the pilots to carry with them during combat sorties. The prayer was a simple prayer asking for God's safety and concluded with the words, "Don't let me screw up." They loved it.[19]

At a typical deployed pace, there were daily exercises donning chemical gear and moving from bunker-to-bunker providing pastoral care to as many as possible. Though everyone present expected the leadership to plan regular exercises, when the horn sounded, no one really knew if it was a real-world attack or an exercise. Fortunately, Chaplain Davidson had the luxury of making his one (and only) mistake and being alive to tell about it.

On one occasion I was ministering to the safety guys. The horn sounded and we headed toward the bunker. We were already in MOPP 2[20] but had forgotten to put on our masks when we heard the siren. As I was running toward the bunker I noticed a large white cloud and thought to myself, "Dear Lord, we've been attacked." Smelling a sulfuric odor I ran even faster. Entering the crowded bunker I rushed to put on my mask. It was dark and noisy from all of the commotion. All the while I thought I was breathing in toxic fumes and would soon be dead. By the time the mask was finally strapped on and my eyes had adjusted to the darkness I heard the all-clear. As I walked out of the bunker I learned that the alarm sounded because an unidentified aircraft flew dangerously close to the installation. Had it been a chemical attack,

19 Written narrative from Charlie Davidson to Michael Whittington (March 22, 2013).

20 Mission Oriented Protective Posture (MOPP) is a protective gear used by military personnel in chemical, biological, radiological, or nuclear strike. In MOPP level 2, the suit and boots are worn, with the gloves and mask at the ready.

I would have died. I returned to my office (an old tin trailer near the runway) and wept from the thought of never seeing my family again. From that moment, I never treated the assignment quite the same. The game was on and I was in the game.[21]

There were multiple fighter jets at Al Udeid, to include the sleek F-117 Nighthawk – a single-seat, twin-engine stealth ground-attack fighter. All of the military chaplains assigned to the forward operating base prayed with the pilots before the day's sorties, but when the phone rang at 0330 hours on 20 March 2003, Davidson knew something was up. On the other end of the line was the 8th Fighter Squadron commander, telling the chaplain to report immediately to squadron Headquarters. Upon arrival, Chaplain Davidson was briefed that two F-117 Stealth Fighters were flying a mission to Baghdad, Iraq to bomb "vital targets of opportunity."[22] As the commander would later write, "This AF mission would in fact start the air campaign into Baghdad, Iraq and begin *Operation Iraqi Freedom*."[23] The commander continued,

> [I asked] Chaplain Davidson to lead the squadron in prayer ... [He] addressed the squadron. He quoted from Prov 21:31, "The horse is prepared for the day of battle but [victory] comes from the Lord." He also stated that our mission is for freedom, it was in the US national interest that we are fighting against an evil regime that must be removed and that he believed the Lord would give us complete victory.

Ch. Davidson offering prayer and words of encouragement to American military forces on the border of Iraq (2003).

---

21 Davidson (March 22, 2013).

22 In an official letter of appreciation written by MATTHEW P. MCKEON, Lt Col, USAF, Commander, 8th Fighter Squadron entitled "OPERATION IRAQI FREEDOM." The letter is in the hands of Charlie Davidson.

23 *Ibid.*

[He then asked] that all bow for a moment of silence, offered a prayer asking for God's presence, guidance, and wisdom in what lay ahead. Chaplain Davidson prayed for the safety of the two fighter pilots and for the success of their mission. He then invited the squadron to close in repeating the Lord's Prayer.[24]

In his personal journal, Davidson added "As we prayed the Lord's Prayer, there were tears on every face."[25]

Soon after, the chaplain joined other squadron personnel watching the attack on a large television screen, reported by the Cable News Network (CNN). The relentless bombing continued for two days. Known to the world as *Shock and Awe*, U.S. and allied forces launched 1,700 air sorties (504 using cruise missiles).[26] Davidson had prayed for all of the aviators, but the faces and names of the two Nighthawk pilots were forever etched in his memory.

Ch. Davidson and A1C Timothy Tabiz- Unit Ministry Team (UMT) Deployed January-May 2003

---

24   *Ibid.*

25   Davidson (March 22, 2013).

26   USCENTAF, "Operation Iraqi Freedom - By the Numbers, Assessment and Analysis Division," (April 30, 2003) at http://www.globalsecurity.org/military/library/report/2003/uscentaf_oif_report_30apr2003.pdf (accessed April 10, 2013).

Easter Celebration at Baghdad International Airport – The Second Leg

Shock and Awe had accomplished its mission. The enemy targets were destroyed or severely compromised and the ground campaign ensued. In the meantime, Chaplain Davidson had been promoted to Lieutenant Colonel and the Air Force relocated him to Prince Sultan Air Base, Kingdom of Saudi Arabia as the 484th Air Expeditionary Wing Chaplain. Within days of arrival, the commander met with Davidson and told him he was responsible for providing ministry to the Air Special Operation Squadron (ASOS) in the Area Of Responsibility (AOR). After the Unit Ministry Team (UMT) – Lieutenant Colonel Davidson and his chaplain assistant Airman First Class (A1C) Timothy Tabiz – was issued the appropriate war gear, they boarded the first aircraft headed for the Iraqi border. Though the UMT enjoyed a great ministry of presence at the classified border location, Davidson and Tabiz needed to move forward to continue ministry to other troops but especially to his ASOS people. He and Tabiz were able to board a C-130 flight headed directly to Saddam Hussein International Airport. Davidson noted,

Chaplain Davidson conducting worship services on the border of Iraq

Through the darkness, I looked out the small porthole windows of the C-130 and saw the red and yellow flashes of the bombs exploding. I immediately thought of Francis Scott Key watching the bombardment of the American forces at Fort McHenry. The lyrics raced through my mind as we approached the runway, "And the rockets' red glare, the bombs bursting in air, gave proof through the night that our flag was still there." The team prepared itself for a combat landing which meant no lights and back hatch opened. No sooner had the wheels touched the runway than a special operations troop wearing night vision goggles grabbed us and hollered "Come with me." We jumped in the bed of a military truck with about 15 other personnel and drove around looking for the communications building. Once located, we rolled out of the truck and ran to the building.[27]

The next few days found Chaplain Davidson and A1C Tabiz moving from building to building where they knew American forces were located. Told to follow the secure paths – the ones proven safe from unexploded ordnance – the UMT visited hundreds of airmen, marines, and soldiers. American tanks rumbled over the flight line and Blackhawk helicopters filled the sky above the tarmac. Prayer and worship followed the chaplain team everywhere they went. Chaplain Davidson would later reflect,

> I learned a long time ago people may not show up for a sermon, especially mine, but would always come for prayer and communion. As I was moving from building to building, I overheard one of the soldier's say, "We will be safe now, the chaplain is here." I can tell you I was really humbled by those words and had to fight back the tears. They knew I was a Baptist minister but I answered to whatever title they wanted to give me, even "Father." I spread the word that we would celebrate worship services on Sunday and to my surprise the Catholic soldiers attended. I explained my take on the Lord's Supper and read from 1 Corinthians 11. We had no wine or grape juice, and no bread of any kind. I told the guys, it's up to you if you want to take communion but the Lord invites all of us to come to the Table. So there we were, sitting on the tarmac of the Baghdad International Airport on Easter Sunday using Kool Aid and crackers taken from an MRE to celebrate the risen Savior.[28]

Upon sharing the story with his co-author, Davidson would later confide, "I am sure there are some religious people out there that would say we were

---

27 Davidson (March 22, 2013).

28 *Ibid.*

wrong to use these as communion supplies but I truly believe my God was okay with it."[29]

Kirkuk, Iraq – The Final Leg

With the airport secure Chaplain Davidson and Airman Tibiz boarded another aircraft and flew north to Kirkuk. Sleeping in an "old, dirty, one-level building with no windows was 'cold and spooky' for both of us. Each night I would say a prayer for my God to protect us and lead us to places He wanted us to go."[30]

Following Kirkuk, Davidson caught a flight back to Prince Sultan Air Base to report to the commander. Word had already spread to the commander that some Air Force "combat chaplain" had traveled through the AOR ministering to American forces. The 484th Air Expeditionary Wing commander didn't need the name; he knew it was Charlie. After a few days of rest, Chaplain Davidson boarded a C-17 and returned to San Antonio, Texas. He had traveled through Jordan, Kuwait, Qatar, Saudi Arabia, and Iraq, providing a "visible reminder of the Holy" to hundreds of American heroes – ninety-three of whom accepted Jesus Christ as their personal Savior.

Having distinguished himself by meritorious achievement under combat conditions Lieutenant Colonel Davidson was awarded the Bronze Star on November 7, 2003. At the time of the award, he was the Wing Chaplain for Eielson Air Force Base, Alaska. Soon after the presentation, Davidson attended the Command Chaplain's Conference at Hickam Air Force Base, Hawaii, where Colonel Whittington, standing before all of the senior chaplains in the Pacific Command, publicly thanked Charlie for his deployed ministry and selfless service to God and country. As for the recognition in front of his peers, Davidson laughed and said, "Only fitting! After all, it was my buddy Mike [as the Lackland Wing Chaplain] who sent me to Iraq in the first place."[31]

---

29 *Ibid.*

30 *Ibid.*

31 *Ibid.*

Photo of Wing Chaplain Lt Col Charlie Davidson awarded Bronze Star by his Wing Commander. Eielson AFB, Alaska, November 7, 2003

Mission Complete:

Ministry of Presence:

Qatar, Saudi Arabia,

Jordan, Kuwait, Iraq

Visitation:

5,000 Joint/Coalition Forces

432 Counseling Cases

52 Worship Services

93 Men/Women accepted Jesus Christ as Savior

TO GOD BE THE GLORY

Summary of Ch, Lt Col Davidson and A1C Tabiz ministry report following OIF deployment to Iraq. The UMT provided battlefield "ministry of presence" to troops in Jordan, Kuwait, Qatar, Saudi Arabia, and Iraq (2003).

Conclusion

With the frequently used phrase, "Foxholes are everywhere," your authors hope every reader will grasp the obvious – you don't have to be in the middle of a firefight to be with the soldier in his time of need. You do, however, have to leave the comfort of the chapel in order to fulfill your calling from God and your commission as a military chaplain.

One may never have the privilege to provide communion to Special Forces securing an enemy runway or pray with a pilot at 0200 hours before a combat sortie, but there will be ample opportunities for the Christian chaplain to reflect the light of Christ in military trenches at home and overseas – from isolated bomb dumps to arctic maintenance hangars. The chaplain must be willing, however, to serve America's warriors where few want to go and at those ungodly hours when most others want to sleep. Successful ministry is intentional. Foxholes are everywhere!

EPILOGUE

Matters of Conscience proposed a twofold thesis: the success of the military chaplaincy – indelibly linked to the First Amendment – is in direct proportion to the freedom of speech extended to its own chaplains; and in order for the evangelical chaplain to fulfill his calling from God, his ultimate allegiance must reside in Jesus Christ or his commitment to the Constitution is disingenuous. Both of these foundational theses address the future of the chaplaincy exposed in one of two possible scenarios.

Demise of Religious Freedom

The worst case scenario signals a dangerous path where political and judicial leaders distance themselves from the moral values embedded in our nation's history and grounded in Holy Scripture. With a total disregard of America's Judeo-Christian heritage, they dismiss the historical past as irrelevant, or worse, rewrite it altogether.

Presently, military regulations protect the religious freedoms of its chaplains but the Department of Defense is duty-bound to reflect government policy. Considering the political climate in our nation's capital it is not too difficult to envision a future where the evangelical chaplain is no longer allowed to preach or counsel according to his faith and conscience.

Forcing military chaplains to redefine moral issues based upon government policy (or resign their commission) would breach the First Amendment on two counts: (1) the government would come dangerously close to establishing a federal clergy – contravening the Establishment Clause; and (2) it would penalize dissension – breaking the Free Exercise Clause. God forbid that day should ever come; if it does, more will be lost than a few hundred conservative chaplains. The far greater injury will be the demise of our religious freedom, and with it, the hallmark of our founding era.

Facilitating Religious Freedom

However, it need not be that way. If political, judicial, and military leaders stand firm on the First Amendment, ensuring the religious rights of all soldiers and equally extending the same freedom to the conservative Christian chaplain without prejudice, the military chaplaincy will do what the Founders envisioned – facilitate the free exercise of religion to America's citizen-soldier.

So where does that leave the Bible-believing Christian citizen? Other than peaceably assembling and petitioning the government for a redress of grievances (guaranteed in the First Amendment) the Christian can live a stellar life! The Apostle Peter's advice to the first-century Church is important to the twenty-first century Christian.

> Respect the authorities, whatever their level; they are God's emissaries for keeping the order. It is God's will that by doing good [deeds] you might cure the ignorance of the fools who think you're a danger to society. Exercise your freedom by serving God, not by breaking the rules. Treat everyone you meet with dignity. Love your spiritual family. Revere God. Respect the government.[1]

As for the evangelical chaplain who believes the Bible is inspired by God, listen to the Word of the Lord:

> I want you to get out there and walk – better yet, run! – on the road God called you to travel. I don't want any of you sitting around on your hands. I don't want anyone strolling off, down some path that goes nowhere. And mark that you do this with humility and discipline – not in fits and starts, but steadily, pouring yourselves out for each other in acts of love, alert at noticing differences and quick at mending fences. You were all called to travel on the same road and in the same direction, so stay together, both outwardly and inwardly. You have one Master, one faith, one baptism, one God and Father of all, who rules

---

1   1 Pt. 2:13-17 (*The Message*)

over all, works through all, and is present in all ... We take our lead from Christ, who is the source of everything we do.[2]

Two promises are made by the Christian chaplain. The first is a confession of faith: "I believe that Jesus Christ is the Son of God."[3] The second is an oath of office: "I do solemnly swear that I will support and defend the Constitution of the United States against all enemies, foreign, and domestic ...."[4] These promises should prove complementary, but if the time ever comes when the servant of God is forced to choose between the two, the chaplain would do well to remember the eternal trumps the temporal.

2 Eph. 4:2-5, 16 (*The Message*)

3 *Cf.* Acts 8:37

4 "Oaths of Enlistment and Oaths of Office," *Center of Military History, United States Army at* http://www.history.army.mil/html/faq/oaths.html.

MEET THE AUTHORS

DR. MICHAEL C. WHITTINGTON
CHAPLAIN, COLONEL, USAF (RETIRED)

Dr. Whittington retired from the United States Air Force in 2005 as a colonel with 30 years of active duty. As a senior leader in the Air Force Chaplain Service, he served as: Chief of the Education Division and Director for the USAF Chaplain Service Institute, command chaplain for the Pacific Air Forces, and senior staff chaplain for the USAF Academy. He was assigned to overseas duty for twelve years serving in four military theaters – the Middle East, Europe, the Pacific, and the Far East. Colonel Whittington is a 3-time recipient of the *Legion of Merit* medal (2 Bronze Oak Leaf Clusters) – the 6th highest medal in precedence of United States military decorations.

Following his military service he moved to Nashville, Tennessee where he presently divides his time between extensive writing in the field of chaplaincy studies and working with Liberty University as an Assistant Professor of Chaplaincy Ministry, subject matter expert, and mentor for doctoral candidates.

He earned a Bachelor of Arts (1974) from Oklahoma Christian University. His graduate degrees include a Master of Science (1977) and a Master of Divinity (1979) from Abilene Christian University, and a Master of Strategic Studies (2000) from the United States Air Force Air University. He completed his doctoral studies at Saint Paul School of Theology, earning a Doctor of Ministry in 1989. He is a graduate of Air Command & Staff College *with honors* (1990) and Air War College (2000) – both earned in residence at Air University. While at Air War College his essay entitled "A Separate Space Force – An Eighty Year Old Argument" received special recognition and was published as *Maxwell Paper # 20.*

Married in 1972, Michael and his wife, Debbie, reside in Nolensville, Tennessee. He enjoys a good book, woodworking, plays the guitar to relax, and appreciates the company of friends on the golf course. His greatest joys, however, come from his family – his wife, three married sons, daughters-in-law, and five fun-loving grandkids who call him "Pop." In his own words, "Apart from one's faith, family, and friends ... nothing else much matters."

DR. CHARLIE N. DAVIDSON
CHAPLAIN, LIEUTENANT COLONEL, USAF (RETIRED)

Dr. Davidson presently serves Liberty University as Director for the Doctor of Ministry degree, Associate Professor and Director of the Master of Divinity Chaplaincy Program, and the chaplain endorsing agent for Liberty Baptist Fellowship for military and corporate chaplains. Dr. Davidson retired from the United States Air Force in 2006 as a lieutenant colonel with over 20 years of active duty and four years of reserve duty. Ordained in 1984 by Dr. Jerry Falwell and endorsed by Liberty Baptist Fellowship, he was commissioned a chaplain in July 1986 and served in chaplain leadership as senior protestant chaplain, branch chief chaplain, and wing chaplain – at CONUS and overseas assignments.

He delivered the opening prayer that initiated the Iraqi air campaign in March 2003 while deployed to Qatar. Soon after, he accompanied the Air Special Operation Squadron (ASOS) into Baghdad and earned the distinction of being the first Air Force chaplain awarded the Bronze Star medal "under combat conditions in hostile and dangerous situations" (7 Nov 2003) during *Operation Iraqi Freedom* (OIF).

Additionally, he is an associate pastor of congregational care for Thomas Road Baptist Church. His professional memberships include the Evangelical Theological Society, staff member of the American Association of Christian

Counselors, and a member of the Board of Directors for the Bristol Motor Raceway Ministries.

He earned a Bachelor of Science (1982), Master of Divinity (1984), and a Doctor of Ministry (2001), from Liberty University. His Professional Military Education (PME) includes Air Force Squadron Officer School (1990) and Air Command & Staff College (2001) from the Air University. He also earned four units of Clinical Pastoral Education (CPE) while in a one-year residence at Walter Reed Medical Center, Washington D.C. (2001).

An avid sportsman, Dr. Davidson has enjoyed hunting and fishing all over the United States and Canada. He and his wife Roydene live in Lynchburg, Virginia. Their three grown children also live in Lynchburg allowing them the daily joy of seeing their son, two married daughters and sons-in-law, and six grandchildren. He believes his life's goal of *"Training Champions for Christ"* – Liberty University's motto – begins with his family.

SELECTED BIBLIOGRAPHY

BOOKS, ARTICLES, ESSAYS

Adams, John. *The Works of John Adams, Second President of the United States,* IX, with notes and illustrations by Charles Francis Adams. Boston: Little, Brown and Company, 1854.

Aerts, Diederik, *et al. World Views – From Fragmentation to Integration.* Brussels: VUB Press, 1994.

Apps, Jerold W. *Ideas for Better Church Meetings.* Minneapolis: Augsburg Publishing House, 1963.

Bainton, Roland H. *Here I Stand: A Life of Martin Luther.* New York: Abingdon-Cokesbury Press, 1950.

Bauknight, Brian Kelley. *Body Building: Creating a Ministry Team Through Spiritual Gifts.* Nashville: Abingdon Press, 1996.

Behm, J. *"metanoéō,"* ed. Geoffrey W. Bromiley, in *Theological Dictionary of the New Testament: Abridged in One Volume,* 641-646. Grand Rapids, Michigan: William B. Eerdmans Publishing Company, 1985).

Bergen, Doris, ed. *The Sword of the Lord.* Notre Dame, Indiana: Notre Dame University Press, 2004.

Bettenson, Henry. *The Early Christian Fathers.* New York: Oxford University Press, 1958.

Biehl, Bobb. *Master-Planning – The Complete Guide For Building A Strategic Plan For Your Business, Church, or Organization.* Nashville: Broadman & Holman, 1997.

Bonomi, Patricia, and Peter R. Eisenstadt. "Church Attendance in the Eighteenth-Century British American Colonies," *William and Mary Quarterly* 39: 2 (April 1982), 245-286.

Bruce, F.F. "Lessons from the Early Church," *In God's Community,* eds. David J. Ellis and W. Ward Gasque, 153-168. Wheaton, IL: Harold Shaw Publishers, 1978.

Bultmann, R. "*Alētheia*," ed. Geoffrey W. Bromiley, *Theological Dictionary of the New Testament: Abridged in One Volume,* 37-40. Grand Rapids, Michigan: William B. Eerdmans Publishing Company, 1985.

Butler, Jon, "Why Revolutionary America Wasn't a 'Christian Nation,'" in *Religion and the New Republic,* ed. James H. Hutston, 187-202. Lanham, Md: Rowman & Littlefield, 2000.

Cappon, Lester J. ed. *The Adams-Jefferson Letters,* vol. 2. Chapel Hill: University of North Carolina Press, 1959.

Carter, Stephen L. *The Culture of Disbelief.* New York: Harper Collins Publishers, 1993.

Chambers, S. David. "The Protestant Problem," *Military Chaplains' Review* (Fall 1987), 81-88.

Clausewitz, Carl von. *On War,* eds. and trans. Michael E. Howard, and Peter Paret. Princeton, NJ: Princeton University Press, 1976.

Conger, Jay A. *Learning to Lead – The Art of Transforming Managers into Leaders.* San Francisco: Jossey-Bass Publishers, 1992.

Cousina, Don, Keith Anderson, and Arthur MacDonald. *Mastering Church Management.* Kansas City: Watterich Publishers, 1956.

Dix, Gregory. *Shape of the Liturgy.* London: Dacre Press, 1970.

Drazin, Israel, and Cecil B. Currey. *For God and Country: The History of a Constitutional Challenge to the Army Chaplaincy.* Hoboken, NJ: KTAV Publishing House, 1995.

Ebener, Dan R. *Servant Leadership Models for your Parish.* Mahwah, NJ: Paulist Press, 2010.

Fea, John. *Was America Founded as a Christian Nation?* Louisville, KY: John Knox Press, 2011.

Friedrich, Gerhard, "εὐαγγελίζομαι," *Theological Dictionary of the New Testament,* II, ed. Gerhard Kittel, trans. Geoffrey W. Bromiley, 707-721. Grand Rapids: Wm. B. Eerdmans Publishing Company, 1964.

Gales, Joseph, ed. *The Debates and Proceedings in the Congress of the United States,* Vol. I. Washington: Gales & Seaton, 1834.

Greenleaf, Robert K. *Seeker and Servant: Essays by Robert Greenleaf,* eds. Anne T. Fraker, and Larry C. Spears. San Francisco: Jossey-Bass Publishers, 1996.

— . *The Servant Within: The Transformative Path,* eds. Hamilton Beazley, Julie Begs, and Larry C. Spears. Mahwah, NJ: Paulist Press, 2003.

Hadley, Donald W., and Gerald T. Richards. *Ministry with the Military.* Grand Rapids, MI: Baker Book House, 1992.

Hauck, Frederick. "*Koinōn,*" in T*heological Dictionary of the New Testament,* III, ed. Gerhard Kittel, trans. Geoffrey W. Bromiley, 804-809. Grand Rapids: Wm. B. Eerdmans Publishing Company, 1965.

Hesse, Herman. *Journey to the East,* trans. Hilda Rosner. New York: The Noonday Press, 1957.

Howard Fielding. "John Adams: Puritan, Deist, Humanist," *Journal of Religion,* 20:1 (January 1940), 33-46.

Hughes, Robert B. and Carl J. Laney. *Tyndale Concise Bible Commentary.* Wheaton, Ill: Tyndale House Publishers, 2001.

Hutcheson, Jr., Richard G. *The Churches and the Chaplaincy.* Atlanta: John Knox Press, 1975.

Hutson, James H. *Forgotten Features of the Founding: The Rediscovery of Religious Themes in the Early American Republic.* New York: Lexington Books, 2003.

—. *Religion and the Founding of the American Republic.* Washington: Library of Congress, 1998.

—. "Thomas Jefferson's Letter to the Danbury Baptists: A Controversy Rejoined," *William and Mary Quarterly,* 61 (October 1999): 788-790.

Isaacson, Walter. *Benjamin Franklin: An American Life.* New York: Simon & Schuster, 2003.

Jamieson, Robert, and A.R. Fausset, David Brown, *A Commentary, Critical and Explanatory, on the Old and New Testaments.* Oak Harbor, WA: Logos Research Systems, Inc., 1997.

Jeremias, Joachim. *The Eucharistic Words of Jesus.* Philadelphia: Fortress Press, 1966.

Jones, W. Paul. *Theological Worlds – Understanding the Alternate Rhythms of Christian Belief.* Nashville: Abingdon Press, 1989.

Jungman, Josef A. *The Early Liturgy to the Time of Gregory the Great,* trans. Francis A. Brunner. London: Darton, Longman & Todd, 1960.

King Jr., Martin Luther. *Strength to Love.* New York: Harper & Row, 1963.

Kramnick, Isaac, and R. Laurence Moore, *The Godless Constitution: The Case Against Religious Correctness.* New York: W.W. Norton Publishers, 1996.

Kuhn, Karl Georg, "Προσήλυτος," *Theological Dictionary of the New Testament,* VI, ed. Gerhard Friedrich, trans. Geoffrey W. Bromiley, 727-744. Grand Rapids: Wm. B. Eerdmans Publishing Company, 1968.

Küng, Hans. "Is Christ's Table Divided"? *International Christian Digest* 1:7 (September 1987): 37-38.

Laing, John D. *In Jesus' Name.* Eugene, Oregon: Resource Publications, 2010.

Lambert, Frank. *The Founding Fathers and the Place of Religion in America.* Princeton, NJ: Princeton University Press, 2003.

Latourette, Kenneth Scott. *A History of Christianity.* New York: Harper & Row, 1953.

Lawson, Kenneth. "Doctrinal Tension: The Chaplain and Information Operations," *Military Intelligence Professional Bulletin* 35:2 (April-June 2009), 24-31.

Longmore, Paul K. *The Invention of George Washington.* Berkeley CA: University of California Press, 1988.

MacArthur, John. *The MacArthur Study Bible.* Nashville: Word Pub., 1997.

Marty, Martin E. *Righteous Empire: The Protestant Experience in America.* New York: Dial, 1970.

Maxwell, John C. *Developing the Leader Within You.* Nashville: Thomas Nelson Publishers, 1993.

—. *The 21 Irrefutable Laws of Leadership.* Nashville: Thomas Nelson Publishers, 1998.

McCarthy, Barry. *A Parliamentary Guide for Church Leadership.* Nashville: Broadman Press, 1976.

McCullough, David. *John Adams.* New York: Simon & Schuster Paperbacks, 2001.

—. *Truman.* New York: Simon & Schuster Paperbacks, 1992.

McDonnell, Charles. "Multi-Cultural and the Unit Ministry Team," *Military Chaplain's Review* (Fall 1987): 77-80.

McGrath, Alister E. *Christianity: An Introduction.* Malden, MA: Blackwell Publishing, 2006.

McIntosh, Gary L. *Staff Your Church for Growth-Building Team Ministry In The 21st Century.* Grand Rapids: Baker Book House Co, 2000.

Meacham, Jon. *American Gospel.* New York: Random House, 2006.

—. *Thomas Jefferson – The Art of Power.* New York: Random House, 2013.

Michaelis, Wilheim. "*Protōs,*" ed. Geoffrey W. Bromiley, in *Theological Dictionary of the New Testament: Abridged in One Volume,* 965-968. Grand Rapids, Michigan: William B. Eerdmans Publishing Company, 1985.

Montoya, Alex D. "Approaching Pastoral Ministry Scripturally," in *Pastoral Ministry: How to Shepherd Biblically,* ed. John MacArthur, 47-63. Nashville: Thomas Nelson, 2005.

Newmann, Barclay Moon and Philip C. Stine, *A Handbook on the Gospel of Matthew.* New York: United Bible Societies, 1992.

Nickols, James P. "Religious Pluralism: A Challenge to the Chaplain Corps," *Military Chaplains' Review* (Fall 1986), 86-92.

Noyce, Gaylord. *Church Meetings That Work.* Herndon, VA: The Alban Institute, 1994.

Oates, Wayne E. *Nurturing Silence in a Noisy Heart.* Garden City, New York: Doubleday & Company, Inc., 1979.

Oden, Thomas C. ed. *Parables of Kierkegaard.* Princeton NJ: Princeton University Press, 1978.

O'Donnell, Joseph F. C.S.C. "Clergy in the Military – Vietnam and After: One Chaplain's Reflections," in *The Sword of the Lord: Military Chaplains from the First to the Twenty-First Century,* ed. Doris L. Bergen, 215-232. Notre Dame, Indiana: University of Notre Dame Press, 2004.

Osborn, Alex. *Applied Imagination.* New York: Charles Scribner's Sons, 1963.

Otterstein, Paul "Theological Pluralism in the Air Force Chaplaincy," *Military Chaplains' Review* (Fall 1987), 889-121.

Padover, Saul K. ed. *The Complete Jefferson.* New York: Duell, Sloan & Pierce, 1943.

Proctor-Smith, Marjorie. "Worship, the World and Work," *Liturgy* 6:4 (Spring 1987), 61-65.

Reisman, W. Michael, and Chris T. Antoniou. *The Laws of War.* New York: Vintage Books, 1994.

Rengstorf, K H. "διδασκαλία," *Theological Dictionary of the New Testament, Abridged In One Volume,* ed. Geoffrey W. Bromiley, 161-166. Grand Rapids, MI: William B. Eerdmans Publishing Company, 1985.

Schaeffer, Francis A., and C. Everett Koop, *Whatever Happened to the Human Race?* In T*he Complete Works of Francis A. Schaeffer: A Christian Worldview,* V. Westchester, Illinois: Crossway Books, 1982.

Schaff, Philip. *History of the Christian Church,* Vol. 4. Peabody, MA: Hendrickson Publishers, Inc., c.1885, 2006.

Schwarzkopf, H. Norman. *It Doesn't Take A Hero.* New York: Bantam Books, 1992.

Smart, Ninian. *The Religious Experience of Mankind.* New York: Charles Scribner's Sons, 1969.

Smith, Gary Layne. *Letters from Boerdonk.* Dripping Springs, Texas: HighPoint Publishing, Inc., 2007.

Sofield, Loughlan, and Donald H. Kuhn. *The Collaborative Leader – Listening to the Wisdom of God's People.* Notre Dame, Indiana: Ave Marie Press, 1995.

Strong, James. *The Exhaustive Concordance of the Bible: Showing Every Word of the Text of the Common English Version of the Canonical Books, and Every Occurrence of Each Word in Regular Order,* electronic edition. Ontario: Woodside Bible Fellowship, 1996.

Swanson, James, Allen Wikgren, Bruce M. Metsger, Carlo M. Martini, and Matthew Black. *The Swanson New Testament Greek Morphology: United Bible Societies' Fourth Edition.* Bellingham, WA : Logos Research Systems, Inc., 2003.

Tocqueville, Alexis de. *Democracy in America,* eds. and trans. Harvey C. Mansfield and Delba Winthrop. Chicago: University of Chicago Press, 2000.

Toulouse, Mark G. *God in Public: Four Ways American Christianity and Public Life Relate.* Louisville: Westminster John Knox Press, 2006.

Townley, Cathy. *Missional Worship.* St. Louis: Chalice Press, 2011.

Towns, Elmer, C. Peter Wagner and Thom S. Rainer, *The Every Church Guide to Growth.* Nashville: Broadman & Holman Publishers, 1998.

Walker, Brent. *Church-State Matters: Fighting for Religion Liberty in our Nation's Capital.* Macon, Georgia: Mercer University Press, 2008.

Warren, Rick. *The Purpose Driven Church.* Grand Rapids: Zondervan Publishing House, 1995.

Webber, Robert E. *Worship Is A Verb.* Peabody, Massachusetts: Hendrickson Publishers, Inc., 1985.

—. *Worship Old & New.* Grand Rapids, MI: Zondervan Publishing House, 1982.

—. "The Modes of God's Presence," *Liturgy* 6:4 (Spring 1987), 79-83._

Westing, Harold J. Church Staff Handbook – *How to Build an Effective Ministry Team.* Grand Rapids: Kregel Publications, 1997.

Wiersbe, Warren W. T*he Bible Exposition Commentary.* Wheaton, Ill.: Victor Books, c1989, 1996.

Wilckens, U. "*Hypokritēs*," *Theological Dictionary of the New Testament: Abridged in One Volume,* ed. Geoffrey W. Bromiley, 1235-1236. Grand Rapids, Michigan: William B. Eerdmans Publishing Company, 1985.

William, William and Arthur Farstad, *Believer's Bible Commentary: Old and New Testaments.* Nashville: Thomas Nelson, 1997, c1995.

Wilson, William. *Wilson's Old Testament Word Studies.* McLean, VA: MacDonald Publishing Co., n.d.

Wolf, Herbert. *Theological Wordbook of the Old Testament,* eds. R. Laird Harris, Gleason L. Archer, Jr., and Bruce K. Waltke. Chicago: Moody Press, 1980.

Workman, H.B. *Persecution in the Early Church.* Cincinnati: Jennings and Graham, 1906.

SELECTED INTERNET SOURCES

Adams Family Papers in The Massachusetts Historical Society, An Electronic Archive: http://www.masshist.org/digitaladams/aea/index.html (accessed February 5, 2012).

Federalist Papers. FoundingFathers. http://www.foundingfathers.info/ federalistpapers (accessed January 10-20, 2012).

Jefferson, Thomas 1743-1826. *Letters,* Electronic Text Center, University of Virginia Library, http://etext.virginia.edu/toc/modeng/public/JefLett.html (accessed February 10-20, 2012).

"Uniform Code of Military Justice Legislative History in Military Legal Resources," http://www.loc.gov/rr/frd/Military_Law/UCMJ_LHP.html (accessed March 24, 2013).

United States A*ir Force Chaplain Official Website:* www.ChaplainCorps.AF.mil

United States *Army Chaplain Official Website:* www.ChapNet.Army.mil

United States House of Representatives: T*he Office of the Chaplain,* http://Chaplain.House.gov/Chaplaincy/History.html

United States *Navy Chaplain Official Website:* www.Chaplain.Navy.mil

CPSIA information can be obtained
at www.ICGtesting.com
Printed in the USA
BVHW021324220223
659001BV00004B/339